THE ALLGEMEINE-SS

A COLLECTOR'S GUIDE TO:

THE ALLGEMEINE-SS

ROBIN LUMSDEN

Ian Allan
PUBLISHING

Acknowledgements

Thanks are due to the directors and staff of the following institutions, for their generous help in supplying documentary and photographic material: Berlin Document Centre, Berlin; Hoffmann Bildarchiv, Munich; Imperial War Museum, London; Ullstein Bilderdienst, Berlin; US Army, Washington.

In addition, special appreciation goes to Alan Lauder of Norval (Photographers) Ltd, Dunfermline, Fife, for his skilful assistance in photographing surviving examples of SS regalia from my own collection.

Cairneyhill
July 1991   *Robin Lumsden*

First published 1992 as *The Collector's Guide to the History and Regalia of the Black Corps*
This impression 2002

ISBN 0 7110 2905 9

Published by Ian Allan Publishing

an imprint of Ian Allan Publishing Ltd, Hersham, Surrey KT12 4RG.
Printed by Ian Allan Printing Ltd, Hersham, Surrey KT12 4RG.

Code: 0201/3

Front cover, top:
Early pattern SS death's head.

Front cover, bottom left:
Allgemeine-SS enlisted man's/NCO's peaked cap.

Front cover, bottom right:
Presentation casket for copies of Hitler's *Mein Kampf* distributed at ss weddings.

Back cover:
A unique oil painting of Heinrich Himmler painted by the renowned German artist Hommel c1943.
Courtesy of the US Arny Captured War Art Collection

Contents

Introduction

In an age of multinational companies and cross-border economic communities, when bureaucratic acronyms and initials have simultaneously become so complex and commonplace that specialist dictionaries have had to be devised for the benefit of those wishing to decypher them, the letters 'SS' are still instantly recognised worldwide, even after half a century, as denoting the very embodiment of terror and the Police State. It has to be said, however, that this concept owes much to the popular outpourings of cinema and television. Make simple mention of the SS and the man-in-the-street, continuously subjected to the ever-repeated products of the wartime moguls of Hollywood, will probably conjure up visions of black uniforms, death's heads and the dreaded 'three o'clock knock' with unfortunate innocents being dragged out of their beds in the middle of the night and hauled away to concentration camps, never to be seen again.

Such is the popular mythology surrounding the SS. It does, of course, have an element of truth about it. But the real SS story is far more complicated and almost defies belief. It is a story of intrigue and nepotism, of archaeology and Teutonism, of art and symbolism. It is the story of an organisation led by a man who was motivated by a genuine belief that he was the spiritual reincarnation of the Saxon King Heinrich I, founder of the German Reich. It is the story of street fighters and convicted criminals becoming Ministers of State and Police Commanders; the story of charitable works and mass extermination being administered from the same building; the story of boy generals directing vast heterogeneous armies on devastating campaigns of conquest. Here, indeed, fact is stranger than fiction.

The SS originated as Hitler's personal bodyguard, and after the Nazi consolidation of power began to develop rapidly. Three specialist fulltime armed groups soon emerged. Firstly, the bodyguard section grew to regimental strength and became the elite unit of the entire organisation, assuming the title Leibstandarte-SS 'Adolf Hitler'. Secondly, the SS-Verfügungstruppe were formed as barracked quasi-military forces to bolster the new regime in the event of political turmoil or counter-revolution. Finally, the SS-Totenkopfverbände were recruited to guard the growing number of concentration camp inmates. These three groupings of the SS were amalgamated to a certain extent during the war, becoming the first three divisions of the Waffen-SS, and much has been written about them in that regard. The Waffen-SS itself, which expanded as a fourth branch of the Wehrmacht to encompass almost 40 field divisions by 1945, has also been prodigiously covered in postwar literature.

The purpose of this book is to relate the history of the rest of the SS, those men and women who came to be covered by the blanket — and somewhat disparaging — term Allgemeine-SS, or General SS. Some had tried, and failed, to gain entry to the Leibstandarte, Verfügungstruppe or Totenkopfverbände. Others, for whatever personal or domestic reasons, chose to remain with the largely part-time and usually unpaid local units. In any event, while the more visible armed SS naturally received all the publicity, especially during the war, it was the rather faceless Allgemeine-SS which actually wielded the real power. Its membership included the entire spectrum of the German civil population, from farm labourers to the landed aristocracy. Its academics in the Sicherheitsdienst or SD, the SS Security Service, engaged upon intelligence gathering activities which had a great influence on both the domestic and foreign policies of the Third Reich. The government, industry, commerce, education and, particularly, the police all came to be dominated by the Allgemeine-SS. In occupied western Europe volunteer native units, known as the Germanic-SS, were set up in Flanders, Holland, Norway and Denmark to support the local police in guarding the various Home Fronts. By 1943, the Allgemeine-SS had evolved from a part-time provincial police reserve to a force which influenced, through its highly placed members, much of the political, racial, cultural and economic face of Europe. In October of that year, Himmler lectured his Generals on the future of the SS. He said:

'After the war, we shall really build up our Order, that Order to which we, the Old Guard, imparted its most important principles 19 years before the war. We shall continue for 20 years after the war so that a tradition can be established, a tradition that will last for 30, 35 or 40 years – a whole generation. Then our Order will march into the future as an élite which will unite the Germanic people and the whole of Europe. It will produce the leaders to direct industry, agriculture, politics and the activities of the mind. We have always subjected ourselves to the law of the élite, selecting the highest and abandoning the lowest. When we no longer apply to ourselves this fundamental law, we shall be condemned to death and perish like every other human organisation.'

The Reichsführer and his SS, then at the height of their power, had 18 months to live.

1 Origins and Early Development of the SS

WORLD WAR 1

The early history of the SS is inextricably linked with the events and aftermath of World War 1. This epic conflict had a profound effect on Adolf Hitler who, after years of aimless drifting in Vienna, suddenly found his true vocation soldiering on the Western Front. Thrown into the mincing machine as a trench messenger, he daily ran the gauntlet of British and French machine guns, was gassed, temporarily blinded and emerged with the Iron Cross 1st Class, an unusually high award for an enlisted man and one which he wore proudly until the day of his death. The crushing terms of the Versailles Settlement, and the theory that the undefeated German Army had been stabbed in the back by the civilian politicians in 1918, created an ideal breeding ground for extreme right wing parties and paramilitary groups of demobilised professional soldiers and nationalist ex-servicemen who aimed to put the country 'back on the rails'. In the early days, Hitler considered that frontline combat experience was a prerequisite for any position of leadership in his new National Socialist party, and the regimented organisation and military terminology used by the first Nazis was directly carried over from their army service.

From the outset, the German Army of World War 1 allowed and encouraged initiative among NCOs and privates. Unlike the British, who had an average of 25 officers per battalion, the Germans had only seven, and tasks which were normally undertaken by a subaltern in the British Army would often be delegated to a junior NCO in the German. So Cpl Hitler and Sgts Ulrich Graf, 'Sepp' Dietrich and their colleagues were more than accustomed to making frontline decisions in their capacities as Offizier Stellvertreter, or deputy officers. This self-reliance amongst the rank-and-file was later to become a cornerstone of SS training.

The Imperial Army was quick to realise the potential of developing élite detachments of hand-picked soldiers to act as assault parties and trench raiders. These men were selected not only for their self-reliance but also for their courage and initiative, and were trained in special techniques necessary to fight in the narrow and dangerous confines of the trench system.

Assault troops wearing the newly-introduced steel helmet were first used in January 1916 at Verdun, and at that time comprised three-man teams called Stosstrupp or shock troops. Their method of attack involved storming a trench in flank, the first of the trio armed with a shield made from a machine gun mounting and a sharpened entrenching tool, followed by the second man carrying haversacks full of short-fused stick grenades and the third soldier armed with a knife, bayonet or club. The Stosstrupp technique proved so successful that the system was further developed during 1916 when assault companies or detachments, the so-called Sturmkompanie or Sturmabteilungen, were formed and attached to divisions on a permanent basis. These assault companies each comprised an officer and 120 other ranks and were organised into three platoons, one of which was attached to each regiment in the division. By 1918, most armies on the Western Front had expanded units known as Sturmbataillone or assault battalions, comprising four assault companies, an infantry artillery company armed with a 37mm field howitzer, a light trench mortar detachment, a flame-thrower detachment, a machine gun company and an HQ company. When not in action, these men served as instructors training new recruits for the units. They received better rations than ordinary soldiers and were usually excused trench-holding duties. The storm troops were looked upon with the same respect that modern armies give their paratroops or special forces.

Officially, special insignia for the storm troops was frowned upon, but many varieties of locally adopted badges were worn. These typically featured bayonets, hand grenades and steel helmets. The most popular badge taken up by the storm troops, however, was the totenkopf or death's head, a skull over crossed bones, which was initially worn by flamethrower units and became representative of a devil-may-care attitude in the face of constant danger and high casualties. It was also seen as an élite badge due to its old associations with the Prussian Royal Bodyguard and famed Brunswick Hussars.

The new élite formations of the emerging German Air Arm were the flights of fast fighters which escorted and protected unwieldy reconnaissance units. They generally worked on a ratio of 1:3 with reconnaissance aircraft and were sometimes grouped together as aerial shock troops for the purpose of attacking ground targets. Because of their primary duties, they were given the title of protection squadrons or Schutzstaffeln, Schustas for short. Prominent Schusta members included Hermann Göring, Josef Kiermaier, later to become head of Himmler's personal security during the Third Reich, and the so-called Black Knight, Eduard Ritter von Schleich, who later commanded SS-Fliegerstaffel Süd and was a Hitler Youth General in the 1930s.

The terms Stosstrupp, Sturmabteilung and Schutzstaffel, devised to describe the crack German forces of land and air, were soon adopted by the Nazis for their own paramilitaries and were to take on an entirely new significance in the postwar era.

THE FREIKORPS

The formation of Freiwilligenkorps or Freikorps, Volunteer or Free Corps, had a long tradition in Germany, dating from the mercenary bands of the Middle Ages. These irregular troops tended to be mustered in times of crisis and during the 18th Cen-

Plate 1 Freikorps troops in Munich, 2nd May 1919. Note the Death's Head emblem painted on the front of their armoured car. *Hoffmann*

Plate 2 Items belonging to Willy Wietfeld of Benteler, Westfalen, a former World War 1 assault trooper and Freikorps freebooter, and one of the NSDAP and SS Old Guard. These include: his Stahlhelm ex-servicemen's association membership book and veteran's badge; the Silesian Eagle, for actions against Polish insurgents during 1919-20; the commemorative award for attending the Nazi rally at Brunswick on 17-18 October 1931, when the SA, purged after the Stennes Putsch, united nationally for the first time behind Hitler; the NSDAP Golden Party Badge; and a ribbon bar indicating an award of the SS 12-Year Long Service Decoration.

Plate 3 The Freikorps Memorial in Munich was unveiled by the city's Lord Mayor, SS-Obergruppenführer Karl Fiehler, on 9 May 1942. *Imperial War Museum (IWM)*

tury were used in various conflicts, their main task being to disrupt communications behind enemy lines.

In November 1918, Germany faced disaster. The war had been lost, the Kaiser had abdicated and the government had collapsed. The armed forces were, in effect, disbanded and groups of demobilised left-wing soldiers with no prospects roamed the streets calling for a Bolshevik uprising like that which had just taken hold in Russia. The country was also under extreme pressure from the civilian Spartacist revolutionaries, and Polish insurgents threatened to invade the eastern Baltic territories of the Reich.

To meet these challenges, new ad hoc Freikorps units were hastily formed by right-wing troops who found themselves anxious to defend their Father-land and its traditional values but without a proper army in which to do so. Still in possession of their wartime uniforms, weapons and transport, they banded together to follow local heroes or well-known military personalities. The usual method of recruitment was simply for an ex-officer to circulate literature or display posters inviting former soldiers to attend at a specified location on a given date and join his Freikorps. In many cases thousands turned up, eager to enlist whether for payment or not.

As well as the promise of action, a big attraction was the fact that discipline in the Freikorps was very lax in comparison to that of the Imperial Army. Officers were commonly referred to by their fore-names and enlisted men saluted only those officers whom they personally respected or admired. The troops paid little or no attention to formal instructions issued by the weak provisional government and gave their loyalty totally to their Freikorps commander, whom they referred to as their Führer or leader. To these destitute soldiers, units and comrades became homes and families.

The State was in desperate need of trained military men to assert control and these Freikorps free-booters provided the experienced manpower at just the right time. Dedicated above all to preventing Germany becoming a Bolshevik regime, they smashed riots, kept order in the streets, protected public buildings and became a mainstay of the law until they were dissolved in 1919, at least on paper, by the Treaty of Versailles which laid down the conditions for the setting up of the Reichswehr, the reconstituted and much reduced army of the Weimar Republic. Those Freikorps men who were n ot accepted back into the new army tended to drift into right-wing paramilitary groups such as the Stahlhelm and Reichskriegsflagge of the National-ists, and the Nazi SA. Such men included Himmler himself and the future SS Generals Kurt Daluege, 'Sepp' Dietrich, Reinhard Heydrich, Friedrich-Wil-helm Krüger, Karl Wolff and Udo von Woyrsch among many others.

In all, during the period 1919-20, there were some 250 individual Freikorps units in existence, comprising more than 70,000 men. They created their own range of over 1,000 medals, badges and insignia and prominent amongst these were the swastika of the Ehrhardt Brigade and the death's head, borrowed from the Imperial storm troops.

EARLY NAZIS AND THE SA

In December 1918, Adolf Hitler was discharged from the military hospital at Pasewalk near Stettin where he had been recovering from a gassing. He volunteered for guard duty at a prisoner-of-war camp at Traunstein, but by January 1919 its last inmates had left. At a loose end, still in uniform, he made his way to Munich and joined the Bavarian Freikorps which had just been formed by the war hero Franz Ritter von Epp to liberate the city from its new Marxist government. This it did with much bloodshed.

All over Germany nationalist groups were spring-ing up with the objective of ridding the country of the 'November Traitors' who had brought the dis-grace of the dictated peace, and of the Communists whose first loyalty was to Russia. Nationalists came from every level of society and at the lower end of the Munich social scale was Anton Drexler's tiny German Workers' Party, one of whose meetings Hitler attended as a military observer on 12 Septem-ber 1919. He joined the Party and, through his pow-ers of oratory, virtually took it over from the outset, changing its name to the National Socialist German Workers' Party (Nationalsozialistische Deutsche Arbeiterpartei or NSDAP) and giving it a nationalis-tic, anti-Semitic, anti-Capitalistic programme where, hitherto, it had possessed only a vague set of ideals. Hitler's greatest aim was to replace the Party's small discussion groups with mass meetings and the first, at the Festsaal of the Munich Hof-bräuhaus on 20 February 1920, attracted nearly 2,000 people.

Hitler's speeches soon found a loud echo in the ranks of the Freikorps and their units provided the new Nazi Führer with his first large followings. Hauptmann Ernst Röhm, von Epp's adjutant, who also headed his own Freikorps known as the Reich-skriegsflagge, sent Hitler an incessant flood of officers, NCOs and men and in October 1920 the veterans of the Ehrhardt Brigade and Iron Division went over en masse to the new Party, bringing with them their swastika and death's head badges. Tak-ing a leaf from the Communists' book, Hitler began to hire lorries and had them filled with Party mem-bers who drove noisily through the streets to meet-ings. The difference was that while the Communists wore a curious assortment of dress the Nazis, most of them ex-soldiers, sat bolt upright, wore smart Freikorps uniforms and seemed the very epitome of law and order reinstated. They were invariably cheered as they passed.

The military nature of the Party grew with the setting up of the Sturmabteilungen or SA during

1921. This was the work of Röhm and the ex-Naval Leutnant Hans-Ulrich Klintzsch, who created the SA as a new Freikorps to hammer the Reds and fend off opponents at political meetings. However, although the SA was affiliated to the Party, it did not initially come under Hitler's personal authority, for its members had little respect for the finesse of politics. It took its orders from its own Führer, its appointed commander-in-chief Oberstleutnant Hermann Kriebel, who thought that 'the best thing political blokes could do would be to belt up'. Originally confined to Munich, the SA made its first important foray outside the city when, on 14-15 October 1922, it took part in a 'German Day' at Coburg which resulted in a pitched battle with the Communists who controlled the town. The 800 SA men present succeeded in breaking the hold of the Red Front on Coburg and press coverage of the incident served to make Hitler's name known to a wider public.

The first national rally of the NSDAP was held on 28 January 1923, when some 6,000 SA men paraded before Hitler who presented standards to the first four full SA regiments, entitled 'München', 'München II', 'Nürnberg' and 'Landshut'. There were sufficient recruits during the next month alone to form a fifth regiment and, in an effort to better control the rapidly growing organisation, Hitler appointed a new man of politics, the former air ace Hauptmann Hermann Göring, to lead it. Göring brought with him the prestige of a great wartime hero, the last commander of the von Richthofen squadron, victor of 22 aerial dog-fights and holder of Germany's highest gallantry decoration the Order 'Pour le Merite', but he was, by nature, lazy and self-indulgent. The true driving force behind the SA remained Röhm, who continued to use his military and Freikorps connections to supply the SA with arms. So, in spite of Göring's appointment, the SA in 1923 was far from being submissive. Its independence, upheld by the former leaders of the Freikorps, compelled Hitler to set up a small troop of men, from outside the SA, which would be entirely devoted to him. Thus was born the SS.

THE FIRST SS

In March 1923, Hitler ordered the formation of a Munich-based bodyguard known as the Stabswache whose members swore an oath of loyalty to him personally and owed no allegiance to the leaders of the Freikorps or SA. Two months later, to avoid confusion with an SA unit of the same name which protected Röhm and Göring, the Stabswache was renamed the Stosstrupp Adolf Hitler and, like the shock troops of the Great War, it adopted the death's head as its distinctive emblem. The Stosstrupp Hitler was led by Hauptmann Julius Schreck and Leutnant Josef Berchtold, both veterans

of the Ehrhardt Brigade. Its headquarters were located in the Torbräu public house and there met the first members of Hitler's bodyguard who were destined to remain faithful to him at all times and follow his way up the political ladder. They included Josef 'Sepp' Dietrich, Ulrich Graf, Rudolf Hess, Hansjorg Maurer, Emil Maurice, Julius Schaub, Edmund Schneider and Christian Weber. By the time it left for the 'German Day' celebrations in Bayreuth on 2 September, the Stosstrupp numbered 30 men.

Hitler quickly recognised that the volatile atmosphere of 1923 was a transient thing, and he resolved to take advantage of it. He reckoned that his SA and their Freikorps allies might at last be strong enough to seize power in Bavaria and, with luck, march from Munich on Berlin for a final triumph. Similar coups had taken place with varying degrees of success elsewhere in Germany since 1918, and the Fascists under Mussolini had just swept to power in Italy after a march on Rome.

At the beginning of November, the 15,000 men of the SA were put on full alert and a suitable opportunity suddenly occurred on 8 November. On that day the three most powerful men in Bavaria, Prime Minister von Kahr, local army commander Lossow and police chief Seisser, attended a political meeting in the Munich Burgerbräukeller where they could be handily seized by a strongarm squad. The Reichskriegsflagge Freikorps was having a 'social' in the Augustiner Beer Cellar when its commander, Röhm, was ordered in his SA capacity to seize the Reichswehr Ministry on the Leopoldstrasse. His troops immediately set off, led by a young former army officer cadet, Heinrich Himmler, who carried an Imperial War Flag, the banner of the Freikorps which bore its name. Meanwhile, armed SA men surrounded the Burgerbräukeller and Hitler had von Kahr, Lossow and Seisser bundled into a side room. They managed to escape, however, and sped off to organise resistance to the Nazi Putsch.

On the morning of 9 November, the main force of the SA under Röhm was besieged in the War Ministry by regular army units summoned by Lossow. Hitler and Göring organised a relief column of 2,000 SA men and, accompanied by the former General Erich Ludendorff, marched through the streets of Munich. They ran into the first cordon of Seisser's police on the Ludwig Bridge but brushed them aside. A second police cordon on the edge of the Odeonplatz, however, gave them a different reception. They were in a strategic spot outside the Feldherrnhalle war memorial and were determined not to retreat. Ulrich Graf who, with the rest of the Stosstrupp Hitler, was present to protect his Führer, stepped out and shouted to the police officer in charge, 'Don't shoot! His Excellency Ludendorff is here!' But this was the police, not the army, and Ludendorff's name had no magic sound. A volley of shots rang out. Many Nazis, including Göring, fell seriously wounded. Josef Berchtold collapsed under a hail of bullets. The swastika standard bearer was in his death throes, drenching the silk of the flag with his blood. The tattered artifact was rapidly gathered up to be piously preserved as the famed Blutfahne or Blood Banner. Hitler had locked his left arm with the right of his close confidant Max Erwin von Scheubner-Richter, and when the latter fell mortally wounded he pulled Hitler to the pavement with him. Instantly, the faithful bodyguard Graf threw himself on his leader and was at once peppered by a dozen bullets which might otherwise have killed Hitler. Somehow, Graf survived it. Sixteen Nazis lay dead and the rest dispersed or were captured, but the Stosstrupp had fulfilled its primary duty – Hitler's life was preserved. The firing outside the Feldherrnhalle finally ended the era of the Freikorps which had started, five years before to the day, with the revolution of 1918. The time for fighting men had now passed, giving way to the politicians.

The reverse experienced at the Munich Putsch and Hitler's subsequent imprisonment, far from harming the cause of the Party and its leader, merely served to get them better known. Yet there were still plenty of troubles ahead. Following the Putsch, the NSDAP was banned and the SA dissolved. Those of its leaders who managed to avoid arrest fled to other German States where Bavarian Law could not touch them. Refugees from Munich set up personal clandestine SA units under the name Frontbanne, the largest being Frontbann 'Nord' centred around Berlin and commanded by Kurt Daluege. Hitler, cooped up in jail with his bodyguards penning 'Mein Kampf', realised that an armed insurrection against a government which commanded the loyalty of both the police and the army would be doomed. Henceforth, he determined to employ only legal methods.

On his release from prison on 20 December 1924, Hitler began to rebuild his Party and in February 1925 the NSDAP was reconstituted and the SA reactivated. Hitler the politician now categorically forbade the SA to bear arms or function as any form of private army. Its purpose was solely to clear the streets of his political enemies, a role hotly contested by Röhm who envisaged the SA as a citizen army which could bolster and ultimately supersede the Reichswehr, like the old Freikorps. The disagreement between the two became so bitter that Röhm eventually resigned from the Party and quit Germany for a military advisor's post in Bolivia. His job as Chief of Staff of the SA fell to the former Freikorps leader Franz Felix Pfeffer von Salomon, but the latter failed to enjoy Hitler's confidence and Röhm was duly reinstated in a stronger position than ever.

In April 1925, Hitler formed a new bodyguard commanded by Schreck, Schaub and his other Stosstrupp favourites. The guard, which came under the auspices of the SA High Command, was known first as the Schutzkommando, then the Sturmstaffel, but on 9 November, probably at the suggestion of Göring, it adopted the old fighter squadron title of Schutzstaffel or Schusta, soon commonly abbreviated to SS.

From the start, it was laid down that the SS, unlike the SA, should never become a mass organisation. In September 1925, Schreck sent a circular to all regional groups of the NSDAP asking them to form a local SS, the strength of which was fixed at one officer and 10 men. This was the beginning of the so-called 'Zehnerstaffeln' or 'Groups of Ten'. Not anybody could join, because the seeds of élitism had already been sown. Applicants had to be between 25 and 35 years of age, have two sponsors, be registered with the police as residents of five years standing and be sober, disciplined, strong and healthy. Habitual drunkards and gossip-mongers were not to be admitted. The reason for all this was simple. Hitler and his followers were tirelessly campaigning to increase membership of the NSDAP and were beginning to travel outside Bavaria into areas where Nazi allegiance was local rather than to Hitler himself. The Führer needed a small hand-picked bodyguard on which he could rely wherever he went.

In April 1926, Schreck was nominated personal bodyguard and chauffeur to the Führer, and Josef Berchtold re-emerged to take over command of the SS, which then numbered about 1,000 men. On 4 July, in a gesture symbolising his intention that the SS should become the true guardian of Nazi values, Hitler solemnly handed over the Blood Banner from the Munich Putsch into their safekeeping and appointed Jakob Grimminger from the Munich SS detachment to be official bearer of the Blutfahne at all subsequent special Party rituals.

Despite the extension of its numbers and theoretical prestige, the SS remained a limited organisation subordinated to the SA. When von Salomon attempted to absorb the SS completely in March 1927, Berchtold resigned and was replaced by his deputy, Erhard Heiden, who managed to maintain its partial autonomy. However, the SA kept a jealous eye on SS expansion and local SA commanders consistently used the SS under their control for the most demeaning tasks such as distributing propaganda leaflets and recruiting subscribers to the Party newspaper, the *Völkischer Beobachter.* By the end of 1928, morale in the SS was at an all-time low and membership had fallen to 280. On 6 January 1929, a dejected Heiden resigned his titular position as Reichsführer der SS in favour of his timid young deputy, Heinrich Himmler. The SA leadership were cock-a-hoop. This colourless bureaucrat posed little threat and was just the man to command the SS and ensure its continued subordination to the SA. They were in for a rude awakening.

Plate 6 Hitler on the election trail in the autumn of 1932, accompanied by, from left to right, Julius Schaub, 'Sepp' Dietrich and Kurt Daluege.

14

Plate 4 The Stosstrupp Hitler leaving for 'German Day' in Bayreuth, 2 September 1923. Josef Berchtold stands leaning on the cab, beside von Salomon and Ulrich Graf. Julius Schreck, with goggles, is seated at the left of the front row. *Hoffmann*

Plate 5 A group of the Reichskriegsflagge Freikorps behind the Bavarian War Ministry on 9 November 1923. From left to right in the foreground: Weickert; Kitzinger: Himmler (with Imperial War Flag); Seidel-Dittmarsch; and Röhm. *Hoffmann*

HIMMLER'S CONSOLIDATION OF POWER

From the day he took command, Himmler was the SS and the SS Himmler. The organisation's progress became bound up with the career of its Reichsführer who obtained one important post after another until by 1945 he had concentrated more power in his person than any other man except Hitler. Wherever Himmler secured a position, he took the SS with him. The SS became both the basis and the instrument of his strength. At the height of his power, Himmler was Chief of Police, Reich Minister of the Interior, an NSDAP Reichsleiter, Member of the Reichstag, Reich Commissioner for the Consolidation of Germanism Abroad, Commander-in-Chief of the Home Army, Chief of Military Armament and Commander of Army Groups on the Rhine and Vistula. In effect, he and his SS controlled all forces, military, paramilitary and police, on the German Home Front during World War 2.

There was no sign of this future greatness in 1929, however. The new SS leader was rather non-descript, pale, mild-mannered and prim with spectacles and prematurely receding hair. Born on 7 October 1900, he was a member of the best Bavarian society and was named after his Godfather, Prince Heinrich of Bavaria, to whom his schoolmaster father was tutor. He had welcomed the outbreak of World War 1 with enthusiasm, and reported for duty as an officer cadet with the 11th Bavarian Infantry Regiment in January 1918. However, he was sent to the Front just at the moment when the Armistice was signed and never saw action, something he always regretted.

On 17 December 1918, Himmler was discharged from the army but he retained his military connections by joining the Oberland Freikorps in 1919. He gained an agricultural degree in 1922, then secured employment as a technical assistant with a fertiliser company, only to see his salary lose half its value to inflation in a single month. In August 1923, he became a member of the NSDAP and two months later enrolled in Röhm's Reichskriegsflagge and participated in the Munich Putsch, an act which cost him his job. After the subsequent dissolution of the Party, Himmler took it upon himself to reorganise the NSDAP in Lower Bavaria to prepare for the elections of 1924. He spent much of his time riding around the countryside on an old motorcycle indoctrinating the locals. Himmler soon became known for his energy, enthusiasm and organising ability and on 12 March 1925 he was summoned by Hitler who appointed him Gauleiter in Lower Bavaria. He was one of the first to join the new SS at the end of the year, and in 1926 became responsible for Nazi propaganda throughout Germany, directly under Hitler's orders. Once he had become the Führer's direct partner, Himmler persisted in putting forward his notion that the SS should become an élite force within the Party, and one which would be totally devoted to Hitler. At a time when the SA was becoming increasingly rebellious, the notion appealed and Hitler approved Himmler's succession to Heiden as Reichsführer der SS.

In April 1929, Himmler persuaded Hitler and von Salomon to approve a recruiting plan designed to create a truly élite body out of the SS. In contrast to the SA, which took all comers, only properly selected candidates would be accepted for the SS, based primarily upon their voluntary discipline. There were none of the racial standards imposed on later recruits, but the early SS men had to demonstrate their willingness to be ready for any sacrifice. At that time, recruits were liable to purchase their own uniforms, which could cost up to 40 Marks, an enormous expense for an unemployed man, and that factor alone was enough to deter many. However, high personal standards had a great appeal to ex-soldiers and young nationalists, and veterans of the Freikorps joined up in large numbers. By the beginning of 1930 the SS had grown to 2,000 men, which worried von Salomon. Yet it was still technically subordinated to the SA High Command, despite Hitler's instruction that no SA officer was authorised to give orders to the SS during their day-to-day duties.

Whereas the SS grew steadily, the SA exploded completely. Its sole purpose was to be a mass organisation of pro-Nazi street fighters, and by 1930 60% of its membership were unemployed ruffians who owed allegiance to their local SA Generals, not Hitler. In the north, the SA split down the middle when the new Party Head in Berlin, the flamboyant intellectual Dr Joseph Goebbels, arrived to take charge of the city. The Berlin SA began to complain that Hitler and his Bavarian friends were living in the lap of luxury while their comrades in the inner cities were starving. Röhm was recalled to take charge, but the SA leaders in Berlin, under SA Oberführer Walther Stennes, rebelled. On 1 April 1931, Kurt Daluege, now in charge of the SS in Berlin, alerted Hitler that all the Berlin SA had taken sides for Stennes against him. The next day, Stennes' men chased Gauleiter Goebbels out of his office and took over the premises of his newspaper, *Der Angriff*. The revolt spread throughout the whole of northern Germany. The SA Generals in Brandenburg, Hesse, Silesia, Pomerania and Mecklenburg supported Stennes and Hitler's fall was widely prophesied. However, the uprising lacked organisation and money and died as quickly as it had been born. Göring purged the SA of Stennes' supporters and the SA throughout the north was reorganised. Hitler issued his public congratulations to the Berlin SS, which alone had remained loyal to him and Goebbels during the crisis. The devotion of the SS to their Führer had been demonstrated in deeds as well as words. In recognition, Hitler appointed Himmler security chief for the NSDAP headquarters, the Brown House in Munich, on 25 January 1932. In effect, he was now Head of the Party Police.

During 1932, the political struggle in Germany rapidly took on the form of a Civil War. The Com-

16

munist Party and Socialists set up armed militias and the SA and SS responded. The Brüning government ordered the disbanding of paramilitaries and the prohibition of political uniforms, but it then collapsed and the 'Cabinet of Barons' set up under Franz von Papen lifted the ban. Ten members of the SS were killed in 1932 and several hundreds wounded during street battles with the Red Front. As the crucial 1933 elections approached, it suited the Nazis to create the impression that Germany was on the verge of anarchy and that they had all the solutions. Not surprisingly, they won a great electoral victory and on 30 January the old Field Marshal Paul von Hindenburg, President of the Reich and a sort of 'Ersatz Kaiser' since 1925, entrusted Hitler with the post of Chancellor and the responsibility of forming a government. On 28 February, less than a month after the assumption of power, the Reichstag building was razed to the ground and the Communists were blamed. The next day, Hitler issued a decree 'For the Protection of People and State' giving police powers to the SA and SS. Firearms were issued to 25,000 SA and 15,000 SS acting as Hilfspolizei or Auxiliary Policemen, and left-wing opponents began to be arrested and herded into makeshift prisons and camps. Soon, 27,000 people were being held in protective custody. In March, Himmler became Police President of Munich and a new SS Stabswache went on duty at the Chancellery door in Berlin, replacing the traditional army guard unit. From then on, the men in black were never to be absent from Hitler's side. The high time of the SS was at hand.

THE SUPREMACY OF THE SS

In May 1933, a number of company-sized SS detachments were armed and put on a full time paid footing. The Chancellery Stabswache, under 'Sepp' Dietrich, was reformed as the SS Sonderkommando Zossen and designated as an élite paramilitary formation which, in addition to its guard duties, could be used for armed police and anti-terrorist tasks. After four months, it was merged with the SS Sonderkommando Jüterbog and received its final title, Leibstandarte-SS 'Adolf Hitler' or LSSAH, the name invoking memories of the Imperial Prussian and Bavarian Life Guards. On 9 November 1933, in front of the hallowed Feldherrnhalle before which, exactly 10 years previously, the Munich Putsch had met its end, the Leibstandarte took an oath of loyalty unto death to its Führer.

After the Leibstandarte-SS 'Adolf Hitler', the first SS formation to be armed and live in barracks, Himmler set up other military units known as the SS Politische Bereitschaften or PB, Political Reserve Squads. Their purpose was to bolster the régime in the event of civil unrest or counter-revolution. Each PB was of battalion size and as their numbers grew

they were amalgamated to form three regiments entitled 'Deutschland', 'Germania' and 'Der Führer'. All of these formations came to be known by the collective designation SS-Verfügungstruppe or SS-VT, political troops at the special disposal of the Nazi régime.

To answer the immediate threat of violent subversion and to house the thousands of leftists being arrested after the Reichstag fire, Himmler opened the first concentration camp or Konzentrationslager (KL) at Dachau near Munich in March, 1933. The purpose of the camp, which was really a roughly organised labour camp, was to provide protective custody for persons who had not been legally sentenced to prison by a court of law. Other camps were soon established at Sachsenhausen outside Berlin and Buchenwald by Weimar. The guarding of these camps was entrusted to yet another new branch of SS volunteers, the Wachverbände, later known as the Death's Head Units or Totenkopfverbände (SS-TV) because they wore the skull and crossbones on their collar patches. The first 150 SS-TV men were selected on 17 March 1933. Like the Leibstandarte and SS-VT recruits, they signed up for 12 years, all of which were considered military service, and they were paid in accordance with army rates. Each Totenkopf Hundertschaft, or Century, was organised like an army rifle company, and the death's head formations were quickly grouped into three regiments named after the areas in which they served, 'Oberbayern', 'Brandenburg' and 'Thüringen'. Their overall commander was SS–Gruppenführer Theodor Eicke, a former policeman and World War 1 officer.

While the SS was consolidating its situation and controlling its membership and recruitment by a constant purging process, the brown shirted SA began to throw its weight about noisily. Denied a position in the State to which it felt entitled, the SA talked of a 'Second Revolution' which would sweep away the bourgeois in the Party and the reactionaries in the Reichswehr. Among the SS, the SA leaders became known as 'fleischschnitten' or 'beef steaks' because they were brown on the outside but red on the inside. Röhm, who now commanded a force over 40 times the size of the regular army and which included SA cavalry regiments, SA marine battalions and SA aviation squadrons, demanded the formation of a people's army in which the SA would simply replace the Reichswehr. Röhm, of course, would be commander-in-chief. The army Generals called upon Hitler to intervene and the Führer could not refuse their request. Ever since November 1918, the Reichswehr had been the very incarnation of continuity in the State, which had been maintained despite defeat, revolution and civil war. Hitler knew he would never achieve supreme power without the backing of the Reichswehr, and decided that the SA had to be cut down to size. The danger it posed was just too great – not simply the threat of a Putsch but the ever-present disorder created by the very men who should have been setting an example of good order. Their incessant brawling, drinking, violence and irresponsible conversation, to say nothing of Röhm's homosexual antics, provoked profound discontent in public opinion. The confidence ordinary Germans had in the new régime was in danger of collapsing altogether.

On 28 June 1934, Hitler took the final decision to eliminate the SA leadership. Two days later he personally directed operations at Munich and Bad Wiessee, where Röhm and his subordinates had peacefully gathered at their Führer's request. Following a carefully co-ordinated plan, SS men of the Leibstandarte and Totenkopfverbände arrested and executed Röhm and 16 senior SA commanders. The SS also seized the opportunity to settle its scores with old enemies, including the former Bavarian Prime Minister von Kahr, who was found in a peat bog with his head smashed in. A hundred or so victims paid with their lives for their opposition to the SS in this bloody purge which came to be known as the 'Night of the Long Knives'. The SA suffered a loss of power and 'face' from which it never fully recovered. The new head of the SA, Viktor Lutze, Police President of Hannover, had an ability to get on with the army and SS which was surpassed only by his obsequious loyalty to Hitler. The rank and file of SA members was reduced from 4 million to 1,200,000 of the 'better elements', and they were stripped of their arms.

On 20 July 1934, in thanks for its duties during the Putsch, Hitler declared the 200,000-strong SS an independent formation of the NSDAP and removed it completely from SA control. Its position of ascendancy was now assured and it entered a period of consolidation in which it developed a new command structure under Himmler whose rank as Reichsführer-SS for the first time actually meant what it implied and made him directly subordinate to Hitler. He immediately shed some 60,000 SS men who had been recruited at a time when the SS was competing for members with the SA, but who now did not conform to the SS image of élitism. The Leibstandarte, Verfügungstruppe and Totenkopfverbände developed their status as separate military branches, eventually amalgamating and expanding during World War 2 under the all-embracing title of Waffen-SS or Armed SS, which will be covered in a later chapter and about which much has been written elsewhere.

From the middle of 1934 the traditional non-military SS, the backbone of the organisation, began to be known as the Allgemeine-SS or General SS to distinguish it from the armed branches. It is on that body that the remainder of this book will concentrate.

Plate 7 SS men prepare to set fire to a collection of placards and flags seized from Berlin Communists, March 1933. *IWM*

2 General Organisation of the Allgemeine-SS

THE REICHSFÜHRER-SS

Prior to becoming a separate element in July 1934, the SS was subordinate to the SA and its Stabschef or Chief of Staff, Ernst Röhm. There was no proper independent SS command structure and the most senior SS leaders, including Himmler, were attached to the SA Supreme Command, the Oberste SA-Führung. Up until that time, Himmler was ranked merely as an SS–Obergruppenführer who held the post, not the rank, of Reichsführer der SS. He was, therefore, on an equal footing with any of the other SS or SA Generals and enjoyed no privileged position. Indeed, his lack of frontline experience during World War 1 led to his being despised by many of the old campaigners who looked upon him as being a figure of fun who had weaseled his way to the top. The leader of SS Group 'Ost' for example, SS-Gruppenführer Kurt Daluege of Stennes Putsch fame, had by 1934 acquired considerable powers with Göring's patronage and felt himself to be so strong that he refused to deal with anyone but Hitler and Röhm, and certainly not with "that Bavarian chicken-breeder Himmler". He was by no means unique in his attitude. The fall of Röhm, however, altered the situation completely. Himmler's elevation to the newly-created rank of Reichsführer-SS, or RfSS, which set him above all others, suddenly made him untouchable.

Yet so far as the Armed SS units were concerned Himmler was soon Reichsführer in name only for, despite their origins, the Leibstandarte-SS 'Adolf Hitler', SS-Verfügungstruppe and SS-Totenkopfverbände came to be regarded not as being in the official employ of the Party but as specially regulated public services of the Reich, on the model of the army. The Leibstandarte in particular, under 'Sepp' Dietrich, became a complete law unto itself, a state of affairs which Hitler supported by writing to Himmler in 1938, 'Dietrich is master in his own house which, I would remind you, is my house'. Young officers such as Hubert Meyer, Joachim Peiper and Max Wünsche were recruited for their military potential rather than their political reliability, and went on to enjoy fine careers in the Armed SS although none of them ever joined the NSDAP. By 1940, the Waffen-SS had developed into a fourth branch of the Wehrmacht, with its divisions coming under the tactical control of Army Generals, and its expenses were a charge on the State. In effect, its most important ties with Himmler and the party were severed. The Reich Finance Minister, Lutz Graf Schwerin von Krosigk, maintained his impartiality in the allocation of national funds to the Waffen–SS by consistently refusing Himmler's offers of honorary SS rank.

In contrast, the Allgemeine-SS always retained its political status as an independent Gliederung, or organisation, of the NSDAP and it was never maintained by the State. Its expenses were paid solely from Party funds and its finances were ultimately controlled by the Reichsschatzmeister der NSDAP or Party Treasurer, Franz Xaver Schwarz, who was renowned as a fist-grasping administrator. However, Schwarz, a veteran of the Munich Putsch, was also very close to Himmler, who made him the highest ranking General Officer in the whole SS, second on the seniority list only to the Reichsführer himself. Consequently, the Party never actually exercised any close independent supervision over Allgemeine-SS funds. Through his mutual back-scratching exercises with Schwarz, Himmler ensured that the Allgemeine-SS got any cash it needed, often at the expense of other Party branches like the SA and NSFK. So the Allgemeine-SS, unlike the military side of the organisation, remained totally under the Reichsführer's control until 1945, immune from outside State interference. Himmler's position at the top of the Allgemeine-SS hierarchy was, therefore, unchallenged and his power unbridled by any potential financial constraints. As a result, the highest levels of the Allgemeine-SS organisation centred around him personally.

THE REICHSFÜHRUNG-SS AND THE SS HAUPTÄMTER

During the autumn of 1934, Himmler quickly went about the business of organising his own high command structure. The Reichsführung-SS was set up as the supreme authority comprising two staffs, the Kommandostab RfSS an executive administrative staff at Himmler's personal headquarters; and the Persönlicher Stab RfSS, a much larger and more loosely organised body consisting of a number of advisory officials including the heads of the main SS departments and certain other special offices. The fresh administrative burdens later imposed by the war made it necessary to create a much larger and more complex command structure than had sufficed during peacetime. By 1942, subject to Himmler's controlling authority and that of the Reichsführung-SS, the day-to-day work of directing, organising and administering the SS was carried out by the eight main departments, or Hauptämter, listed on the next page. Each will duly be described in turn.

In addition, there were a number of minor offices and departments not of Hauptamt status.

By 1945, the Hauptamt system had become a vast and complex network of intertwining bureaucratic empires, each vying for supremacy over the others and for the attention of their Reichsführer. Having said that, there is no doubt that they always functioned effectively, even if not efficiently. The spirit of competition between them, which Himmler actively encouraged, ensured that everything dealt with by each department was recorded, checked and double checked to avoid error. If another Hauptamt had an interest, it too would record, check and

20

(i)	Hauptamt Persönlicher Stab RfSS	—	Himmler's Personal Staff
(ii)	SS Hauptamt	—	SS Central Office
(iii)	SS Führungshauptamt	—	SS Operational HQ
(iv)	Reichssicherheitshauptamt	—	Reich Central Security Office
(v)	SS Wirtschafts-und Verwaltungshauptamt	—	SS Economic and Administrative Department
(vi)	SS Rasse-und Siedlungshauptamt	—	SS Race and Settlement Department
(vii)	Hauptamt SS Gericht	—	SS Legal Department
(viii)	SS Personalhauptamt	—	SS Personnel Department

double check. The result was the most detailed system of manual files ever compiled, not just on the SS organisation but on every aspect of life in the Third Reich. The SS Personalhauptamt alone housed 150 million individual documents, and the Reichssicherheitshauptamt even maintained secret and potentially incriminating dossiers on Hitler himself and on all the other Nazi leaders, Himmler included. This attention to detail and ability to come up with all sorts of information gave the impression of an all-seeing, all-knowing command structure which ensured that, right up until the capitulation, the Reichsführung-SS and SS Hauptämter successfully managed to control and administer the vast SS organisation. That was not an insignificant achievement considering that, at its peak, the SS operated across an area from the Channel Islands to the Black Sea and from the Arctic Circle to the Mediterranean, with a generally hostile population.

THE HAUPTAMT PERSÖNLICHER STAB RFSS

As the core of the Reichsführung-SS, the personal staff of the Reichsführer-SS (Pers. Stab RfSS) had its main offices at 8 Prinz-Albrecht-Strasse, Berlin. Its members were designated 'i.P.St.' (on the Personal Staff) and were subordinated directly to Himmler. The Pers. Stab RfSS consisted of:

(i) Heads of the SS Hauptämter, who were ex-officio members

(ii) SS officials in certain offices and departments integrated into the Pers. Stab

(iii) SS officials appointed or attached to the staff for special advisory or honorary purposes

Besides being an advisory and co-ordinating body, the Pers. Stab was responsible for all business in which the Reichsführer-SS was concerned that did not come into the province of any of the other SS Hauptämter. In addition, it liaised with government and Party offices. The Chief of the Personal Staff was SS-Obergruppenführer Karl Wolff, who served as Himmler's adjutant from 1934. In 1943 Wolff was also appointed Supreme SS and Police Commander in Italy, in effect Military Governor of the country, but he always retained his post as Chief of the Personal Staff and, with it, all the powers and disciplinary prerogatives of a Hauptamtschef.

Much of the administrative work generated by the Pers. Stab was processed through the Kommandostab RfSS which operated during the war on a mobile basis under the title Feldkommandostelle RfSS, or Field Headquarters of the Reichsführer-SS. It was by then organised like a military HQ and accompanied Himmler on his numerous tours of the occupied territories. Together with attached SS units including a signals section, an escort battalion and a flak detachment, the Feldkommandostelle eventually numbered over 3,000 men.

THE SS HAUPTAMT

Based at 7 – 11 Douglasstrasse, Berlin-Grünewald, the SS Hauptamt or SS-HA, the SS Central Office, developed from the original SS-Amt under SS-Gruppenführer Kurt Wittje which co-ordinated SS operations prior to 1935. It was the oldest of the SS main departments and its bare title of Hauptamt without further qualification indicated in itself the fundamental part it originally played in the administration of the SS. As late as 1940, under SS-Obergruppenführer August Heissmeyer, it maintained its supremacy. At that time there were still only three Hauptämter proper, the other two being the Rasse-und Siedlungshauptamt and the Reichssicherheitshauptamt. With the exception, therefore, of the specialist functions carried out by these two departments, the SS-HA was responsible for all the varied tasks involved in the general administration of the whole SS.

The expansion of the SS as a result of wartime mobilisation, however, made the multiplicity of functions converging on the SS-HA too great a burden for one department and in August 1940 a major reorganisation of the central administration of the SS took place. Two existing SS-HA branches, the Personalamt (Personnel Office) and the SS Gericht (Legal Department) were detached and themselves raised to Hauptamt status, becoming the SS Personalhauptamt and the Hauptamt SS Gericht. In addition, two further Hauptämter were created, namely the SS Führungshauptamt and the SS Wirtschafts- und Verwaltungshauptamt by taking certain responsibilities away from the SS-HA. Several other functions of the

21

SS-HA were also transferred or absorbed elsewhere, an example being the supervision of SS radio communications and signals which was taken over by the Chief of Communications on the Persönlicher Stab RfSS. The result of this reorganisation was that the SS-HA lost eight of its 13 offices. At one stroke it was completely deprived of the commanding position it had previously enjoyed. The main importance still attaching to the SS-HA under its new chief, SS-Obergruppenführer Gottlob-Christian Berger, was its responsibility for recruitment and the maintenance of records on non-commissioned personnel.

The subsequent recovery of the SS-HA during 1941-45 was almost entirely due to the continued expansion of the Waffen-SS and the extension of the area of Allgemeine-SS influence into occupied territories. From 1941, the Waffen-SS increasingly recruited both individual Germanic volunteers and complete Germanic units from western Europe and Scandinavia. At the same time efforts were made in Flanders, Holland, Norway and Denmark to raise native Allgemeine-SS formations, the so-called Germanic-SS, to assist in policing these countries. In both of these tasks, the SS-HA played a leading part.

THE SS FÜHRUNGSHAUPTAMT

The SS Operational Headquarters or Führungshauptamt (SS-FHA), under SS-Obergruppenführer Hans Jüttner, was located at 188 Kaiserallee, Berlin-Wilmersdorf. It grew from the Operations Department of the SS Hauptamt, becoming a separate entity in August 1940, and developed into the biggest of all the SS Hauptämter with a staff of 40,000 in 1945. The reason for its rapid growth was the expansion of the Waffen-SS, which imposed an administrative burden on the SS for which there was no parallel before the war. However, while the greater operational needs of the Waffen-SS made the administration of that branch by far the most important function of the SS-FHA, the latter was never intended to be the headquarters solely of the Waffen-SS. It was, in fact, the Operational HQ of the whole SS, and included as one of its departments the Allgemeine-SS Headquarters (Kommandoamt der Allgemeinen-SS) under SS-Gruppenführer Leo Petri, which was responsible for the control and operational deployment of the Allgemeine-SS as well as its general organisation, supplies, training and mobilisation.

THE REICHSSICHERHEITSHAUPTAMT

The Reichssicherheitshauptamt or RSHA, the Reich Central Security Office, was set up in September 1939 to bring together the security police forces of both the Party and the State.

The RSHA was responsible for both domestic and foreign intelligence operations, espionage and counter-espionage, combatting political and common law crime, and sounding out public opinion on the Nazi régime. It will be covered in more detail in Chapter 5: The SS and the Police.

THE SS WIRTSCHAFTS- UND VERWALTUNGSHAUPTAMT

Formed in 1942, the SS Wirtschafts- und Verwaltungshauptamt or SS-WVHA, the SS Economic and Administrative Department, was headed by SS-Obergruppenführer Oswald Pohl and was based at 126-135 Unter den Eichen, Berlin-Lichterfelde. This department dealt primarily with supply and equipment and with the financial administration of the SS. It controlled a large number of SS industrial and agricultural undertakings, carried out housing and construction programmes, and administered the concentration camps. The SS-WVHA will be covered in detail in Chapter 9: The SS Economy.

THE SS RASSE- UND SIEDLUNGSHAUPTAMT

The SS Rasse-und Siedlungshauptamt or RuSHA, the SS Race and Settlement Department, achieved Hauptamt status on 30 January 1935, having grown from the SS Race and Settlement Office set up at the end of 1931 under SS-Obergruppenführer Richard Walther Darré. It was subsequently commanded by Günther Pancke, who later became Senior SS and Police Commander in Denmark, and finally by Richard Hildebrandt, and had its offices at 24 Hedemannstrasse, Berlin.

RuSHA looked after the ideological and racial purity of all SS members. It was the authority for all matters of genealogy, and issued lineage certificates and marriage permits within the SS. In addition, it was responsible for executing the policy of settling SS men, especially ex-servicemen, as colonists in the conquered eastern territories, and thus translated into practice the 'Blood and Soil' theories of Darré and the other SS racial teachers.

RuSHA will be covered in more detail in Chapter 6: The Racial Concept.

THE HAUPTAMT SS GERICHT

The Hauptamt SS Gericht or HA SS Gericht, the SS Legal Department, situated at 10 Karlstrasse, Munich, administered the disciplinary side of the special code of laws to which members of the SS and police were subject. It controlled the SS und Polizei Gerichte (SS and Police Courts) in the larger towns of Germany and the occupied countries, and the Strafvollzugslager der SS und Polizei (SS and Police Penal Camps) also came under its jurisdiction. The department was headed by SS-Gruppenführer Paul Scharfe until his death in 1942, when he was succeeded by SS-Obergruppenführer Franz Breithaupt.

The Hauptamt SS Gericht was an extension of the older SS Gericht, an office which carried out on behalf of the Reichsführer-SS investigations within the ranks of the SS into disciplinary offences and infringements of the SS code of honour. It prepared and prosecuted cases and was responsible for the execution of penal and disciplinary sentences and for the remission or reprieve of such sentences. In addition, as supreme authority within the SS on matters of law and discipline, it was the channel of liaison between the SS and all other legal bodies of the State and Party.

THE SS PERSONALHAUPTAMT

The SS Personalhauptamt or SS Personnel Department was based at 98-99 Wilmersdorferstrasse, Berlin-Charlottenburg and co-ordinated the work of the personnel branches of the various Hauptämter. It was the ultimate authority responsible for all questions of SS personnel, but its primary concern was with officers only, as the SS Hauptamt retained records concerning NCOs and other ranks. The SS Personalhauptamt was commanded by SS-Obergruppenführer Walter Schmitt until 1942, and thereafter by SS-Obergruppenführer Maximilian von Herff.

OTHER OFFICES AND DEPARTMENTS

In addition to the regular SS Hauptämter, there were a number of other smaller offices and departments which had their places in the SS command structure.

The Hauptstelle der Hauptamt Ordnungspolizei was a department representing the uniformed civil police at Himmler's headquarters. It advised the Reichsführer on all matters concerning the Ordnungspolizei, which was commanded by Himmler's old rival Kurt Daluege and which will be covered in Chapter 5: The SS and the Police.

The Hauptamt Dienststelle Heissmeyer, an office attached to the staff of SS-Obergruppenführer August Heissmeyer in his capacity as Senior SS and Police Commander for the Berlin District, was responsible for supervision of the Nationalpolitische Erziehungsanstalten (NPEA or Napola), the National Political Educational Institutes set up to train the future Germanic élite. These will be covered in Chapter 8: The SS and Education.

The Stabshauptamt der Reichskommissar für die Festigung des deutschen Volkstums in Ausland, or Hauptamt RKF, Himmler's Staff HQ in his capacity as Reich Commissioner for the Consolidation of Germanism Abroad, was based at 142-3 Kurfürstendamm, Berlin-Halensee, and commanded by SS-Obergruppenführer Ulrich Greifelt. It had a general interest in all matters affecting the maintenance of the racial qualities of the German population and the protection and enlargement of the German race as a whole. Its principal activity was to promote settlement by Germans of the annexed eastern territories of the Reich.

The Hauptamt Volksdeutsche Mittelstelle or VOMI, the Department for the Repatriation of Racial Germans, was operated from offices at 29 Keithstrasse, Berlin, and led by SS-Obergruppenführer Werner Lorenz. In contrast to the Hauptamt RKF, its main function was the organised return to the Reich of the descendants of older generations of German colonists and settlers in Russia and southeast Europe.

Both the Hauptamt RKF and VOMI will be covered in greater detail in Chapter 6: The Racial Concept.

'DAS SCHWARZE KORPS'

From 1935, the Reichsführung-SS published a weekly newspaper called Das Schwarze Korps or 'The Black Corps'. Set up on Heydrich's initiative and directed by SS-Standartenführer Gunter d'Alquen, descendant of a Huguenot family, it was printed by the NSDAP publishing house of Eher Verlag, Munich, and had its editorial offices at 88 Zimmerstrasse, Berlin. By 1939, circulation had reached 500,000 copies.

Das Schwarze Korps was a sharply written paper, very neo-pagan, and specialised in the exposure of those the Reichsführung-SS considered social miscreants whom the courts could not reach. It was the only organ of the German press which was not censored and, although rigorously orthodox at the ideological level, was also the only newspaper that gave any indication of having a critical or non-conformist spirit. From its very first number, the originality of Das Schwarze Korps was emphasised by its aggressiveness to the rest of Goebbels' Press. It took sides against the tyranny of the leaders of the Party, attacked bourgeois Ministers such as Alfred Rosenberg who had been short-sighted enough to shun Himmler's offers of honorary SS rank, and denounced inadequacies in the Administration. Private enterprise and initiative were favoured by the paper because they aided progress, particularly in wartime.

After 1939, the write-up of SS and police military heroes became an increasingly important feature, particularly when d'Alquen was made commander of the SS War Correspondents' Regiment and Kurt Eggers took over the paper.

As the war progressed and the need grew for all sections of the régime to be seen to act as one, the old criticisms of the excesses of the Party leaders disappeared. By 1945, **Das Schwarze Korps** had degenerated from a lively and controversial weekly to a propaganda sheet expounding the exploits of Waffen-SS soldiers on the battlefront.

THE OBERABSCHNITTE

On a level immediately below the SS Hauptämter were the Oberabschnitte (Oa.) or Regions, the bases of Allgemeine-SS territorial organisation. Initially there were five Oberabschnitte, formed in 1932 from the existing SS Gruppen. By 1944, their number had risen to 17 within Germany proper and each corresponded almost exactly to a Wehrkreis or Military District. The SS Regions were generally known by geographical names, but it was also customary to refer to them by the Roman numeral allocated to the corresponding Wehrkreis.

Each Oberabschnitt was commanded by an SS-Obergruppenführer, Gruppenführer or Brigadeführer designated Führer des Oberabschnittes (F.Oa.). He was usually also Himmler's representative at the military headquarters of the local Wehrkreis and, in addition, held the post of Höhere SS- und Polizeiführer or HSSPf, the Senior SS and Police Commander in the Region. In the few cases where the HSSPf was not the Führer of the corresponding Oberabschnitt it was because the latter, though filling some other active appointment, was allowed to retain the titular leadership of the Oa. on personal grounds. For example, during the war, SS-Obergruppenführer August Heissmeyer found himself appointed HSSPf for Oberabschnitt Spree because the nominal Führer of that Region, 'Sepp' Dietrich, was fully committed with the Waffen-SS on the battlefront.

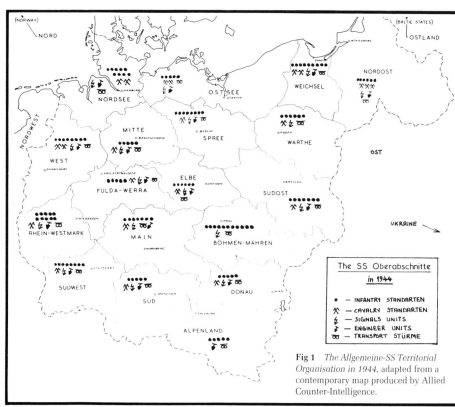

The SS Oberabschnitte
in 1944

● — INFANTRY STANDARTEN
✕ — CAVALRY STANDARTEN
⚡ — SIGNALS UNITS
✦ — ENGINEER UNITS
⬚ — TRANSPORT STÜRME

Fig 1 *The Allgemeine-SS Territorial Organisation in 1944*, adapted from a contemporary map produced by Allied Counter-Intelligence.

24

Directly subordinated to the F. Oa., or HSSPf, was the Stabsführer der Allgemeinen-SS (Allgemeine-SS Chief of Staff) who was responsible to him for the general conduct and control of the Allgemeine-SS within the Oa. The Regional headquarters was staffed primarily by Hauptamtlicher Führer (full-time officers) together with a number of Nebenamtlich (part-time) or Ehrenamtlich (honorary) officials. The full-timers included the Leiter der Verwaltung or Verwaltungsführer (Administrative Officer), the Oberabschnittsarzt (Medical Officer), the Oberabschnittsausbildungsführer (Training Officer), the Oberabschnittspersonalchef (Personnel Officer) and the Nachrichtenführer (Signals Officer). Part-timers were generally below the rank of Sturmbannführer and were not paid for their services.

The 17 SS Oberabschnitte situated within Germany were named and numbered as follows.

Oberabschnitt	HQ	Wehrkreis
Alpenland	Salzburg	XVIII
Donau	Wien	XVII
Elbe	Dresden	IV
Fulda-Werra	Arolsen-Waldeck	IX
Main	Nürnberg	XIII
Mitte	Braunschweig	XI
Nordost	Königsberg	I
Nordsee	Hamburg	X
Ostsee	Stettin	II
Rhein-Westmark	Wiesbaden	XII
Spree	Berlin	III
Süd	München	VII
Südost	Breslau	VIII
Südwest	Stuttgart	V
Warthe	Posen	XXI
Weichsel	Danzig	XX
West	Düsseldorf	VI

(NB: There were no SS Oberabschnitte corresponding to Wehrkreise Nos XIV, XV, XVI and XIX).

In addition to these, there were six foreign Oberabschnitte which evolved during the war, as listed below:

Oberabschnitt	HQ	Region
Böhmen-Mähren	Prague	Czechoslovakia
Nord	Oslo	Norway
Nordwest	The Hague	Holland
Ost	Krakow	Poland
Ostland	Riga	Baltic States
Ukraine	Kiev	Ukraine

Of these six, only Oa. Böhmen-Mähren, which included the Sudetenland, existed long enough to develop an organisation strictly comparable to the Oberabschnitte inside Germany. Oa. Nord and Nordwest co-ordinated police operations and those of the relatively small contingents of Germanic-SS in Norway, Denmark, Holland and Flanders, while Oa. Ost, Ostland and Ukraine directed the miscellaneous security and anti-guerrilla forces in their respective areas.

THE ABSCHNITTE

Each SS Oberabschnitt in turn comprised an average of three Abschnitte or Districts, again distinguished by Roman numerals. They were also referred to by the names of the areas which they covered or by the location of their headquarters. The Abschnitt commander or Führer des Abschnittes (F. Ab.) was generally an officer of the rank of SS-Oberführer or Standartenführer. In 1944, the following Abschnitte were listed:

Abschnitte No	District
I	München/Landshut/Ingolstadt
II	Dresden/Chemnitz/Plauen
III	Berlin-Steglitz
IV	Hannover/Braunschweig/Celle/Göttingen
V	Duisberg/Düsseldorf/Essen/Köln
VI	Breslau/Frankenstein/Glogau
VII	Königsberg/Insterburg/Elbing
VIII	Linz
IX	Würzburg/Nürnberg/Ansbach/Schweinfurt
X	Stuttgart/Tübingen/Ulm
XI	Koblenz/Trier/Darmstadt/Wiesbaden/Bingen
XII	Frankfurt (Oder)/Senftenberg
XIII	Stettin/Köslin/Schneidemühl
XIV	Oldenburg/Cuxhaven/Bremen
XV	Hamburg-Altona/Hamburg-Harburg
XVI	Dessau/Magdeburg/Stassfurt
XVII	Münster/Detmold/Bielefeld/Buer
XVIII	Halle (Saale)/Leipzig/Wittenberg
XIX	Karlsruhe
XX	Kiel/Flensburg
XXI	Hirschberg/Mährisch Schönberg/Jägerndorf/Troppau
XXII	Allenstein/Memel/Zichenau
XXIII	Berlin-Wilmersdorf/Neuruppin/Eberswalde/Potsdam
XXIV	Oppeln/Beuthen/Kattowitz
XXV	Dortmund/Bochum/Hagen
XXVI	Danzig/Zoppot/Marienwerder/Marienburg/Neustadt/Elbing
XXVII	Weimar/Gotha/Gera/Meiningen/Erfurt
XXVIII	Bayreuth/Regensburg/Bamberg
XXIX	Konstanz
XXX	Frankfurt (Main)/Kassel/Giessen
XXXI	Wien/Krems/Znaim
XXXII	Augsburg/Lindau
XXXIII	Schwerin/Greifswald
XXXIV	Saarbrücken/Kaiserslautern/Heidelberg
XXXV	Graz/Klagenfurt/Leoben
XXXVI	Salzburg/Innsbruck
XXXVII	Reichenberg/Trautenau/Brüx/Aussig
XXXVIII	Karlsbad/Eger/Asch
XXXIX	Brünn/Iglau/Prag
XXXX	Bromberg/Tuchel

8

Plate 8 Secret memorandum dated 31 October 1935 from Himmler to the SS-Personalbüro, forerunner of the SS Personalhauptamt, concerning the suitability of SS-Obergruppenführer Friedrich-Wilhelm Krüger to command an SS Oberabschnitt.

9

10

Plate 9 Copy of *Das Schwarze Korps* dated 29
September 1938, the date of the infamous Munich
Agreement which gave the Sudetenland to the
Germans. The cartoon satirises the 'behind the scenes'
machinations of Stalin, his Foreign Minister Litvinov
and their 'pet monkey', President Benes of
Czechoslovakia, while the triumphant headline
proclaims 'An End To The Terror' hitherto endured by
the Sudeten Germans.

Plate 10 Himmler, Wolff and SS-Gruppenführer
Heinrich Schmauser, Führer of Oberabschnitt Süd,
inspecting men of the 34th SS Fuss-Standarte at
Weilheim in December 1934. *Hoffmann*

Plate 11 A detachment from an SS Fuss-Standarte,
preceded by its band and traditional musicians'
'Schellenbaum' or 'Belltree' standard, c1934. *IWM*

Plate 12 An SS reservist poses proudly with his son.
IWM

Abschnitte No	District
XXXXI	Thorn/Kulm
XXXXII	Gnesen/Posen
XXXXIII	Litzmannstadt/Kalisch/Leslau
XXXXIV	Gumbinnen/Memel/Zichenau
XXXXV	Strassburg/Colmar

NB: the expansion of SS membership in a few towns and cities resulted in their being split between two Abschnitte

FUSS-STANDARTEN

The organisation of the Allgemeine-SS in respect of formations below the level of the Abschnitte was on a more flexible unit rather than territorial basis, although each unit itself related to, or was recruited from, a particular area.

The typical Abschnitt controlled an average of three SS Fuss-Standarten, the equivalent of foot or infantry regiments. As the name suggests, the Standarte was the standard unit of the Allgemeine-SS and had been firmly established as such by 1929, long before the SS regional system fully evolved. Every regiment was represented by a 'Deutschland Erwache' feldzeichen or banner, which was itself also known as the regimental 'standarte'. Each

September, at the annual NSDAP rally, Hitler presented these feldzeichen to the commanders of newly-formed Standarten in a semi-religious ceremony during which the flags were touched by the famed blood banner, so linking in spirit the most recent SS members with the martyrs of the Munich Putsch.

Prior to the war, the average Fuss-Standarte comprised around 2,000 men, but corresponding numbers fell to around 1,600 in 1941 and 400 in 1944 due to Allgemeine-SS members being drafted into the Wehrmacht and Waffen-SS. Each regiment was commanded by a Führer des Standartes (F. Sta.) who was assisted by a small staff and part-time headquarters unit. Depending on unit size, the regimental commander could be an SS-Standartenführer, Obersturmbannführer or Sturmbannführer. By 1943, it was common for two of the smaller adjacent Standarten to be placed together under a single acting commander.

Standarten were numbered consecutively from 1 to 126. A select few also bore the names of celebrated SS men who had died or been killed, and such honour titles were similarly extended to a number of Stürme or Companies with certain Standarten.

The following table lists all of the SS Fuss-Standarten with their regimental numbers and locations and, where applicable, Standarte or Sturm honour titles.

Standarte No	Location	Standarte Honour Title	Sturm Honour Title
1.	München	'Julius Schreck'	1. 'Karl Ostberg'
			2. 'Casella'
			5. 'Hellinger'
			10. 'Karl Laforce'
2.	Frankfurt (Main)		4. 'Josef Bleser'
3.	Nürnberg		
4.	Hamburg-Altona		
5.	Luxemburg		
6.	Berlin-Charlottenburg		6. 'Eduard Felsen'
			8. 'Oskar Goll'
			9. 'Kurt von der Ahe'
7.	Plauen	'Friedrich Schlegel'	3. 'Paul Fressonke'
			6. 'Paul Teubner'
8.	Hirschberg		
9.	Stettin		
10.	Kaiserslautern		
11.	Wien	'Planetta'	
12.	Hannover		
13.	Stuttgart		
14.	Gotha		
15.	Neuruppin		
16.	Breslau		
17.	Celle		
18.	Königsberg		
19.	Münster		
20.	Düsseldorf	'Fritz Weitzel'	1. 'Karl Vobis'
			3. 'Kurt Hilmer'
			5. 'Werner Hannemann'
			11. 'Friedrich Schreiber'

Standarte No	Location	Standarte Honour Title	Sturm Honour Title
21.	Magdeburg		
22.	Schwerin	'Friedrich Graf von der Schulenburg'	
23.	Beuthen		
24.	Oldenburg		
25.	Essen		1. 'Garthe'
			3. 'Friedrich Karpinski'
			4. 'Arnold Guse'
			5. 'Leopold Paffrath'
26.	Halle (Saale)		1. 'Paul Berck'
27.	Frankfurt (Oder)		
28.	Hamburg		1. 'Henry Kobert'
			9. 'Hans Cyranka'
29.	Lindau		
30.	Bochum		1. 'Fritz Borawski'
			3. 'August Pfaff'
			11. 'Adolf Höh'
31.	Landshut		4. 'Faust'
			12. 'Andreas Zinkl'
32.	Heidelberg		
33.	Darmstadt		
34.	Weilheim		
35.	Kassel		
36.	Danzig		
37.	Linz		
38.	Graz		
39.	Köslin		
40.	Kiel		1. 'Radke'
			8. 'Martens'
41.	Bayreuth		
42.	Berlin		4. 'Fritz Schulz'
43.	Frankenstein		
44.	Eberswalde		
45.	Oppeln		
46.	Dresden		
47.	Jena		
48.	Leipzig		8. 'Gutsche'
49.	Braunschweig		1. 'Gerhard Landmann'
50.	Flensburg		
51.	Göttingen		
52.	Krems		
53.	Heide		
54.	Landsberg (Warthe)	'Seidel-Dittmarsch'	
55.	Lüneburg		
56.	Bamberg		
57.	Meiningen		
58.	Köln		2. 'Franz Müller'
59.	Dessau	'Loeper'	
60.	Insterburg		
61.	Allenstein		
62.	Karlsruhe		
63.	Tübingen		
64.	Berent		
65.	Freiburg (Br.)		
66.	Bartenstein		
67.	Erfurt		12. 'Fritz Beubler'
68.	Regensburg		
69.	Hagen (Westf.)		
70.	Glogau		
71.	Elbing		1. 'Ernst Ludwig'

Standarte No	Location	Standarte Honour Title	Sturm Honour Title
72.	Detmold		
73.	Ansbach		
74.	Greifswald		
75.	Berlin		8. 'Edmund Behnke'
76.	Salzburg		
77.	Schneidemühl		
78.	Wiesbaden		
79.	Ulm		
80.	Berlin		
81.	Würzburg		2. 'Hans Purps'
82.	Bielefeld		
83.	Giessen		
84.	Chemnitz		4. 'Grobe'
			9. 'Steinbach'
			11. 'Ludwig Frisch'
85.	Saarbrücken		
86.	Offenburg		
87.	Innsbruck		
88.	Bremen		
89.	Wien	'Holzweber'	
90.	Klagenfurt	'Franz Kutschera'	
91.	Wittenberg		
92.	Ingolstadt		
93.	Koblenz		
94.	Leoben		
95.	Trautenau		
96.	Brüx		
97.	Eger		
98.	Mährisch Schönberg		
99.	Znaim		
100.	Reichenberg		
101.	Saaz		
102.	Jägerndorf		
103.	Aussig		
104.	Troppau		
105.	Memel		
106.	Augsburg		
107.	Brünn		
108.	Prag		
109.	Posen		
110.	Hohensalza		
111.	Kolmar		
112.	Litzmannstadt		
113.	Kalisch		
114.	Lesslau		
115.	Zichenau		
116.	Bromberg		
117.	Konitz		
118.	Pr. Stargard		
119.	Graudenz		
120.	Kulm		
121.	Strasburg		
122.	Strassburg		
123.	Kolmar		
124.	Scharley		
125.	Metz		
126.	Marburg/Drau		

NB: a few of the larger towns and cities had more than one Fuss-Standarte.

REITERSTANDARTEN

As well as the Fuss-Standarten, there were 22 Allgemeine-SS cavalry units of regimental size, the Reiterstandarten. Each comprised from five to eight Reiterstürme (Cavalry Companies), a Sanitätsreiterstaffel (medical squad) and a Trompeterkorps (trumpet corps). The Reiterstandarten were never concentrated in their HQ city, the component Companies usually being dispersed amongst smaller towns of the Abschnitte. They were always basically ceremonial in function, and were seldom if ever used to assist the Fuss-Standarten and police in domestic crowd control.

The Inspector of SS Cavalry Training was the equestrian SS–Brigadeführer Christian Weber, one of the old guard Stosstrupp men and veteran of the Munich Putsch. He set up the Main SS Cavalry School, or SS-Hauptreitschule, in Munich which was commanded by Hermann Fegelein until 1939. After the outbreak of war, the majority of members of the Reiterstandarten were conscripted into army cavalry units, or into the hastily mustered SS-Totenkopfreiterstandarten for frontline service. In 1941, the latter amalgamated to form the Waffen-SS Cavalry Brigade which by 1942 had expanded to become the SS-Kavallerie-Division, named 'Florian Geyer' in 1944. All of these formations were commanded during the various stages of their development by Fegelein.

The Allgemeine-SS Reiterstandarten were numbered from 1 to 22, each being prefixed by the letter 'R' to distinguish them from the Fuss-Standarten. Their headquarters were located as follows.

Standarte No	HQ
R.1	Insterburg
R.2	Danzig
R.3	Treuburg
R.4	Hamburg
R.5	Stettin
R.6	Düsseldorf
R.7	Berlin
R.8	Pelkum
R.9	Bremen
R.10	Arolsen
R.11	Breslau
R.12	Schwerin
R.13	Frankfurt (Main)
R.14	Stuttgart
R.15	München
R.16	Dresden
R.17	Regensburg
R.18	Wien
R.19	Graudenz
R.20	Tilsit
R.21	Hannover
R.22	Posen

NB: Several of these locations were former garrison towns of Imperial cavalry regiments and consequently had excellent equestrian facilities.

STURMBANNE AND LOWER FORMATIONS

Each SS Standarte was composed of three active Sturmbanne or battalions, one Reserve-Sturmbann for men between the ages of 35 and 45, and a Musikzug or marching band. A Sturmbann was usually commanded by an SS-Sturmbannführer, assisted by an adjutant. The full peacetime strength of a Sturmbann ranged from 500 to 800 men and, as it was considered the basic tactical unit of the Allgemeine-SS, it was planned that the SS Sturmbann would be able to operate as an independent entity in time of strife or revolt.

The three active Sturmbanne of a Standarte were numbered in Roman numerals from I to III, for example the third Sturmbann of the 41st Standarte was abbreviated 'III/41'. The Reserve-Sturmbann was distinguished by the prefix 'Res.', in this case 'Res./41'.

Each active Sturmbann was in turn composed of four Stürme or Companies, a Sanitätsstaffel (medical squad) and a Spielmannszug (fife-and-drum corps). The full peacetime strength of a Sturm was 120 to 180 men, under an SS-Hauptsturmführer, Obersturmführer or Untersturmführer. During wartime, one of the four Stürme served locally as a Wachkompanie or Guard Company protecting bridges, important buildings and so on. Another stood by as a civil defence Alarmsturm or Emergency Company for use during air raids, and the remaining two were assigned to general patrol duties. A Reserve-Sturmbann generally comprised two Reserve-Stürme, numbered 'Res.1' and 'Res.2', and a Reserve-Sanitätsstaffel.

Within each Standarte, the four Stürme of Sturmbann I were numbered 1, 2, 3 and 4. Those of Sturmbann II were numbered 5, 6, 7 and 8 and those of Sturmbann III were numbered 9, 10, 11 and 12. Thus the 1st Sturm of the 2nd Sturmbann of the 3rd Standarte, ie the 5th Sturm in the 3rd Standarte, would be referred to within the Standarte as '5/II' and outwith the Standarte as '5/3'.

Every Sturm was divided into three or four Truppen (platoons) each composed of three Scharen (sections). A Schar generally numbered 10 to 15 men and was used to patrol blocks of houses within cities and guard official buildings. The Schar itself comprised two or three Rotten (files), the smallest units of the Allgemeine-SS numbering about five men. Depending on their size, Truppen and Scharen were commanded by NCOs of the ranks between SS-Hauptscharführer and Unterscharführer, while Rotten were led by experienced enlisted men known as Rottenführer.

NACHRICHTENSTURMBANNE

Each SS Oberabschnitt was assigned one Nachrichtensturmbann or Signals Battalion, responsible for

SS communications in the Region. These Signals Battalions were numbered consecutively from 1 to 19, in Arabic rather than Roman numerals, prefixed by the letters 'Na.'. Their headquarters were located as follows:

Sturmbann No	HQ
Na.1	München
Na.2	Stuttgart
Na.3	Arolsen
Na.4	Düsseldorf
Na.5	Braunschweig
Na.6	Hamburg
Na.7	Königsberg
Na.8	Berlin
Na.9	Dresden
Na.10	Breslau
Na.11	Nürnberg
Na.12	Stettin
Na.13	Wiesbaden
Na.14	Wien
Na.16	Danzig
Na.17	Posen
Na.19	Prag

NB: No records remain of the locations of Nachrichtensturmbanne Nos 15 and 18

PIONIERSTURMBANNE

Pioniersturmbanne or Engineer Battalions were again organic components of the Oberabschnitte and were equipped to carry out emergency construction work such as road and bridge repairs, and maintenance of public utilities including gas, electricity, water and the like. Each Pioniersturmbann was numbered consecutively from 1 to 16, prefixed by the letters 'Pi.'. Their headquarters were located as follows:

Sturmbann No	HQ
Pi.1	München
Pi.2	Stuttgart
Pi.3	Arolsen
Pi.4	Köln
Pi.5	Harburg-Wilhelmsburg
Pi.6	Stettin
Pi.7	Königsberg
Pi.8	Berlin
Pi.9	Dresden
Pi.10	Breslau
Pi.11	Nürnberg
Pi.12	Magdeburg
Pi.13	Frankfurt (Main)
Pi.14	Wien
Pi.15	Salzburg
Pi.16	Danzig

THE RÖNTGENSTURMBANN SS-HA

The Röntgensturmbann SS-HA, or SS Hauptamt X-Ray Battalion, was composed of 350 full-time SS men and toured all the Allgemeine-SS Oberabschnitte carrying out routine health checks on SS personnel. It utilised portable X-ray equipment and was primarily employed to detect pulmonary diseases among factory workers who were part-time SS members.

The battalion was formed by SS-Obersturmbann-führer Konrad Perwitzschky and was later commanded by SS-Oberführer Dr Hans Holfelder, Professor of Medicine at the University of Frankfurt (Main). The only unit of its kind, its services could be summoned in times of epidemic by any of the NSDAP Gauleiters and it also co-operated with local officials of the German Labour Front. During the war, the Röntgensturmbann was absorbed into the medical branch of the Waffen-SS.

SANITÄTSSTÜRME

In addition to the Sanitätsstaffel attached to every Sturmbann, each Abschnitt contained at least one Sanitätssturm or Medical Company. A group of several such Stürme, or a single large Sturm, was often termed a Sanitätsabteilung (Medical Detachment). These units were referred to by the Roman numeral of the Abschnitt in which they were located.

KRAFTFAHRSTÜRME

SS Kraftfahrstürme or Motor Transport Companies were composed of Staffeln or Squads, one Kraftfahrstaffel being allotted to each Abschnitt. They were responsible for the motorised transport of SS personnel within the District. In addition, a motorcycle company was at the disposal of each Oberabschnitt commander to be used for relaying urgent despatches. Kraftfahrstürme were numbered from 1 to 19, prefixed by the letter 'K'. The areas they covered are listed below:

Sturm No	Area
K.1	München/Augsburg
K.2	Erfurt
K.3	Berlin/Senftenberg
K.4	Hamburg/Kiel/Bremen
K.5	Düsseldorf/Buer/Dortmund
K.6	Dresden/Chemnitz
K.7	Königsberg
K.8	Linz/Wien
K.9	Breslau
K.10	Stuttgart/Karlsruhe/Freiburg

Sturm No	Area
K.11	Magdeburg/Hannover
K.12	Bamberg/Schweinfurt/Nürnberg
K.13	Schwerin/Stettin
K.14	Frankfurt (Main)/Wiesbaden/Pirmasens
K.15	Graz/Innsbruck
K.16	Danzig/Elbing
K.17	Posen/Litzmannstadt
K.19	Asch/Reichenberg/Brünn

NB: No record exists of a Kraftfahrsturm No 18

THE SS-FLIEGERSTURM

The SS-Fliegersturm or SS Flying Company was formed in November 1931 at Munich and remained active until absorbed by the Deutscher Luftsport Verband (DLV), the forerunner of the Luftwaffe, in September 1933. It was responsible for flying Hitler and other senior Nazi personalities around Germany and its most celebrated commander was Eduard Ritter von Schleich, the famed Black Knight of World War I.

THE STREIFENDIENST

What amounted to a military police force for the Allgemeine-SS was brought into being in 1935 with the creation of the SS Streifendienst or Patrol Service. Its functions were policing the SS contingents at Party rallies, checking SS documentation at railway stations and the like, and rooting out any petty criminal elements in the organisation. Streifendienst units were fairly small and mobile and their members were specially selected from amongst the most reliable SS men. Whilst on duty, they wore a gorget bearing the legend 'SS Streifendienst'.

SPORTABTEILUNGEN

Each Oberabschnitt contained a Sportabteilung or Sports Detachment which was responsible for the physical fitness of SS personnel. It also trained with the Hitler Youth and the Allgemeine-SS Reserve.

STAMMABTEILUNGEN

In addition to the regular and specialist SS units, and the first-line reserve of those between the ages of 35 and 45, each Oberabschnitt also contained an independent Stammabteilung or Supplementary Reserve Detachment composed partly of unfit or older men over the age of 45, and partly of younger men whose duties to the State or Party debarred them from taking an active part in the SS. For example, it was customary for full-time regular police officers to be assigned to the Stammabteilung upon receiving SS membership. The Stammabteilung carried the name of the corresponding Oberabschnitt and was divided into Bezirke or sub-districts, each Bezirk working in conjunction with a Standarte and bearing the Arabic numeral of the latter.

As their title indicated, these additional second-line reservists supplemented the rest of the Allgemeine-SS in the various functions where normal duty personnel and first-line reserves might be overtaxed, as in the case of large national parades and celebrations, or major disasters. They were readily distinguishable by the fact that a reverse colour scheme was employed on their uniform insignia, ie a light grey background to collar patches and cuff titles with black or silver numbers and script. For a short time, members of the Stammabteilungen also wore light grey rather than black borders on their armbands.

HELFERINNEN

During the war, German women were called to 'do their bit' in all spheres of life. As more men were conscripted, their work places were taken over by women and in this respect the SS was no exception.

SS Helferinnen, or Female SS Auxiliaries, were first recruited in 1942 to relieve male SS personnel who were more urgently needed at the front. The designation SS Helferin was used only for those who had been accepted as SS members proper and trained at the Reichsschule-SS at Oberehnheim in Elsass, primarily for the Communications Branches of the Allgemeine-SS and Waffen-SS. All other female auxiliaries engaged by the SS, ie those who were not full SS members, were termed Kriegshelferinnen or War Auxiliaries.

Originally, the SS Oberabschnitte were responsible for recruiting SS Helferinnen but in May, 1944 that responsibility was transferred to the SS Hauptamt. Enrolment as an SS Helferin was on a voluntary basis. Official recruiting through newspaper advertisements, radio and cinema was forbidden since careful selection was necessary. Close cooperation was maintained with the Reichsjugendführung and most of the recruiting was done through the Bund Deutscher Mädel or BDM, the female equivalent of the Hitler Youth. All women between the ages of 18 and 35 were eligible to apply. Upon enrolment, the applicant was interviewed by the Senior SS and Police Commander of the Oberabschnitt in which she resided, in the presence of a BDM Liaison Officer, and a medical examination took place the same day. Next, the applicant signed a statement declaring that she had not observed any signs of pregnancy or serious illness, as well as a statement of her racial suitability. No individual could be accepted until a thorough investigation had been completed by the Sicherheitsdienst.

The Reichsschule-SS at Oberehnheim in Elsass had the task of instructing the female auxiliaries for the Communications Branch of the SS. This included their training as teleprinter operators, telephonists and wireless operators. Instruction was also given in domestic science so that SS Helferinnen would be capable of assuming responsibility for SS nurseries and other similar establishments if and when necessary. Upon satisfactory completion of the course, the girls were assigned in groups to the various headquarters of the SS in Germany, Alsace, Lorraine, Luxembourg, Holland, Poland and Russia. During 1943 alone, 422 SS Helferinnen were trained at the Reichsschule.

THE FÖRDERNDE MITGLIEDER

Not all who desired could become members of the SS, but those who wished, for public or private reasons, to stand well with the new élite and who could afford to pay for the privilege were allowed to become Fördernde Mitglieder (FM), or Patron Members.

All Aryan Germans of both sexes were eligible to join the FM organisation, and Party membership was not a necessary qualification. When accepted, each patron was presented with an FM membership book and badge, and bound himself or herself to pay a monthly contribution to SS funds. The contribution varied with the income of the member and could be as low as 1 Reichsmark. The money thus levied from bankers, industrialists, businessmen and shopkeepers strengthened the economic base of the SS, and at the same time the contacts secured in German society enlarged SS influence. The FM members themselves were promised the protection of the SS against 'revolutionary tendencies'. In effect, the FM organisation became a sort of 'old boys network' through which members could secure business deals, promotion or employment, and in the Third Reich virtually replaced the outlawed Society of Freemasons.

By 1935, there were 500,000 Fördernde Mitglieder and there were probably over 1 million in 1943.

An extension to the FM was the practice of appointing selected members of the government or important public figures to high rank in the SS, as Ehrenführer or Honorary Officers. While these appointments had no functional significance, the new members felt their importance enhanced by their semi-military ranks, and the SS secured influential and well-placed allies. The Ehrenführer will be covered in more detail in Chapter 10: The SS and Public Life.

Plate 13   An ornate wine cooler, in hammered silver plate, given to a member of the Nachrichtenzug, 2nd Sturmbann, 3rd SS Fuss-Standarte, as a 27th birthday present from eight of his colleagues.

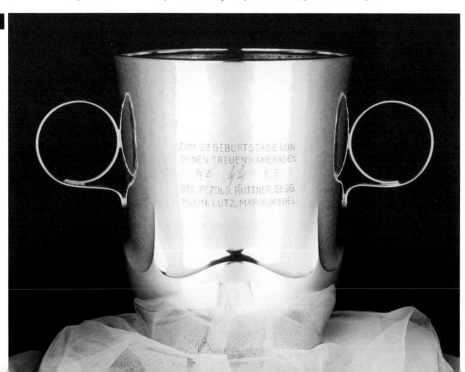

3 Conditions of Service

DUTIES OF THE ALLGEMEINE-SS

Officially, the first and foremost duty of the entire SS organisation was the protection of Adolf Hitler. In 1931, after Hitler had lost the Presidential election to von Hindenburg, Himmler described the SS as 'Des Führers ureigenste, erlesene Garde', the Führer's most personal, selected guards. However, while it is true to say that the earliest Stosstrupp and SS men in the 1920s were indeed directly employed only as Hitler's bodyguards and then as 'Rednerschutz' to protect other leading Nazi orators, the vast majority of the Allgemeine-SS in the 1930s and 1940s never even came into the close proximity of members of the political hierarchy, far less that of the Führer himself whose SS protection after 1933 was the responsibility of the Leibstandarte-SS 'Adolf Hitler' alone. Nevertheless, even in later years the primary SS duty of guarding Hitler was still stressed, the Organisationsbuch der NSDAP declaring in 1937: 'It is the fundamental and most noble task of the SS to be concerned with the safety of the Führer'.

After the advent of the Leibstandarte, whose members worked full-time to a rota system and accompanied Hitler on his journeys throughout the Reich, the part-time SS men who had originally been recruited on a local basis to protect Hitler during his trips around Germany found that aspect of their work taken from them. Consequently, it was decided that as of 1933 the main day-to-day function of these highly-disciplined Allgemeine-SS volunteers would be to bolster the régime by supporting the Police in maintaining public order, especially as some of the Police themselves were politically unreliable. Their immediate success as Hilfspolizei during the mass arrests of Communists and other dissidents after the Nazi assumption of power led to the rapid expansion of the SS organisation and the formation of new Allgemeine-SS Standarten trained and equipped to combat any internal uprising or counter-revolution which might take place within Germany. It was planned that, in such an event, the Allgemeine-SS Fuss-Standarten and Stammabteilungen would act as Police reinforcements in conjunction with the heavily-armed SS-Verfügungstruppe and SS-Totenkopfverbände, while the Nachrichtensturmbanne, Pioniersturmbanne and Kraftfahrstürme of the Allgemeine-SS would take over the operation of the Post Office and national radio network, public utilities and public transport, respectively. However, the anticipated civil unrest never came about and so the Police duties of the Allgemeine-SS before the outbreak of the war were generally restricted to overseeing crowd control at Party rallies and other celebrations, including national holidays and state visits of foreign dignitaries.

After 1939, members of the Allgemeine-SS who had not been called up for military service took a more active Police support role. They were frequently lectured on the work of the Police and SD, and in many cities special SS Wachkompanie and Alarmstürme were detailed to protect factories, bridges, roads and other strategic points and assist the Luftschutz or Civil Defence during air-raids. On the borders of the Reich, SS men worked as Auxiliary Frontier Personnel or Hilfsgrenzangestellte (HIGA) in conjunction with the Customs Service. Others helped with the harvest, supervised foreign labourers and engaged upon welfare work among the families and dependants of deceased SS servicemen. During 1944-45, the cadres of the Allgemeine-SS spread throughout Germany were trained to co-ordinate the short-lived guerrilla fighting which took place against Allied occupation troops.

In winter, the routine activity of the Allgemeine-SS comprised instruction in military matters, indoor shooting, specialist and technical training, lectures on propaganda, political topics and German culture, and talks on the general history and work of the SS and NSDAP. In summer there were route marches, parade and field drill, and manoeuvres. At Party rallies and assemblies the SS always took a prominent role, and in processions had the place of honour at the end of the parade.

The ordinary Allgemeine-SS unit which regularly mustered for training was the Trupp or, in the more populous districts, the Sturm. Larger musters of the SS were possible only as an exceptional procedure. There were periodic gatherings of the Standarten and conferences of Abschnitte officers, when speeches and propaganda displays helped to foster corporate spirit and preserve SS ideology. However, the vast majority of meetings usually took place on a local basis once or twice a week in the evening or at the weekend and gave those attending a feeling of 'belonging' and importance which made a welcome break from the humdrum of their daily lives working in the fields and factories of the Reich.

The great reduction in the number of active part-time personnel which resulted from the war and their temporary enlistment in the Wehrmacht and Waffen-SS considerably reduced the day-to-day activities of the Allgemeine-SS. Even among the members still at home in reserved occupations, long working hours and additional war service drastically cut down attendance at company parades. By 1943, it had become the rule to find SS NCOs in command of Stürme and even Sturmbanne, and for duty parades to be confined to one or two hours per week. Under such circumstances, musters were frequently attended by only a dozen or fewer members.

RECRUITING AND TRAINING

From the day he took charge of the SS in 1929, Himmler set himself the task of creating an aristocracy within the Nazi Party, an élite which he later

Plate 14   SS men guarding Hitler during a speech at Elbing, 5 November 1933. *IWM*

Plate 15   Fanfare trumpeters of the Leibstandarte at the opening ceremony for the Berlin Horse Show in 1934. *IWM*

Plate 16   Anwärter of the Leibstandarte-SS 'Adolf Hitler' take the oath of allegiance in front of the Feldherrnhalle in Munich, 9 November 1934. *IWM*

called his 'Deutsche Männerorden' or Order of German Manhood. The qualifications on which he initially based his policy of selection were those of discipline and high personal standards, but after 1933 racial and political attributes became increasingly important. Whosoever possessed the requisite qualities, whatever his background, class or education, could find a place in the SS.

Many of the first SS men were former members of the Freikorps who had fought against Communist revolutionaries and Allied occupation troops after World War I. They were followed by unemployed labourers, farmers, disillusioned teachers, white collar workers and ex-officers and men of the defeated Imperial armies, all of whom went into the SS during the late 1920s and early 1930s with no aim other than the betterment of their current difficult existence. The year 1933, which Himmler called 'the time of the great influx and flood tide of all those opportunists wishing to join the Party and its various organisations', was the turning point so far as SS recruiting was concerned. After Hitler's election as Chancellor on 30 January that year, everyone suddenly wanted to join the SS and there was a rush at the recruiting offices. Himmler maintained his standards by immediately closing ranks and instituting a vigorous weeding-out process among those already admitted. Between 1933 and 1935, 60,000 SS officers and men were expelled from the organisation because of petty criminal convictions, homosexuality, alcoholism, poor health, inadequate physique, questionable racial or political backgrounds, or simple lack of commitment. The result was an Allgemeine-SS numbering about 210,000 only 0.4% of whom were now unemployed, which did actually constitute the élite Himmler required. It was inevitable, because of this policy, that the ordinary SS units were scattered widely throughout Germany. Concentration would have meant a lowering of standards. As a result, the organisation was spread very thinly across all the rural districts of the Reich, so much so that Himmler could proudly boast in 1936: 'Many SS Truppen are recruited from several villages, a single village never having more than its two really best boys in the SS'. Not surprisingly, the majority of these 'best boys' found that their SS membership, while unpaid, had a real and beneficial knock-on effect on their chosen civilian careers.

After 1933, the Hitler Youth (Hitlerjugend or HJ) was the main source of recruitment for the Allgemeine-SS, excepting of course honorary members, specialists, and those in affiliated bodies such as the police. Potential SS recruits were singled out by local units while still in the HJ, and boys who had proved themselves in the HJ-Streifendienst were made particularly welcome. Out of every 100 applicants, only 10 or 15 were finally admitted. While there were no educational qualifications required, each of these had to demonstrate the good political behaviour of his parents, brothers and sisters, produce a clean police record and an Aryan pedigree dating back to the mid-18th Century, and prove that there was no hereditary disease in his family. A Race Commission composed of SS eugenists and doctors supervised the last and most decisive medical tests. They judged not only the shape of the head and colour of eyes, but also whether the applicant had the right build. Even if he had attained the prescribed minimum height, which altered periodically but was approximately 5ft 10in, he had also to have the correct proportions between the upper and lower leg, and between leg and body. The Commission also considered whether the applicant behaved in a disciplined yet not servile way, and how he answered questions and generally conducted himself. If the applicant satisfied all these requirements of political reliability, racial purity and physique he was officially recognised on his 18th birthday as an SS-Bewerber or SS Candidate, and given a uniform without insignia.

After some preliminary training, the Candidate progressed to the stage of becoming an SS-Anwärter or Cadet on the occasion of the annual NSDAP Reichsparteitag celebrations in Nürnberg the following September. At that time he was provisionally enrolled into the ranks of the SS proper, and received his uniform insignia and Ausweis or membership card. On the following 9 November, the anniversary of the Munich Putsch, he and all other SS-Anwärter appointed that year took the organisation's personal oath of allegiance to the Führer, which ran: 'I swear to you, Adolf Hitler, as Führer and Chancellor of the Reich, loyalty and bravery. I promise to you, and to those you have appointed to have authority over me, obedience unto death.'

Throughout the next few months, the SS-Anwärter continued with his civilian occupation or apprenticeship during the day and attended the set musters of his local Allgemeine-SS Trupp or Sturm in the evenings or at weekends. Much of his training at this stage in his service revolved around his qualifying for the SA Military Sports Badge and the German National Sports Badge, both of which he was expected to win.

Under normal prewar conditions, the SS-Anwärter was thereafter called up first for six months compulsory full-time duty in the Reichsarbeitsdienst or RAD, the Reich Labour Service which worked on public building programmes, and then for his two-year term of conscription in the Wehrmacht. During that period, he almost completely severed his active ties with the Allgemeine-SS. Subsequently, his labouring and military duties finished, he returned to civilian life and to the SS, still as an Anwärter, to receive his final intensive training and indoctrination. This included ideological schooling in the fundamental laws and concepts of the SS, marriage orders and the SS code of honour and discipline.

On 9 November following his return from the Wehrmacht to civilian life, the successful Anwärter was received into the SS as a full SS-Mann. On that solemn occasion he took a second oath, swearing that he and his family would always adhere to the principles of the SS, and was thereafter presented with his SS dagger and the right to use it to defend his honour and that of the Black Corps.

The confirmed SS man remained in the active Allgemeine-SS until his 35th year at which time he was eligible for honourable discharge from the organisation. However, many elected at that stage to apply for acceptance into their local Reserve-Sturm-bann, and at the retirement age of 45 some of those transferred yet again to the Regional Stammabteilung. A series of SS Dienstauszeichnun-gen or long service awards was instituted on 30 January 1938, but these were restricted to the small number of full-time Allgemeine-SS members and to the officers and men of the Leibstandarte, SS-Verfü-gungstruppe and SS-Totenkopfverbände. Part-time members of the Allgemeine-SS, no matter how long their period of service, were eligible to receive only the succession of NSDAP service awards.

Recruiting for the Allgemeine-SS, which was the responsibility of the SS Hauptamt, peaked in 1939 then drastically decreased on the outbreak of war. As early as January 1940, Himmler announced that, of approximately 250,000 regulars in the Allgemeine-SS at the opening of hostilities, 175,000 had since joined the Wehrmacht and Waffen-SS, the majority going to the army. These men retained their Allgemeine-SS membership throughout the war, but due to the commitments of military service were unable to participate in their normal SS duties. By 1944, the total active strength of the Allgemeine-SS had fallen to 40,000 excluding that part of the organisation represented by the German police.

In addition to the general military and political training given to Allgemeine-SS men at local level, at the regular musters of Truppe and Stürme, there were a number of selective and specialist training establishments which members could attend. A batch of NCO and officer candidate schools produced and trained leaders for assignment throughout the whole SS system. As well as the Main Cavalry School at Munich and the Helferinnen Reichsschule at Oberehnheim, there was an SS-Ärztliche Akademie or SS Medical Academy at Graz, an SS-Verwaltungsschule or Administration School at Dachau, a Kraftfahrtechnische Lehranstalt or Motor Technical Training Establishment at Vienna, an SS-Musikschule or Music College at Brunswick, a Pioneer and Mining School at Gisleben, and a Signals School and Security Police Training College at Berlin. There were also a number of special SS-Berufsoberschulen or Higher Technical Schools set up under the auspices of the SS Hauptamt to teach technical skills to candidates for the Allgemeine-SS and Waffen-SS.

One of the less well known but important educational offshoots of the SS were the SS Mannschaft-shäuser or SS Men's Halls. These institutions formed a Dienststelle or branch of the Allgemeine-SS whose function was to train young officers intending to take up civil and non-political professions. They differed, therefore, from the specialist schools of the SS and police and from the Waffen-SS Junkerschulen in that they were designed for SS men who proposed to make their careers in walks of life that had no official connection with the SS, such as the Civil Service, medicine, law, art, science, engineering and the academic field generally. The acknowledged object of their training was to infuse the SS spirit into the higher professions'.

OFFICERS AND PROMOTION

In stark contrast to the Imperial army, promotion in the SS depended upon personal commitment, effectiveness and political reliability, not class or education. 'Das Schwarze Korps' continually denounced the old reactionary military system as typifying that 'middle-class arrogance which excluded the worker from society and gave him the feeling of being a third-class citizen'. Consequently, the SS cadet schools consciously offered something which those of the Wehrmacht never did, an officer's career for men without a middle or upper-class background or formal educational qualifications.

The SS always encouraged self-discipline and mutual respect rather than a brutally enforced discipline, and its general working atmosphere was more relaxed than that of the army, the relationship between officers and men being less formal. Officers were termed 'Führer' or 'leaders', not 'Offiziere' which had class connotations. On duty, the old military rank prefix 'Herr', implying superiority and dominance, was strictly forbidden and even the lowliest SS-Bewerber would address Himmler himself simply as 'Reichsführer', not 'Herr Reichsführer'. Off duty, junior ranks referred to their seniors as 'Kamerad' (Comrade), or 'Parteigenosse' (Party Colleague) if both were members of the NSDAP.

The SS-Führerkorps or Officer Corps of the Allgemeine-SS comprised a number of different categories, mainly dependent upon the nature of the officer's employment. Those below the rank of Sturmbannführer were generally Nebenamtlich or part-time, and unpaid, while higher ranks were usually Hauptamtlich or full-time, and salaried. The main categories of SS officers were as follows:

(i) *Aktive SS Führer* (Active SS Officers)
     All those who held regular part-time or full-time office in the local Allgemeine-SS, SS Hauptämter or other departments, including all officers of the rank of Gruppenführer and above irrespective of employment.

(ii) *Zugeteilte Führer bei den Stäben* (Officers attached to Staffs and Headquarters)
     Officers prevented by reason of their civil, governmental or Party posts from taking an active

39

Plate 17   A newly-commissioned Untersturmführer of the SS-VT, as depicted by Wolfgang Willrich in 1936.

Plate 18   The SS Officers Seniority List, produced in several volumes at the end of 1944.

Plate 19   The first entries in the 1944 Dienstaltersliste, giving relevant details about Himmler and his most senior SS Generals.

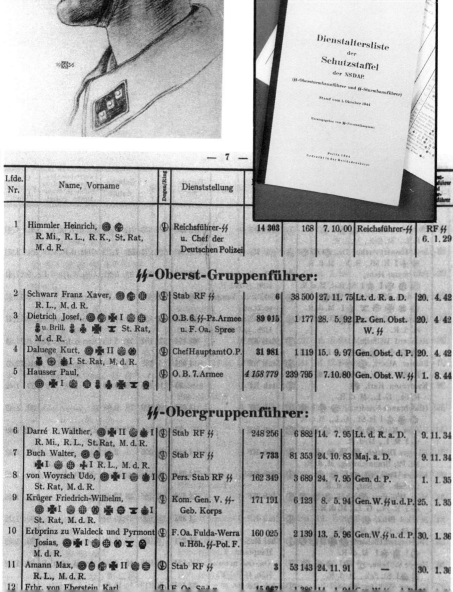

— 7 —

Lfde. Nr.	Name, Vorname	Degen/Ring	Dienststellung				führer	führer
1	Himmler Heinrich, ⊚ ✿ R. Mi., R. L., R. K., St. Rat, M. d. R.	Ⓛ	Reichsführer-SS u. Chef der Deutschen Polizei	14 303	168	7. 10. 00	Reichsführer-SS	RF SS 6. 1. 29

SS-Oberst-Gruppenführer:

2	Schwarz Franz Xaver, ⊚✿⊕ R. L., M. d. R.	Ⓛ	Stab RF SS	6	38 500	27. 11. 75	Lt. d. R. a. D.	20. 4. 42
3	Dietrich Josef, ⊚✿✠I⊕✿ ⚶ u. Brill. ⚶ ✠ ⚶ ✠ St. Rat, M. d. R.	Ⓛ	O.B. 6. SS-Pz.Armee u. F. Oa. Spree	89 015	1 177	28. 5. 92	Pz. Gen. Obst. W. SS	20. 4 42
4	Daluege Kurt, ⊚✠II⊕✿ ✠ ⊕ ✠I St. Rat, M. d. R.	Ⓛ	ChefHauptamtO.P.	31 981	1 119	15. 9. 97	Gen. Obst. d. P.	20. 4. 42
5	Hausser Paul, ⊚✠I⊕⊕⚶✠✠I⊕	Ⓛ	O. B. 7. Armee	4 158 779	239 795	7. 10. 80	Gen. Obst. W. SS	1. 8. 44

SS-Obergruppenführer:

6	Darré R. Walther, ⊚✠II⊕✿I R. Mi., R. L., St. Rat, M. d. R.	Ⓛ	Stab RF SS	248 256	6 882	14. 7. 95	Lt. d. R. a. D.	9. 11. 34
7	Buch Walter, ⊚⊕✿ ✠I⊕ ✠I R. L., M. d. R.	Ⓛ	Stab RF SS	7 733	81 353	24. 10. 83	Maj. a. D.	9. 11. 34
8	von Woyrsch Udo, ⊚✠I⊕✠I Ⓛ St. Rat, M. d. R.		Pers. Stab RF SS	162 349	3 689	24. 7. 95	Gen. d. P.	1. 1. 35
9	Krüger Friedrich-Wilhelm, ⊚✠I⊕⊕⊕✠⚶✠I St. Rat, M. d. R.	Ⓛ	Kom. Gen. V. SS-Geb. Korps	171 191	6 123	8. 5. 94	Gen.W.SS u.d.P.	25. 1. 35
10	Erbprinz zu Waldeck und Pyrmont Josias, ⊚✠I⊕⊕⊕⚶ ✿ M. d. R.	Ⓛ	F. Oa. Fulda-Werra u. Höh. SS-Pol. F.	160 025	2 139	13. 5. 96	Gen.W.SS u.d.P.	30. 1. 36
11	Amann Max, ⊚⊕✿✠II⊕✿ R. L., M. d. R.	Ⓛ	Stab RF SS	3	53 143	24. 11. 91	—	30. 1. 36
12	Frhr. von Eberstein Karl	Ⓛ	F. Oa. Süd...	15 067	1 ...			

part in the SS. They were normally attached as advisers to the Persönlicher Stab RfSS, or to the staffs of the SS Hauptämter or Oberabschnitte HQs.

(iii) *Führer in der Stammabteilung* (Officers in the Supplementary Reserve)
Officers not included in the foregoing two categories who were obliged by reason of age or infirmity to retire honourably from active service in the SS or first-line SS reserve. The majority of full-time police officers given SS membership were also taken into the Stammabteilung as they could not readily be absorbed by the active Allgemeine-SS Standarten.

(iv) *Führer zu Verfügung* (Officers 'On Call')
Officers suspended for disciplinary reasons whom the SS court had put 'on call' for a maximum period of two years, as a term of probation. Within that period, depending upon their behaviour, they were either restored to active service or dismissed from the SS.

Any Allgemeine-SS officer who joined the Waffen-SS during the war retained his Allgemeine-SS position and rank, but usually received a lower Waffen-SS rank until such time as he had gained sufficient military experience to warrant promotion. Thereafter, any promotion he achieved within the Waffen-SS resulted in a simultaneous and level upgrading of his Allgemeine-SS rank. The following regulations governed promotion within the Allgemeine-SS:

(i) Promotion to SS-Gruppenführer and above was decided by Hitler himself, in his technical capacity as Commander-in-Chief of the SS on the recommendation of the Reichsführer-SS.

(ii) Promotion of officers below the rank of Gruppenführer was decided by the Reichsführer-SS at the instance of the SS Personalhauptamt. The heads of the SS Hauptämter, acting as Himmler's representatives, could carry out promotions up to and including SS-Hauptsturmführer.

(iii) Promotion to SS-Hauptscharführer was effected by Oberabschnitte commanders.

(iv) Promotion to SS-Oberscharführer was carried out by Abschnitte commanders.

(v) Other NCOs were promoted by the commanders of the various SS Standarten.

(vi) Nominations for appointment as SS-Mann, Sturmmann and Rottenführer were made by delegated officers of the Standarten concerned.

Technical, administrative and medical personnel were bound by the same regulations as regards promotion and appointment but, in addition had to be approved by the SS Wirtschafts- und Verwaltungshauptamt or the Reichsarzt SS und Polizei, whichever was appropriate.

PERSONNEL RECORDS AND THE DIENSTALTERSLISTE

The SS maintained a thorough system of personnel records, based on cards filled out in triplicate in respect of each member. The cards were reddish-brown in colour and contained a host of personal details including date and place of birth, physical measurements, marriage particulars, names and ages of children, SS and Party membership numbers, promotions, decorations and history of RAD and military service. All fixed information was entered in ink and variable information in pencil. Every Sturm maintained a file holding the original cards made out for each officer and man assigned to it. Duplicate cards, which had broad red diagonal stripes on the reverse, were kept at the HQ of the Standarte to which the Sturm belonged. The third set of cards, with dark green stripes at the back, were filed at the SS Personalhauptamt if they related to officers or at the SS Hauptamt if they referred to NCOs and lower ranks. It was the responsibility of all personnel to ensure that they reported timeously any information relevant to the updating of their records.

Several times a year, the SS Personalhauptamt produced a Seniority List covering all officers in all branches of the SS. As the SS grew so did the list, and by the end of 1944 it comprised several volumes. Known as the 'Dienstalterliste der Schutzstaffel der NSDAP', it was printed by the government publishers in Berlin and was intended for administrative use only within the offices of the SS. Being classified, it was not for personal issue or distribution to non-SS bodies. Above all, it was not to be made available to the public.

The Dienstalterliste went into great detail about each officer listed. Not only did it state his full name and date of birth, it also gave his SS rank, position of seniority, NSDAP and SS membership numbers, current posting, decorations, and any governmental, military, political or police rank held. It even mentioned if he was on long-term sick leave.

In April 1945, the SS made concerted attempts to destroy all existing copies of the Dienstalterliste, but a few volumes fell into Allied hands and these proved invaluable reference material during the postwar de-Nazification process. Many prominent Germans who were by then vigorously denying all association with the NSDAP and its affiliated organisations were suddenly confronted with their names appearing on the Dienstalterliste and were forced to admit their intimate involvement in the Nazi régime. One of those was none other than Josias, Erbprinz zu Waldeck and Pyrmont, the only member of a German royal house to be tried for war crimes. As commander of the Oberabschnitt in which Buchenwald Concentration Camp was situated, he was held to be directly responsible for the conditions which prevailed there and was sentenced to life imprisonment.

THE SS LEGAL SYSTEM, DISCIPLINE AND COURTS OF HONOUR

One of the most important factors to be taken into account when considering the swingeing powers and activities of the various SS and police forces in their role as supreme guardians of law and order during the Third Reich, is that they were themselves placed outside and above the normal German legal system. With the foundation of the SS- und Polizeigerichtsbarkeit (Special Jurisdiction of the SS and Police) during 1939-40, SS men were made responsible only to SS disciplinary officers and SS courts for all crimes and offences committed both inside and outside Germany. The very nature of their work meant that SS members frequently had to infringe the common law in the execution of their duties, and so to achieve its ends the SS hierarchy demanded and ultimately achieved the legal independence necessary to ensure that SS men should not be answerable to the civil courts for unlawful acts committed in the line of duty. The significance of this position cannot be over-emphasized, as it guaranteed the whole SS organisation immunity from normal prosecution and hence the legal right, according to its own code, to arrest, imprison, ill-treat and ultimately exterminate its political and racial opponents.

The original decrees and regulations establishing the Special Jurisdiction of the SS and Police continued to be enlarged and supplemented in the years after 1940. On 1 September 1943, the final and definitive SS Disciplinary and Penal Code (Disziplinarstraf- und Beschwerdeordnung der SS, or DBO) came into effect. It was valid for every member of the SS without exception. All SS officers, NCOs and other ranks, male and female, whether Allgemeine-SS, Waffen-SS, full-time, part-time, trainee, auxiliary, inactive or honorary in status, were liable to trial and punishment only by SS courts for all disciplinary and criminal offences they might commit. Where the offences were military ones, they were tried according to military procedures. In the case of criminal offences, the SS legal officials tried the accused by normal German criminal procedure. The jurisdiction of the DBO extended right across Germany and the occupied territories and the scale of punishments which might be inflicted ranged from simple disciplinary measures and expulsion from the SS to penal servitude and death by hanging, shooting or beheading. The only course of appeal, and then only on special occasions, was to the Führer himself.

While in practice most disciplinary matters were disposed of by the competent SS senior disciplinary officers by direct action or courts-martial, and most criminal matters by the duly appointed SS courts, full disciplinary powers were attached to Himmler personally, as Reichsführer-SS. He was competent to impose all disciplinary penalties allowed by the DBO, although Hitler usually took a personal inter-

est in the punishment of officers from Gruppenführer upwards. In particular, the Reichsführer reserved to himself the rights of:

(i) dismissal from the SS, together with demotion or reduction to the ranks, of any SS officer;

(ii) dismissal from the SS of any SS members from numbers 1 to 10,000 (ie, the Old Guard); and

(iii) prescribing disciplinary punishments in addition to penal sentences passed by the SS courts.

In order to exercise these powers, and also for the purpose of considering appeals against disciplinary sentences passed by the heads of the SS Hauptämter, Himmler could order the setting up of a special court or Disziplinarhof to hear any particular case and report back to him. In times of absence, he could also delegate his disciplinary authority to the Chief of the Hauptamt SS Gericht. In addition, a special legal officer was permanently attached to the Persönlicher Stab RfSS to assist Himmler in dealing with legal matters which came to him for disposal.

The ordinary SS courts were of two types:

(i) the Feldgerichte or Courts-Martial, convened in the normal way by the divisions and higher formations of the Waffen-SS; and

(ii) the SS und Polizei Gerichte or SS and Police Courts, established in Germany and the occupied territories.

By 1943, there were over 40 of these SS und Polizei Gerichte. Outside the Reich they were set up in the capitals and larger towns of conquered countries. Inside Germany there was one in every Oberabschnitt, normally but not invariably at the seat of the Oberabschnitt HQ. They were numbered in Roman figures which, unlike the Oberabschnitte, did not follow Wehrkreis numbering but corresponded to the chronological order in which they were set up. Each SS and Police Court was competent to try all cases which occurred within its area.

In addition, there were two other courts, both based in Munich, which deserve special mention. The first of these was the Oberstes SS und Polizei Gericht, the Supreme SS and Police Court, presided over by SS-Oberführer Dr Günther Reinecke. It tried cases of particular gravity, for example treason, attempts on the life of the Führer or Reichsführer, crimes against the State, and espionage. It was also the only competent tribunal for the trial of SS and police generals of the rank of Brigadeführer and above. The second of the special courts was the SS und Polizei Gericht z.b.V., or Extraordinary SS and Police Court. It was attached directly to the Hauptamt SS Gericht and was a secret tribunal which dealt with delicate and difficult cases which it was desired to keep from the general knowledge even of the SS itself.

In common with the other formations and affiliated organisations of the NSDAP, the SS had its own code of honour enforced by special Courts of Honour or Schiedshofe. This code had two primary objects, firstly to protect the general repute of the SS against the scandal of internal dissension and quarrels, and secondly to provide its individual members with a formal method of defending their own honour with weapons. In dealing with cases which came under the first category, the Courts of Honour had only limited powers, their main function being to reconcile differences by means of arbitration. As regards cases in the second category, their purpose was to see that 'affairs of honour' were settled according to due form. In principle, all SS men were entitled to demand satisfaction with pistol or sword for affronts to their honour and integrity. However, the Schiedshofe usually intervened to prevent matters proceeding to an actual duel, particularly as Hitler had long set his face against the practice.

A special class of SS legal officers or SS Richter existed to administer SS law. Full-time officials held their commissions directly from the Führer and their status and independence were guaranteed by the Reichsführer-SS. Their main duty was to prepare cases and conduct proceedings in court. These SS Richter were helped, and on occasion represented, by assistant legal officers or SS Hilfsrichter. SS protocol officers and NCOs (SS Beurkundungsführer und Unterführer) dealt with the preparation of documents, and examining officers (Untersuchungsführer) interviewed witnesses. All of these officers were subordinated to the Hauptamt SS Gericht. Their initial training and subsequent examinations took place at the Hauptamt and all appointments and promotions were issued from there.

As soon as the Special Jurisdiction of the SS and Police was legally established, measures were taken to provide the SS organisation with facilities for carrying out sentences imposed by its courts. For this purpose punishment camps for the SS and police (Straflager der SS und Polizei) were set up at Dachau, near to the concentration camp, and at Karlsfeld. Moreover, prison camps (Strafvollzugslager) were instituted at Danzig and Ludwigsfelde.

Minor periods of detention were generally completed in the relatively comfortable surroundings of the prison quarters of the SS barracks at Munich. Longer terms of imprisonment were served in one of the Strafvollzugslager. Execution of such sentences might at any time be postponed and the prisoner remitted to a Straflager, which represented an intensification in the severity of the sentence in that conditions at the punishment camps were worse than those in the prisons and the period served in the Straflager did not count towards the legal term of imprisonment still pending.

For men dismissed from the SS during the war, and simultaneously sentenced to a term of impris-

onment, another possibility was open. They might choose to be handed over to one of the following two special formations of the Waffen-SS, in an attempt to redeem themselves while working out part of their sentence.

(i)   The Rehabilitation Detachment (Bewährungs Abteilung) at Chlum in Bohemia. After a period of initial training there, the men were sent to units employed as fighting troops in the frontline.

(ii) The Labour Detachment (Arbeits Abteilung) based at Debica in Poland. Members of that unit did not normally bear arms but were employed on heavy and dangerous work at the front, including bridge repair and minefield clearance.

For men dismissed from the police there was a similar formation attached to the SS-Police-Division, officially entitled the Sondereinheit der SS-Polizei-Division but colloquially known as the 'Verlorene Haufen' or VH, the 'Lost Souls'. Members of these special units did not rank as SS or police men and did not wear SS or police insignia on their uniforms.

MEDICAL AND WELFARE SERVICES

The Reichsarzt SS und Polizei or Chief SS and Police Medical Officer, SS-Obergruppenführer Prof Dr Ernst-Robert Grawitz, was responsible for the general supervision of all the medical services of the SS and police, for medical research and training, and for the control and distribution of medical supplies and equipment. He was assisted by two senior officials, the Chief Medical Quartermaster, SS-Gruppenführer Dr Carl Blumenreuter, and the Chief Hygiene Officer, SS-Oberführer Prof. Dr Joachim Mrugowsky. Grawitz was also Business President of the German Red Cross and used that position to ensure that the SS kept up to date with all the latest international medical developments. Moreover, Himmler purposely gave senior SS rank to many German doctors of renown, including Karl Gebhardt, head of the famous Hohenlychen Orthopaedic Clinic, and Leonardo Conti, the Reich Minister of Health. In this way, the SS was kept at the forefront of medical technology and the Sanitätsstürme and Sanitätsstaffeln attached to Abschnitte and Sturmbanne were able to provide the best treatment possible to ailing SS members and their families.

The whole relationship between the SS and most medical men came to be soured during the war, however, when Himmler was persuaded by his hard pressed Waffen-SS battlefield surgeons and certain military scientists to allow live research to take place amongst condemned inmates of concentration camps. The Luftwaffe doctor Sigmund Rascher was one of those 'researchers' with the most sinister reputation. He carried out meaningless medical experiments at Dachau on the effects of decompression on prisoners, and thereafter turned his attention to the problems of survival in cold conditions, then survival in extreme heat. Eventually the SS concluded that Rascher was nothing more than a dangerous charlatan evading frontline service, and sentenced him to death in April 1945. However, not all medical studies carried out at the camps were of such a fantastic nature. One of the benefits others provided was the development of haemostatic and coagulant products which did much to help wounded men in the Wehrmacht during World War 2 and, indeed, injured soldiers of all nations thereafter. Nevertheless, even the ordinary doctors of the Allgemeine-SS, whose only concern was the welfare of their men and who had nothing whatsoever to do with these matters, eventually came to be tarred with the same brush as Rascher and his accomplices in the minds of the postwar public.

Medicine apart, the main welfare activities of the Allgemeine-SS were administered by the Rasse- und Siedlungshauptamt and financed from the private funds of the SS. The concept of the SS as 'one big family' resulted in considerable care being devoted to the provision of financial help for those members in need of it. Even in the early days of the organisation, before the profits of office and established position put the finances of the SS on a sound footing, a special Economic Assistance Section was set up under the auspices of the Persönlicher Stab RfSS to provide help to SS men who had suffered material loss during the struggle for power. It also loaned money to poorer SS members to enable them to purchase items of uniform and equipment and, in some cases, liquidated their debts. In November 1935, Himmler put the matter on a more businesslike basis by instituting a savings fund to which all future SS recruits in employment and all serving full-time officers and men were to contribute according to their means. In this way, the SS was able to build from its own resources the necessary financial reserve from which assistance could be given or loans made to its members.

All commanders of Oberabschnitte, Abschnitte, Standarten and Sturmbanne had a general duty to look after the welfare of their subordinates and particularly of the widows and orphans of deceased SS men. Each Abschnitt and Standarte had a welfare official or Fürsorgereferent, usually an NCO, who was the primary local authority to which SS men and their relatives could appeal. Questions outside his competence were referred to the Sippenpflegestelle (Family Welfare Office) of the Oberabschnitt and, if required, could be passed on up yet again to the Sippenamt or Family Office of the Rasse- und Siedlungshauptamt for a decision. Where an SS man died or was killed on active service and left a widow and children, the Oberabschnitt appointed a suitable SS man as Berater or family advisor. He then gave as much personal advice and

help as was possible, assumed responsibility for the education of the children and, when necessary, called in the assistance of the welfare official.

SPORTING ACTIVITIES

Sport and fitness were given great emphasis in the day to day training programmes of the Allgemeine-SS, and there were many local SS sports clubs. Members were eligible to win not only the SA Military Sports Badge and German National Sports Badge, which they strove for during their term as SS-Anwärter, but also the Achievement and Championship Badges of the National Socialist Physical Training League, the Heavy Athletics Badge, the German Motor Sports Badge, Ski Competition Badges, and the various National Equestrian Awards. Many of these decorations had to be competed for annually, ie holders had to pass qualification tests at least once every year in order to retain the right to wear the badges concerned, so training was a continual process.

The Reichssportführer or National Sports Leader was an SA-Obergruppenführer, Hans von Tschammer und Osten, and consequently the SA tended to organise most of the paramilitary competitive sports events during the Third Reich. At these domestic competitions, however, the SS and police teams always figured prominently and invariably dominated the scene. In February 1937, for example, the SS won the Führer's Prize at the NSDAP Ski Championships at Rottach-Egern, and Himmler and von Tschammer und Osten were present to award it. Internationally, too, SS men made their mark. Hermann Fegelein led Germany's famed equestrian squad in the 1936 Olympics, and the SS motorcycle team of Zimmermann, Mundhenke, Patina and Knees, all wearing green leathers emblazoned with the SS runes, won the Six Day Trial at Donnington in England in July 1938. Later the same year, an SD team headed by Heydrich himself and comprising von Friedenfeldt, Hainke, Liebscher and Losert, all graduates of the SS-Fechtschule or SS Fencing School at Bernau, emerged victorious from the International Sabre Competition in Berlin. Finally, in April 1940, Italy's famous Gran Premio di Brescia motor racing event was won by the SS driver von Manstein in a BMW 328 coupé.

To forge these soldier-athletes, the SS spared no expense. The facilities of the Waffen-SS Officer's School at Bad Tölz, for instance, included a stadium for soccer and track and field events, separate halls for boxing, gymnastics and indoor games, a heated swimming pool and a sauna. The athletics programme emphasised group exercises and SS teams competed successfully against their rivals from the Wehrmacht. Not surprisingly, SS physical training establishments attracted outstanding talent, and at one time eight out of the 12 coaches at Bad Tölz were national champions in their events.

44

THE DEATH'S HEAD

Of all SS uniform trappings and insignia, the one emblem which endured throughout the history of the organisation and became firmly associated with it was the death's head or totenkopf, an eerie motif comprising a skull and crossed bones. It has often been assumed that the death's head was adopted simply to strike terror into the hearts of those who saw it. However, that was not so. It was chosen as a direct and emotional link with the past, and in particular with the élite military units of Imperial Germany.

In 1740, a large right-facing jawless death's head with the bones lying behind the skull, embroidered in silver bullion, adorned the black funeral trappings of the Prussian king, Friedrich Wilhelm I. In his memory, the Leib-Husaren Regiments Nos 1 and 2, élite Prussian Royal Bodyguard units which were formed the following year, took black as the colour of their uniforms and wore a massive totenkopf of similar design on their pelzmützen or busbies. The State of Brunswick followed suit in 1809 when the death's head was adopted by its Hussar Regiment No 17 and the third battalion of Infantry Regiment No 92. The Brunswick totenkopf differed slightly in design from the Prussian one, with the skull facing forward and situated directly above the crossed bones.

During World War 1, the death's head was chosen as a formation symbol by a number of crack German army units, particularly the storm troops, flamethrower detachments and tank battalions. Several pilots of the Schutzstaffeln, including the air ace Leutnant Georg von Hantelmann, also used variants of it as personal emblems. Almost immediately after the end of hostilities in 1918 the death's head could be seen again, this time painted on the helmets and vehicles of some of the finest and most famous Freikorps. Because of its association with these formations it became symbolic not only of wartime daring and self-sacrifice but also of postwar traditionalism, anti-liberalism and anti-Bolshevism. Nationalist ex-servicemen even had death's head rings, cuff links, tie pins and other adornments privately made for wear with their civilian clothes.

It is not surprising, therefore, that members of the Stosstrupp Adolf Hitler eagerly took the totenkopf as their distinctive emblem in 1923, initially acquiring a small stock of appropriate army surplus cap badges. Their successors in the SS thereafter contracted the firm of Deschler in Munich to restrike large quantities of the Prussian-style jawless death's head which they used on their headgear for the next 11 years. As Hitler's personal guards, they liked to model themselves on the Imperial Bodyguard Hussars, who had become known as the 'Schwarze Totenkopfhusaren' or 'Black Death's Head Hussars', and were fond of singing their old regimental song with its emotive verse:

In black we are dressed,
In blood we are drenched,
Death's Head on our helmets.
Hurrah! Hurrah!
We stand unshaken!

When, in 1934, the Prussian-style totenkopf began to be used as an élite badge by the new army panzer units which were, after all, the natural successors to the Imperial cavalry regiments, the SS devised its own unique pattern of grinning death's head, with lower jaw, which it wore thereafter.

The 1934-pattern SS totenkopf ultimately took various forms, right-facing, left-facing, and front-facing and appeared on the cloth headgear of all SS members and on the tunics and vehicles of the SS-Totenkopfverbände and Waffen-SS Totenkopf-Division. It was the centrepiece of the famed SS Death's Head Ring and could be seen on dagger and gorget suspension chains, mess jackets, flags, standards, drum covers, trumpet banners and the SS and police Guerrilla Warfare Badge. Moreover, because of its direct associations with Danzig, where the Prussian Leib-Husaren Regiments had been garrisoned until 1918, it was selected as the special formation badge of the SS-Heimwehr Danzig and the Danzig Police and Fire Services. Himmler wanted his men to be proud of their heritage and there is no doubt that the honourable associations of the German death's head were well used to that end. It became an instant status symbol in the Third Reich and an inspiration to those who were granted the privilege of wearing it.

THE TRADITIONAL UNIFORM

The earliest Nazis wore normal civilian clothing and were distinguished only by their crudely hand-made kampfbinde, or swastika armbands, worn on the left upper arm. With the advent of the paramilitary SA in 1921, however, it became necessary to evolve a uniform specifically for its members. At first, their dress lacked any consistency and was characteristically Freikorps in style, generally taking the form of field-grey army surplus double-breasted windcheater jackets, waist belts with cross-straps, grey trousers, trench boots, steel helmets and mountain caps. Many SA men simply retained the uniforms they had worn during the 1914-18 war, stripped of badges. The swastika armband was the only constant feature, sometimes bearing a metal numeral or emblem to indicate unit identity and a metal 'pip' or cloth stripes to denote rank. In 1923, members of the Stabswache and Stosstrupp Adolf Hitler wore similar garb with the addition of a Prussian-style death's head on the cap, usually surmounted by the 'Reichskokarde', a circular metal cockade in the Imperial colours of black, white and red. After the failure of the Munich Putsch and the banning of the SA and Stosstrupp, the men contin-

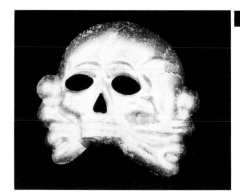

Plate 20 Prussian-style Death's Head, adopted by the Stosstrupp Adolf Hitler in 1923 and worn by the SS until 1934.

Plate 21 Austrian 1916-pattern steel helmet subsequently used by a German Freikorps unit, c1919-20. The large white hand-painted Totenkopf is in the Brunswick style.

Plate 22 1934-pattern SS Death's Head. This particular example is of exceptional quality and was produced by the renowned firm of Deschler in Munich.

Plate 23 SS 1925-pattern armband, of multi-piece construction. The swastika alone comprises six separate silken strips.

Plate 24 Men of the newly-formed SS proudly display an NSDAP Feldzeichen at the end of 1925. Note the wild variety of dress, particularly the short-lived 'Krätzchen' field caps with massive eagle insignia, and the assorted belt buckles. *Hoffmann*

Plate 25 Protected by SS men, NSDAP Treasurer Franz Xaver Schwarz (left, in overcoat) watches a parade in his home town of Günzburg, September 1929. Himmler stands nearest the camera. His kepi features the recently introduced eagle and swastika, and his position of seniority is indicated solely by the three white stripes of an NSDAP Reichsleiter on his SS armband. *Hoffmann*

ued to wear their old uniforms as members of the Frontbanne, adding a steel helmet badge to the centre of the swastika armband.

At the end of 1924 Leutnant Gerhard Rossbach, formerly one of the most famous of the Freikorps and SA leaders, acquired a bargain lot of surplus German army tropical brown shirts in Austria. These items were, in reality, not shirts at all, but blouses with collars and pockets which were worn over an ordinary collarless shirt. When the NSDAP was reconstituted and the SA reactivated in February 1925, Hitler kitted his men out with these readily available shirts and had ties, breeches and kepis made to match. Thus by chance circumstances rather than design, brown became the adopted colour of the SA and the Nazi Party in general.

When the Stosstrupp was reformed in April of the same year, under the titles Schutzkommando then Sturmstaffel, its members too were issued with brown shirts. To distinguish them from the SA, however, they retained their death's heads and wore black kepis, black ties, black breeches and black borders to the swastika armband. By 9 November 1925, when the term Schutzstaffel was adopted, the brown shirt with black accoutrements was firmly established as the 'traditional uniform' of the SS. The vast majority of SS men, who were also members of the NSDAP, wore the Nazi Party Badge on their ties.

On 9 November 1926, the rapidly expanding SA introduced collar patches or Kragenspiegel to indicate unit and rank, replacing the badges and stripes formerly worn on the armband. The right patch bore unit numerals and the left patch a Stahlhelm-style system of rank pips, bars and oakleaves. By contrasting the colour of the patch with that of the numerals, an attempt was made to reflect the State colours of the district in which the unit concerned was located, eg Berlin SA men wore black and white patches, Hamburg SA men red and white, Munich men blue and white, and so on. This arrangement proved difficult to sustain and the colour combinations ultimately underwent a number of changes. SA unit patches were particularly complex, accommodating not only Standarte, specialist and staff appointments but also Sturmbann and Sturm designations.

In August 1929, the SS likewise introduced collar patches to denote rank and unit. As with the SA, rank was shown on the left patch, or both patches for Standartenführer and above, with unit markings on the right patch. However, the SS system was much more simplified than that of the SA. All SS collar patches were black in colour with white, silver or grey numerals, pips, bars and oakleaves. Moreover, the unit collar patches were restricted to indicating Standarte, specialist or staff appointments. To show Sturmbann and Sturm membership, the SS devised their own complicated system of cuff titles, narrow black bands worn on the lower left sleeve. Within every Fuss-Standarte, each Sturmbann was assigned a colour which bordered

the upper and lower edges of the cuff title. The prescribed Sturmbanne colours were:

Sturmbann I	–	Green
Sturmbann II	–	Dark Blue
Sturmbann III	–	Red
Sturmbann IV (Reserve)	–	Light Blue

The number and, if appropriate, honour name of the wearer's Sturm appeared embroidered in grey or silver thread on the title. Thus a member of the 2nd Sturm, 1st Sturmbann, 41st SS Fuss-Standarte would wear a green-bordered cuff title bearing the numeral '2' in conjunction with the number '41' on his right collar patch. A man in the 11th Sturm 'Adolf Höh', 3rd Sturmbann, 30th SS Fuss-Standarte would sport a red-edged cuff title with the legend '11 Adolf Höh',and regimental numeral '30' on the right collar patch. All members of Allgemeine-SS cavalry units had yellow-edged cuff titles while those of signals and pioneer formations had their titles bordered in brown and black, respectively. A relatively small number of cuff titles bore Roman numerals or designations relating to staff or specialist appointments.

During the autumn of 1929, at the same time as the new SS collar patches and cuff titles were being manufactured and distributed, a small sharp-winged eagle and swastika badge, or hoheitsabzeichen, was introduced for wear on the SA and SS kepi in place of the Reichskokarde. SS bandsmen's uniforms were further modified by the addition of black and white military style 'swallow's nests' worn at the shoulder.

At the end of 1931, the SS adopted the motto 'Meine Ehre heisst Treue' ('My Honour is Loyalty') following upon a well-publicised open letter which Hitler had sent to Kurt Daluege after the Stennes Putsch, declaring in his praise: 'SS Mann, deine Ehre heisst Treue'. Almost immediately, a belt buckle incorporating the motto into its design was commissioned and produced by the Overhoff firm of Lüdenscheid to replace the SA buckle hitherto worn by all members of the SS. The new belt buckle was circular in form for officers and rectangular for lower ranks, and continued in wear unchanged until 1945.

In May 1933, shoulder straps or Achselstücke were devised for wear on the right shoulder only. These straps were adornments to be used in conjunction with the collar insignia already in existence and indicated rank level (ie enlisted man or NCO/junior officer/intermediate officer/senior officer) rather than actual rank.

In February 1934, a silver Honour Chevron for the Old Guard (Ehrenwinkel für Alte Kämpfer) was authorised for wear on the upper right arm by all members of the SS who had joined the SS, NSDAP or any of the other Party-affiliated organisations prior to 30 January 1933. Qualification was later extended to include former members of the police, armed forces or Stahlhelm who fulfilled certain conditions and transferred into the SS.

Plate 26 The plain SS Traditional Uniform as worn by Himmler in 1929. (See **Plate 25**)

Plate 27 SS men in formalised Traditional Uniform mount a guard of honour over a comrade killed in street fighting, Berlin 1932. *Hoffmann*

Plate 28 Hand-embroidered collar patch worn by members of the 88th SS Fuss-Standarte, based at Bremen.

Plate 29 Red-edged cuff title indicating membership of the 12th Sturm, 3rd Sturmbann of an SS Fuss-Standarte.

Plate 30 Early SA belt buckle, worn by the SS until 1931.

Plate 31 SS belt buckle for enlisted ranks, introduced at the end of 1931.

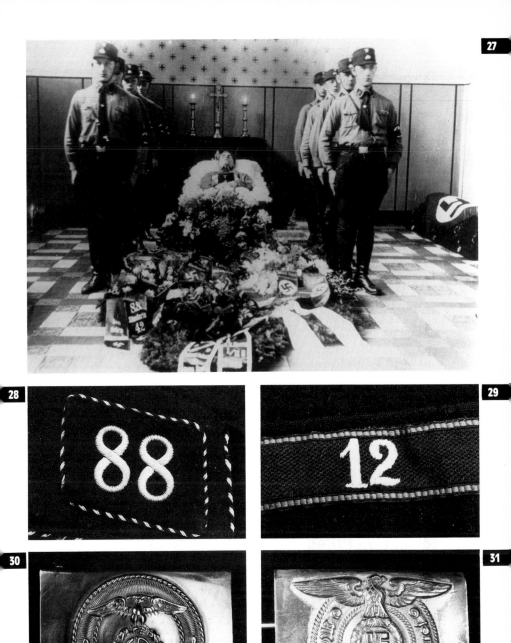

10/3

Abzeichen eines
S.-A.-Mannes
vom Sturm 10 der Standarte 3

II/2

Sturmbannstab II
der Standarte 2

12

Angehöriger des
Stabs der Standarte 12

B.O.

Angehöriger des
Stabs der Untergruppe
Berlin-Ost

R^2/7

Reservesturm 2
der Standarte 7

M^5/2

Motorsturm 5
der Standarte 2

4/2

Nachrichtensturm 4
der Standarte 2

Reitersturm

Flieger

Musikzug

Geldverwalter
Rangabzeichen

Jackenspiegel der S.-S.

Fig 2 *Right Collar Patches worn by the SA and SS, cMay 1934*
At this time the SS was still technically a part of the SA, but while the SA wore multi-coloured regional patches depicting their Sturm, Sturmbann and Standarte numerals, the SS wore only black patches bearing Standarte numbers, such as the '12' patch at upper right, as their Stürme and Sturmbanne were denoted by cuff titles. The runic patch at lower right had just been introduced and, despite the caption underneath, was at that time reserved for wear by the Leibstandarte-SS 'Adolf Hitler' and the SS Politische Bereitschaften. *Reproduced from* Die Uniformen der Braunhemden, *1934*

Fig 3 *Styles of Allgemeine-SS Uniform*
From left to right:
(i) Standard 1932-Pattern Black Service and Parade Uniform for SS-Oberscharführer;
(ii) 'Traditional Uniform' for SS-Unterscharführer. This was the first formalised SS uniform, worn by all ranks until 1932-34 and donned on selected ceremonial occasions thereafter by members of the 'Old Guard';
(iii) Service Uniform with Overcoat for SS-Rottenführer;
(iv) Walking-out Uniform with Raincoat for SS-Sturmbannführer. The raincoat was unpopular and was soon replaced by a heavy leather coat. *Reproduced from the* Organisationsbuch der NSDAP, *1937 edition.*

The traditional brown shirt uniform of the SS therefore developed almost continually over 11 years and incorporated many additions or alterations at specific times. These can be of great assistance in dating period photographs. With the advent of the black uniform, the traditional uniform was gradually phased out and it was not generally worn after 1934, except on special ceremonial occasions by members of the SS Old Guard.

THE BLACK UNIFORM

A major change to SS uniform was made in 1932, in response to a governmental demand that the SA and SS should adopt a more 'respectable' outfit as a condition of the lifting of the ban on political uniforms. On 7 July, a black tunic and peaked cap, harking back to the garb of the Imperial Leib-Husaren, were introduced for the SS to replace the brown shirt and kepi. These items were made available first to officers, then lower ranks, and were worn side-by-side with the traditional uniform during 1933 while all members were being kitted out. By the beginning of 1934, sufficient quantities of the black uniform had been manufactured for it to be in general use.

The new SS uniform was designed by SS-Oberführer Prof Karl Diebitsch, in conjunction with SS-Sturmhauptführer Walter Heck who was responsible for the SS runes emblem. The tunic comprised

Dienst- und Paradeanzug der Allgem. SS — SS-Oberscharführer | Traditionsanzug der SS — SS-Unterscharführer | Dienstanzug, Mantel — SS-Rottenführer | Ausgehanzug mit Regenmantel — SS-Sturmbannführer

Plate 32 SS-Standartenführer Julius Schreck after receiving the Golden Party Badge at the end of 1933. Note the early pattern collar patches and cap insignia. *Hoffmann*

Plate 33 An Allgemeine-SS Schar on parade, 1934. Note the mixture of traditional and black uniforms. *Hoffmann*

Plate 34 SS men at Hamburg Railway Station, c1934-35. Both styles of Death's Head are being worn on the cap during this transitional period. The runic collar patches of the men at the left of each row denote their membership of the Leibstandarte-SS 'Adolf Hitler'. *IWM*

Plate 35 Allgemeine-SS 1932-pattern Black Service Tunic as worn by an Old Guard SS-Oberscharführer in the 12th Sturm, 3rd Sturmbann, 88th SS Fuss-Standarte, c1935. The 'swallow's nests' at the shoulders denote his position as a member of the unit's Drum Corps, and his decorations indicate extensive World War 1 service, including participation with Turkish forces in the Middle East.

Plate 36 Allgemeine-SS NCO's/man's peaked cap, c1935.

Plate 37 SS-Obersturmbannführer Hilmar Wäckerle of the SS-VT Standarte 'Germania', one of the Old Guard, as depicted by Wolfgang Willrich in 1936. The black steel helmet was generally restricted to wear by members of the Leibstandarte, SS-VT and SS-TV during parades or on ceremonial occasions. It was seldom seen after 1939.

a standard four pocket military-style jacket, the lower two pockets being of the slanted 'slash' type, with a four-button front. There were two belt hooks at the sides and two false buttons at the rear to support the leather waist belt. Insignia was the same as that devised for the traditional uniform and the tunic was worn over a plain brown shirt. The new SS peaked caps were again military in appearance, silver piped for generals and silver piped for others, with velvet bands and silver cap cords for officers and cloth bands and leather chin straps for lower ranks. As with the kepi, a 1929-pattern eagle was worn above a Prussian-style death's head on the cap. Several minor variants of the black uniform were produced during 1933, but the whole outfit was formalised and standardised by mid-1934 when the new SS-style totenkopf with lower jaw was introduced.

During the remainder of the 1930s, the black service uniform was developed as the SS organisation expanded. Greatcoats were produced and a series of specialist arm diamonds or Ärmelraute devised for wear on the lower left sleeve. Imperial-style porkpie field caps, known as 'Krätzchen' or 'scratchers' because of their rough texture, forage caps and steel helmets began to be worn from 1934 on military manoeuvres, at drill training and during guard duty. On 21 June 1936 a new and larger SS cap eagle replaced the old 1929-pattern, at the same time as the introduction of a series of SS swords and the SS chained dagger. Also around that period, white shirts were authorised for wear under the black tunic on ceremonial occasions. For evening functions such as parties, dances and so on there were black mess jackets for officers and white 'monkey suits' for waiters, all sporting full SS insignia. Finally, as from 27 June 1939, officers were provided with an all-white version of the service uniform for walking out during the summer period, officially defined as running from 1 April — 30th September each year.

Full-time SS men were regularly issued with items of uniform and equipment. So far as part-timers were concerned, however, all uniform articles had to be purchased by the SS members themselves at their own expense. The only exceptions were replacements for items lost or damaged during the course of duty, which were provided free of charge. If an SS man wished to acquire a new tunic, for example, he could either buy it direct from a tailoring shop which was an approved sales outlet of the Reichszeugmeisterei der NSDAP, ie an authorised dealer in Nazi Party uniforms and equipment, or else place a pre-paid order with his local Trupp or Sturm which would, in turn, arrange to requisition a tunic on his behalf from one of the clothing stores run by the SS administrative department. The latter regularly produced price lists which were circulated to all SS formations for the attention of would-be buyers.

The gradual introduction of the grey service uniform, combined with the sudden reduction in the number of active part-time Allgemeine-SS men because of enhanced conscription at the outbreak of war, led to a surplus of black uniforms building up in SS stores after 1939. In 1942, the police collected most of the unwanted black Allgemeine-SS uniforms in Germany and sent them east to the Baltic States, Poland and the Ukraine for distribution to the hastily-mustered native auxiliary police units or Schutzmannschaft der Ordnungspolizei, the so-called Schuma. Regulations demanded that all SS insignia be removed from the tunics and replaced by distinctive bright 'police-green' lapels, shoulder straps, pocket flaps and cuffs prior to their wear by members of the Schuma. The remainder of the surplus black SS uniforms in Germany were shipped west and issued to the Germanic-SS in Flanders, Holland, Norway and Denmark, who again attached their own badges. Consequently, very few black Allgemeine-SS tunics survived the war with their original German insignia intact.

THE GREY UNIFORM

From 1935, field-grey uniforms in the same style as the black service uniform were issued to members of the Leibstandarte-SS 'Adolf Hitler' and SS-Verfügungstruppe for wear during their everyday duties. Simultaneously, an earth-brown uniform of identical cut was authorised for SS-Totenkopfverbände men serving in concentration camps. The new uniforms immediately proved to be very practical and eminently suited to the nature of the tasks performed by these full-time militarised units. Thereafter, members of the Leibstandarte, SS-VT and SS-TV donned the black SS uniform only on ceremonial occasions and for walking out.

In 1938 the Allgemeine-SS followed suit by introducing a very elegant pale grey uniform for its full-time staff, thus bringing the whole SS organisation into line with the general war footing of the other uniformed services. The new outfit was identical in style to the black uniform, but bore an SS-pattern shoulder strap on the left shoulder as well as one on the right and replaced the swastika armband with a cloth version of the 1936-pattern SS eagle. The idea was to give the appearance of a military rather than

Fig 4 *Specialist Officers Badges*
These were worn on the left sleeve above the cuff title by specialist SS officers. From top to bottom, they denoted expertise in the following:
Recruiting and Training; Race and Resettlement; Germanic Colonisation; Racial German Assistance; Building Administration; Economic Enterprises; Agricultural Administration; Press and War Economy; SS and Police Liaison. *Reproduced from the Organisationsbuch der NSDAP, 1943 edition.*

Fachführerabzeichen

SS-Fachunterführer und SS-Fachführer

Dienststelle		Ärmelabzeichen
SS-Hauptamt (Ergänzung, Erfassung und Schulung)		
SS-Rasse und Siedlungshauptamt (Rasse- und Siedlungswesen)		
Reichskommissariat für die Festigung deutschen Volkstums	Stabshauptamt (Gruppe Siedlung)	
	Volksdeutschenmittelstelle (Gruppe Volkstumsarbeit)	
SS-Wirtschafts- und Verwaltungshauptamt	(Gruppe Bauwesen)	
	(Gruppe Wirtschaftsbetriebe)	
	(Gruppe Landwirtschaftl. Verwaltung)	
Persönlicher Stab Reichsführer SS (Gruppe Presse und Kriegswirtschaft)		
Reichssicherheitshauptamt (Gruppe SS- und Polizeiwesen)		

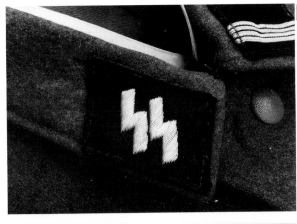

Plate 38 Sig-Runes collar patch, initially restricted to members of the Leibstandarte-SS 'Adolf Hitler', but eventually worn by all Germanic formations of the Waffen-SS.

Plate 39 Willrich print showing Günther Rauert, a peasant farmer from Todendorf serving as a Sturmmann with the SS-VT Standarte 'Germania' in 1936. Note the black side cap worn by personnel of the Armed SS during this period.

Plate 40 Himmler wearing the elegant pale grey Allgemeine-SS uniform introduced in 1938. *Hoffmann*

Plate 41 Woven SS eagle worn on the left sleeve of the field-grey uniform by all members of the Waffen-SS, and with the pale grey uniform by members of the Allgemeine-SS.

Plate 42 Himmler in conversation with SS-Obergruppenführer Dr Hans Lammers, who is wearing the white summer tunic. *IWM*

Dienststellungsabzeichen

Dienststellung	Ärmelabz.	Dienststellung	Ärmelabz.
Führer im Verwaltungsdienst		Schirrmeister	
Führer im Gerichtsdienst		Waffenunterführer	
Arzt		Nachrichtenpersonal	
Sanitätspersonal		Führer im techn. Dienst	
Führer und Unterführer im Veterinärdienst		Musikzugführer	
Hufbeschlagpersonal		Steuermann	

Fig 5 *Trade Badges*
These were worn on the left sleeve above the cuff title by personnel of all ranks who had been trained in certain disciplines or trades. From left to right, top to bottom, they denote the following:
Administrative Officer; Transport NCO;
Legal Officer; Armourer NCO;
Medical Officer; Signaller;
Medical Orderly; Technical Officer;
Veterinarian; Bandmaster;
Farrier; Coxswain. *Reproduced from the*
Organisationsbuch der NSDAP, *1940 edition*

political uniform, thus lending some authority to full-time Allgemeine-SS officers who were, by the nature of their employment, exempt from service in the Wehrmacht.

The pale grey uniform was issued first to Hauptamt personnel and thereafter to others qualified to wear it. During the war, it was gradually superseded by a Waffen-SS style field-grey version, particularly favoured by the SD and senior Allgemeine-SS officers stationed in the occupied territories. Those attached to the highly mobile security police and SD special action groups or Einsatzgruppen in Russia, dedicated to hunting down political functionaries, active Communists, looters, saboteurs, partisans and Jews, often wore a wild mixture of any available SS, army and police clothing. By 1944, most grey SS uniforms were being produced in SS-Bekleidungswerke or SS clothing factories, forming integral parts of the concentration camp system.

Throughout the entire period of the war, the 40,000 or so active part-time members of the Allgemeine-SS, who were almost exclusively engaged in reserved occupations, were never issued with grey outfits and so continued to proudly wear the black uniform whilst on duty in Germany. By 1945, however, that most impressive of all uniforms, which had been such a status symbol in the prewar days, had become an object of derision since its wearers were increasingly thought of as shirking military service. The grey uniform, meanwhile, fulfilled its ultimate function by providing the full-time and senior Allgemeine-SS membership with a shield, albeit a psychological one, which protected them from such criticism.

RANKS AND TITLES

Although the SS became one of the most complex of all Nazi paramilitary organisations, its rank structure remained relatively stable and underwent few major alterations.

The nine initial ranks employed by the SS, based on those of the SA, were:

- SS-Mann
- SS-Scharführer
- SS-Truppführer
- SS-Sturmführer
- SS-Sturmbannführer
- SS-Standartenführer
- SS-Oberführer
- SS-Gruppenführer
- SS-Obergruppenführer

On 19 May 1933, a further eight ranks were created to accommodate the general expansion of the SS, namely:

- SS-Sturmmann
- SS-Rottenführer
- SS-Oberscharführer
- SS-Obertruppführer
- SS-Obersturmführer
- SS-Sturmhauptführer
- SS-Obersturmbannführer
- SS-Brigadeführer

In August 1934, Himmler was elevated to the new rank of Reichsführer-SS and given insignia unique to his position, replacing the SS-Obergruppenführer badges he had worn prior to that time.

On 15 October 1934, further revisions were made to the SS rank system, as indicated below:

- SS-Bewerber was added as the lowest rank
- SS-Anwärter was added as the second lowest rank
- SS-Scharführer became SS-Unterscharführer
- SS-Oberscharführer became SS-Scharführer
- SS-Truppführer became SS-Oberscharführer
- SS-Obertruppführer became SS-Hauptscharführer
- SS-Sturmführer became SS-Untersturmführer
- SS-Sturmhauptführer became SS-Hauptsturmführer

Overleaf:
Fig 6 *Rank Badges of the SA and SS c May 1934*
At this stage, lower ranks had white piped collar patches while junior officers' patches were piped in black and silver and those of senior officers in plain silver. Early terms such as Sturmhauptführer still feature, and there is no special insignia for Himmler who, even though he held the post of Reichsführer der SS, was ranked simply as an SS-Obergruppenführer. *Reproduced from* Die Uniformen der Braunhemden, *1934*

Fig 7 *SS Rank Badges, c October 1934*
New terminology has been introduced, piping standardised, and a special collar patch devised for the rank of Reichsführer-SS. *Reproduced from the* Organisationsbuch der NSDAP, *1937 edition*

Rangabzeichen der S.=A. und S.=S.
auf dem linken Kragenspiegel

S.=A.=Mann

Sturmmann

Rottenführer

Scharführer

Oberscharführer

Truppführer

Obertruppführer
San.=Sturmbannarzt=
Anwärter

Sturmführer
San.=Sturmführer

Obersturmführer
San.=Obersturmführer

Sturmhauptführer
San.=Sturmhauptführer

Sturmbannführer
San.=Sturmbannführer

Obersturmbannführer
San.=Oberstu mbannführer

Standartenführer
San.=Standartenführer

Oberführer
San.=Oberführer

Brigadeführer
San.=Brigadeführer

Gruppenführer
San.=Gruppenführer

Obergruppenführer
San.=Obergruppenführer

Chef des Stabes

(Die Sanitäterabzeichen werden auf beiden Kragenspiegeln getragen)

Dienſtrangabzeichen der Schutzſtaffeln

SS-Mann

Sturmmann

Rottenführer

Unterſcharführer

Scharführer

Oberſcharführer

hauptſcharführer

Unterſturmführer

Oberſturmführer

hauptſturmführer

Sturmbannführer

**Oberſturmbann-
führer**

Standartenführer

Oberführer

Brigadeführer

Gruppenführer

Obergruppenführer

Reichsführer SS

Rank insignia remained unchanged from that point until 7 April 1942, when new collar patches were introduced for:

- SS-Oberführer
- SS-Brigadeführer
- SS-Gruppenführer
- SS-Obergruppenführer

At the same time, a new and senior rank of SS-Oberst-Gruppenführer was created.

The final and definitive Allgemeine-SS rank system, dating from April 1942 and lasting until the end of the war, was as follows:

Mannschaften (Other Ranks)
- SS-Bewerber   Candidate
- SS-Anwärter   Cadet
- SS-Mann   Private
- SS-Sturmmann (Strm.)   Lance Corporal
- SS-Rottenführer (Rotf.)   Senior Lance Corporal

Unterführer (NCOs)
- SS-Unterscharführer (Uschaf.)   Corporal
- SS-Scharführer (Schaf.)   Sergeant
- SS-Oberscharführer (Oschaf.)   Staff Sergeant
- SS-Hauptscharführer (Hschaf.)   Sergeant-Major

(Two senior NCO ranks of Stabsscharführer and Sturmscharführer existed but were generally restricted to the SS-VT and Waffen-SS, not the Allgemeine-SS)

Untere Führer (Junior Officers)
- SS-Untersturmführer (Ustuf.)   2nd Lieutenant
- SS-Obersturmführer (Ostuf.)   Lieutenant
- SS-Hauptsturmführer (Hstuf.)   Captain

Mittlere Führer (Intermediate Officers)
- SS-Sturmbannführer (Stubaf.)   Major
- SS-Obersturmbannführer (Ostubaf.)   Lieutenant-Colonel

Höhere Führer (Senior Officers)
- SS-Standartenführer (Staf.)   Colonel
- SS-Oberführer (Oberf.)   Senior Colonel
- SS-Brigadeführer (Brigf.)   Brigadier
- SS-Gruppenführer (Gruf.)   Major-General
- SS-Obergruppenführer (Ogruf.)   Lieutenant-General
- SS-Oberst-Gruppenführer (Obstgruf.)   General
- Reichsführer-SS (RfSS)   Supreme Commander

As with all NSDAP formations, Hitler himself was ultimately Commander-in-Chief of the SS and held the personal title of 'Der Oberste Führer der Schutzstaffel'.

Allgemeine-SS officers and NCOs who joined the Waffen-SS retained their Allgemeine-SS ranks and had them automatically upgraded if they were promoted to higher levels in the Waffen-SS. Similarly, with the ultimate objective of merging all members of the German police into the Allgemeine-SS, serving police officers were regularly incorporated into the SS and given SS ranks corresponding to their positions in the police. In such cases, Allgemeine-SS ranks took precedence over those of the Waffen-SS and police in official SS correspondence. A man who was a General in both the Allgemeine-SS and the Waffen-SS, for example, would be entitled 'SS-Obergruppenführer und General der Waffen-SS', while a police Colonel accepted into the SS under the provisions of the rank parity decree would be known as 'SS-Standartenführer und Oberst der Polizei'.

DAGGERS

The SS Service dagger, or 'Dienstdolch', was introduced along with its SA counterpart by the interim Chief of Staff of the SA and Himmler's then superior, Obergruppenführer von Krausser, under SA Order 1734/33 of 15 December 1933. Black and silver in colour, it bore the SS motto on the blade and runes and eagle on the grip, and its general design was based on that of a 17th Century Swiss hunting dagger, which was itself derived from a weapon carried by a soldier depicted on the Trajan Column in Rome. Worn by all ranks of the Allgemeine-SS with service and walking out dress, the SS dagger was presented to its owner only at the special 9 November ceremony when he graduated from SS-Anwärter to SS-Mann. It was not issued at any other time, or en masse like the daggers of the plebian SA. Each SS-Anwärter paid the full cost of his dagger, usually in small instalments, prior to its presentation.

On 17 February 1934, SS-Gruppenführer Kurt Wittje, Chief of the SS-Amt and later dismissed because of his homosexual tendencies, forbade the private purchase or 'trading-in' of SS daggers on the open market. Henceforth, daggers could only be ordered from manufacturers through the SS-Amt for issue via the three main SS uniform distribution centres at Munich, Dresden and Berlin, which regularly processed requisitions received from the various Oberabschnitte Headquarters. Moreover, it was made a disciplinary offence for an SS man to dispose of or lose his dagger, on the grounds that it was a symbol of his office. In that way, it was assured that no unauthorised person could buy or otherwise acquire an SS dagger.

Fig 8 *SS Rank Badges, cApril 1942*
This illustration includes the final pattern of collar patches worn by SS and Police Generals, whose badges were altered when the new rank of Oberst-Gruppenführer was created. Shoulder straps for the Allgemeine-SS are also depicted. *Reproduced from the Organisationsbuch der NSDAP, 1943 edition*

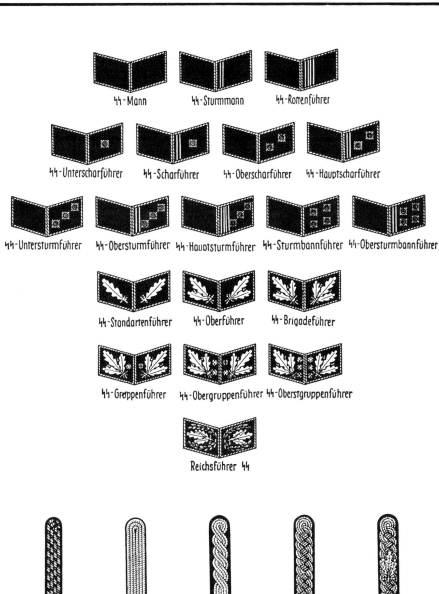

ᛋᛋ-Mann   ᛋᛋ-Sturmmann   ᛋᛋ-Rottenführer

ᛋᛋ-Unterscharführer   ᛋᛋ-Scharführer   ᛋᛋ-Oberscharführer   ᛋᛋ-Hauptscharführer

ᛋᛋ-Untersturmführer   ᛋᛋ-Obersturmführer   ᛋᛋ-Hauptsturmführer   ᛋᛋ-Sturmbannführer   ᛋᛋ-Obersturmbannführer

ᛋᛋ-Standartenführer   ᛋᛋ-Oberführer   ᛋᛋ-Brigadeführer

ᛋᛋ-Gruppenführer   ᛋᛋ-Obergruppenführer   ᛋᛋ-Oberstgruppenführer

Reichsführer ᛋᛋ

ᛋᛋ-Mann
bis
Hauptscharführer   ᛋᛋ-Untersturmführer
bis
Hauptsturmführer   ᛋᛋ-Sturmbannführer
bis
Standartenführer   ᛋᛋ-Oberführer
bis
Oberstgruppenführer   Reichsführer-ᛋᛋ

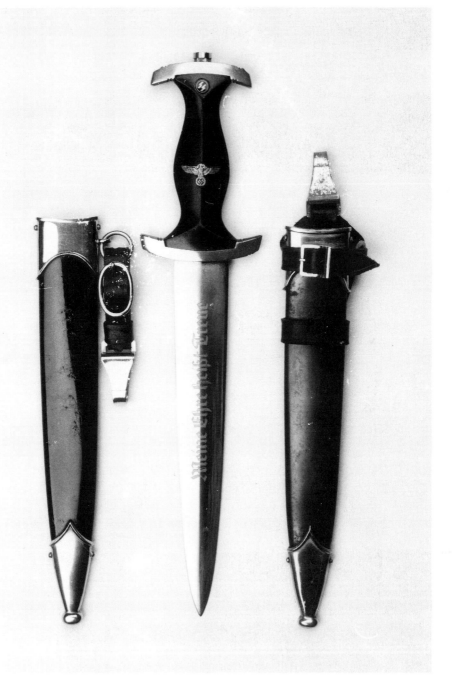

Plate 43   1933-pattern SS dagger, showing the single
strap hanger (left) and vertical hanger (right).

Plate 44 The SS motto, ('My Honour is Loyalty'), etched on all dagger blades.

Plate 45 1936-pattern SS dagger, with regulation portepee knot authorised in 1943 for wear by officers of the Waffen-SS, Sipo and SD.

Plate 46 SS 1936-pattern dagger chain links, bearing the Totenkopf and Sig-Runes. The swirly design of the quadriform suspender was derived from Dark Age Germanic ornamentation.

Plate 47 Police NCO's sword, introduced in 1936. It is identical to its SS counterpart, being distinguished solely by the Police eagle on the grip.

As of 25 January 1935, members dismissed from the SS had to surrender their daggers, even if they were personal property paid for by their own means. In cases of voluntary resignation or normal retirement, however, daggers could be retained and the person in question was given a certificate stating that he was entitled to possess the dagger.

Only the finest makers of edged weapons were contracted to produce the 1933-pattern SS dagger. These included Böker & Co, Carl Eickhorn, Gottlieb Hammesfahr, Richard Herder, Jacobs & Co, Robert Klaas, Ernst Pack & Söhne, and C. Bertram Reinhardt. The earliest pieces from the 1933-35 period featured the maker's trademark on the blade, a dark blue-black anodised steel scabbard, and nickel-silver fittings with the crossguard reverse stamped 'I', 'II', or 'III' to denote that the dagger had passed inspection at the main SS uniform distribution centre responsible for issuing it, viz Munich, Dresden or Berlin, respectively, During 1936-37, makers' marks were replaced by RZM code numbers, scabbards began to be finished with black paint, and the stamped inspection numerals were discontinued as the RZM had by then taken over entirely the regulation of quality control. Finally, from 1938, nickel-silver gave way to cheaper plated steel for the mounts and aluminium for the grip eagle. Yet, despite the lowering standard of materials used, a high quality appearance was always maintained and the daggers were consistent in their fine finish.

The SS dagger was suspended at an angle from a single leather strap until November 1934, when Himmler introduced a vertical hanger for wear with service dress during crowd control. However, the vertical hanger, while more stable, was too reminiscent of the humble bayonet frog and in 1936 the single strap was reintroduced for both the walking out and service uniforms. Thereafter, the vertical hanger was restricted to use on route marches and military exercises.

In September 1940, due to national economies, the 1933-pattern dagger was withdrawn from production for the duration of the war.

A more ornate SS dagger, to be worn only by officers and those Old Guard NCOs and other ranks who had joined the organisation prior to 30 January 1933, was introduced by Himmler on 21 June 1936. Generally known as the 'chained dagger', it was very similar to the 1933-pattern but was suspended by means of linked octagonal plates, ornately embossed with death's heads and SS runes, and featured a central scabbard mount decorated with swastikas. During the 1936-37 period, these chains and fittings, which were designed by Karl Diebitsch, were made from nickel-silver. Later examples were in nickel-plated steel with slightly smaller, less oval-shaped skulls. Chained daggers bore no makers' marks and it is likely that only one firm, probably Carl Eickhorn which manufactured the small number of very special SS honour daggers and which featured the chained dagger in its sales catalogue, was contracted to produce them. Each chained dagger, costing 12.15 Reichsmarks in 1938, had to be privately purchased from the SS administrative department in Berlin via the various Oberabschnitte Headquarters, requisition forms being submitted at the start of every month. Direct orders from individual officers were not entertained.

In the Spring of 1940, SS-Obergruppenführer Fritz Weitzel suggested to Himmler that an army-type dagger should be introduced for wear exclusively by officers of the Waffen-SS, who had performed so well in the western campaign but who were prevented by regulations from wearing the Allgemeine-SS dagger with their field-grey uniform. Three prototype Waffen-SS daggers, produced by the Solingen firms of Alexander Coppel and Peter Krebs and by the SS Damascus School at Dachau, were duly submitted for the Reichsführer's consideration but were rejected out of hand. It was not until 15 February 1943 that Waffen-SS officers were finally permitted to wear the chained dagger with their field-grey walking out dress. As a concession to their military status, they were also given the right to use an army-pattern portepee knot, tied about the grip and crossguard in a new and unique SS style. On 4 June 1943, wear of the SS chained dagger and knot with field-grey uniform was extended to officers of the security police and SD, and thus the SD became the only branch of the Allgemeine-SS whose members were permitted to sport dagger knots. At the same time, direct private purchase of daggers was at last allowed by the SS Wirtschafts- und Verwaltungshauptamt.

Production of the chained dagger had to be discontinued at the end of 1943 because of material shortages, and its wear was subsequently forbidden for the duration of the war.

In addition to the standard 1933-pattern and 1936-pattern SS daggers, several special presentation variants were also produced. The first of these was the so-called Röhm SS Honour Dagger, 9,900 of which were distributed in February 1934 by SA Stabschef Ernst Röhm to members of the SS Old Guard. It took the form of a basic 1933-pattern dagger with the addition of the dedication 'In herzlicher Kameradschaft, Ernst Röhm' ('In heartfelt comradeship, Ernst Röhm') etched on the reverse side of the blade. Following the Night of the Long Knives, 200 similar daggers, etched 'In herzlicher Kameradschaft, H. Himmler', were presented by the Reichsführer to SS personnel who had participated in the bloody purge of the SA. A very ornate and expensive SS honour dagger, with oakleaf-decorated crossguards, leather-covered scabbard and damascus steel blade, was instituted by Himmler in 1936 for award to high ranking officers in recognition of special achievement. When one was presented to the NSDAP Treasurer, Franz Xaver Schwarz, he responded by secretly commissioning the Eickhorn firm to produce an even more elaborate example, with fittings and chain hanger in solid silver, which he then gave to Himmler as a birthday present!

SWORDS

During the 1933-36 era, SS officers and NCOs engaged in ceremonial duties were permitted to wear a variety of privately purchased army-pattern sabres, often with silver rather than regulation gilt fittings. In 1936 however, at the same time as the introduction of the chained dagger, a series of standardised swords in the classic straight-bladed 'degen' style was created specifically for members of the SS and police, emphasising the close relationship between the two organisations. There were minor differences between degen for officers and those for NCOs, while SS swords featured runes on the grip and police examples the police eagle. Personnel attached to SS Reiterstandarten retained the traditional curved sabre for use on horseback.

SS NCOs could readily purchase their swords, via local units, from the SS administrative department in Berlin. The officer's sword, on the other hand, which was referred to as the Ehrendegen des Reichsführers-SS or Reichsführer's Sword of Honour, was given an elevated status and could not be worn automatically by every SS officer. It was bestowed by Himmler only upon selected Allgemeine-SS commanders and graduates of the Waffen-SS Junkerschulen at Bad Tölz and Braunschweig. Each presentation of the Ehrendegen was accompanied by a citation in which the Reichsführer instructed the recipient: 'I award you the SS sword. Never draw it without reason, or sheathe it without honour!' ('Ich verleihe Ihnen den Degen der SS. Ziehen Sie ihn niemals ohne Not! Stecken Sie ihn niemals ein ohne Ehre!') However, despite Himmler's dramatic exhortations, the sword never became a cult weapon to the same extent as the revered SS dagger and it fell into general disuse during 1940. Manufacture of the Ehrendegen ceased on 25 January 1941 for the duration of the war, and SS officers commissioned after that date frequently reverted to the old practice of carrying army sabres.

Awards of the officer's sword were recorded in the Dienstaltersliste, which reveals that only 86% of even the most senior SS commanders were entitled to wear it at the end of 1944. That percentage can be broken down as follows:

● Standartenführer	–	58%
● Oberführer	–	83%
● Brigadeführer	–	90%
● Gruppenführer	–	91%
● Obergruppenführer	–	99%
● Oberst-Gruppenführer	–	100%

Still more exclusive were the so-called 'Geburtstagsdegen', or 'birthday swords' given by Himmler to SS generals and other leading Nazi personalities as birthday presents. They were made to order by Germany's master swordsmith, Paul Müller, Director of the SS Damascus School at Dachau, and featured hallmarked silver fittings and blades of the finest damascus steel with exquisitely raised and gilded personal dedications from Himmler. The sword gifted to von Ribbentrop on his birthday in 1939, for example, bore the golden legend 'Meinem lieben Joachim von Ribbentrop zum 30.4.39 – H. Himmler, Reichsführer-SS' ('To my dear friend Joachim von Ribbentrop on 30 April 1939 – H. Himmler, Reichsführer-SS') set between two swastikas. Hitler received a similar weapon, the blade inscription of which extolled the virtues and loyalty of the entire SS officer corps. Müller continued producing Geburtstagsdegen on commission from Himmler until 1944.

THE SS DEATH'S HEAD RING

One of the most obscure yet most potent of all SS uniform accoutrements was the Totenkopfring der SS, or SS Death's Head Ring, instituted by Himmler on 10 April 1934. The Totenkopfring was not classed as a national decoration, as it was in the gift of the Reichsführer. However, it ranked as a senior award within the SS brotherhood, recognising the wearer's personal achievement, devotion to duty, and loyalty to the Führer and his ideals.

The concept and runic form of the ring was undoubtedly adopted by Himmler from pagan German mythology, which related how the great God Thor possessed a pure silver ring on which people could take oaths much as Christians swear on the Bible, and how binding treaties were carved in runes on Wotan's spear. The Death's Head Ring comprised a massive band of oakleaves deeply embossed with a totenkopf and a number of symbolic runes. Each piece was cast and exquisitely hand-finished by specially commissioned jewellers, working for the renowned firm of Gahr in Munich, and was finely engraved inside the band with the letters 'S.lb' (the abbreviation for 'Seinem lieben' or, roughly, 'To Dear') followed by the recipient's surname, the date of presentation and a facsimile of Himmler's signature.

Initially, the weighty silver ring was reserved primarily for those Old Guard veterans with SS membership numbers below 5,000 but qualifications for award were gradually extended until, by 1 August 1939, the following persons were eligible to wear it:

(i) Members of any rank whose numbers were below 10,000;

(ii) Officers who joined the SS before 30 January 1933;

(iii) Officers who joined the SS after 30 January 1933 and had served for three years;

(iv) Officers who had served for two years, having been prevented from joining the SS earlier than they did because of their membership of the army or police prior to 30 January 1933;

(v) Officers who had been members of the SS for two years, having transferred directly into the organisation from active uninterrupted membership in the NSDAP, SA, NSKK or HJ;

(vi) Members of any rank holding the Golden Party Badge;

(vii) Members of any rank holding the Coburg Badge;

(viii) Officers and NCOs who were members of both the police and the Nazi Party before 30 January 1933;

(ix) Officers who resided in Austria before the Anschluss and were members of the outlawed Austrian SS during that time, provided they had been officers for at least two years;

(x) Officers who resided in the Sudetenland and became SS members before 31 December 1938, provided they had been officers for at least two years;

(xi) Officers who resided in the Memel District and became SS members before 1 June 1939, provided they had been officers for at least two years;

(xii) Members of any rank who did not fulfil any of the above criteria but were classed as 'Special Cases' by the Reichsführer-SS. This category might include honorary officials, or SS men who had performed particularly arduous tasks.

Award of the ring could be postponed for anything between three months and three years if the prospective holder had been punished during his service by reprimand, detention or demotion for contravention of the SS discipline code. Moreover, SS members who were suspended or being investigated under the Party or SS disciplinary procedures at the time of their becoming eligible for the ring were temporarily excluded from consideration for award.

Certified lists of nominees for the ring, together with their finger sizes, were regularly submitted by SS Abschnitte headquarters to the SS Personalhauptamt in Berlin, which processed the applications and duly awarded rings and accompanying citations on behalf of the Reichsführer-SS. Each citation read as follows:

The ring, which was worn only on the ring finger of the left hand, was bestowed on set SS promotion dates, principally 30 January (the anniversary of the Nazi assumption of power), 20 April (Hitler's birthday), 21 June (Midsummer's Day, a traditional pagan and SS festival), and 9 November (the anniversary of the Munich Putsch). All awards were recorded in the Dienstaltersliste and personnel files of the holders, but it was expressly forbidden to publicise presentations in the Press.

All ring holders who were demoted, suspended or dismissed from the SS, or who resigned or retired, had to return their rings and citations to the SS Personalhauptamt. Those later accepted back into the organisation would again qualify for the ring. When a serving ring holder died, his relatives could retain his citation but had to return his ring to the SS Personalhauptamt, which arranged for its preservation at Wewelsburg Castle in permanent commemoration of the holder. Similarly, if a holder fighting with the Wehrmacht or Waffen-SS was killed in action, his ring had to be retrieved from the body by members of his unit and returned by the unit commander to the SS Personalhauptamt for preservation. In effect, the returned rings of dead SS men constituted individual military memorials and were cared for as such.

The Death's Head Ring became so sought after an honour that many SS and police officers not entitled to wear it had a variety of unofficial 'skull rings' produced in gold and silver by local jewellers and even concentration camp inmates. However, these lacked any runic symbolism and were rather vulgar representations of the real thing.

On 17 October 1944, the Reichsführer-SS cancelled further manufacture and presentation of the Totenkopfring for the duration of the war. By that time 14,000 rings had been awarded. In the Spring of 1945, on Himmler's orders, all the rings which had been returned to the SS Personalhauptamt for preservation as memorials were blast-sealed into a mountainside near Wewelsburg, the precise location of which was kept secret, to prevent their capture by the enemy. To this day, they have never been found.

'I award you the SS Death's Head Ring.
The ring symbolises our loyalty to the Führer, our steadfast obedience and our brotherhood and comradeship.
The Death's Head reminds us that we should be ready at any time to lay down our lives for the good of the Germanic people.
The runes diametrically opposite the Death's Head are symbols from our past of the prosperity which we will restore through National Socialism.
The two Sig-runes stand for the name of our SS. The Swastika and Hagall-rune represent our unshakable faith in the ultimate victory of our philosophy.
The ring is wreathed in oak, the traditional German leaf.
The Death's Head Ring cannot be bought or sold and must never fall into the hands of those not entitled to wear it.
When you leave the SS, or when you die, the ring must be returned to the Reichsführer-SS.
The unauthorised acquisition of duplicates of the ring is forbidden and punishable by law.
Wear the ring with honour!
H. HIMMLER.'

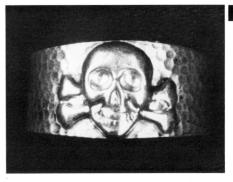

Plate 48 The SS Death's Head Ring.

Plate 49 Unofficial 'Skull Ring', featuring a gold totenkopf on a hammered silver band. Such pieces had been popular since the Freikorps days, and were frequently worn after 1934 by SS and police members who were not entitled to the SS Death's Head Ring.

Plate 50 Himmler placing a wreath at the Feldherrnhalle on the 11th anniversary of the Munich Putsch, 9 November 1934. The Blood Banner, held by Jakob Grimminger, stands in the background. The guard of honour comprises members of the SS-VT, still dressed in black but wearing their distinctive runic collar patches. *Hoffmann*

Plate 51 Preceded by their Feldzeichen, men of the 6th SS Fuss-Standarte march past Berlin Cathedral on their way to a rally at the Lustgarten, 3 April 1938.
Ullstein

FLAGS AND BANNERS

From 4 July 1926, the SS had the distinction of keeping the most revered flag in the Third Reich, the Blutfahne or Blood Banner, which had been carried at the head of the Nazi Old Guard during the Munich Putsch when they were fired upon by the police. It was splattered with the gore of those shot during the encounter and was thereafter considered to be something of a 'holy relic'. SS-Truppführer Jakob Grimminger from the Munich SS detachment, a veteran of the World War I Gallipoli campaign and participant in the 1922 'Battle of Coburg', was accorded the honour of being appointed the first official bearer of the Blood Banner and he retained that position throughout his career. The last public appearance of the Blutfahne was at the funeral of Adolf Wagner, Gauleiter of Munich-Upper Bavaria, in April 1944. By that time, Grimminger had attained the rank of SS-Standartenführer, his association with the mystical flag having assured him a steady succession of promotions.

Every Allgemeine-SS Standarte was represented by a banner or Feldzeichen, which was itself known as the regimental 'Standarte'. Somewhat reminiscent of the ancient Roman vexillum banner, it took the form of a wooden pole surmounted by a metal eagle and wreathed swastika, below which was a black and silver boxed nameplate bearing the title of the SS Standarte on the front and the initials

'NSDAP' on the back. From the box was suspended a red silk flag with a black static swastika on a white circle. The motto 'Deutschland Erwache' ('Germany Awake') was embroidered in bullion on the obverse, with 'Nat. Soz. Deutsche Arbeiterpartei – Sturmabteilung' on the reverse. The whole item was finished off with a black/white/red fringe and tassels. Apart from the black name box, the SS Feldzeichen was identical to that of the SA.

When an SS unit achieved roughly regimental proportions, it was awarded a Feldzeichen in a mass pseudo-religious ceremony which took place each September as part of the annual NSDAP celebrations at Nürnberg. During the proceedings, Hitler would present many new standards to regimental commanders and touch them with the Blutfahne which Grimminger was carrying alongside, so linking in spirit the most recent SS members with the martyrs of the Munich Putsch.

SS Reiterstandarten carried similar but distinctive Feldzeichen which had the 'Deutschland Erwache' flag hanging from a wooden bar fixed at right angles to the standard pole. In place of the name box, these cavalry standards featured a black patch or Fahnenspiegel on the flag cloth, bearing crossed lances and the unit designation in silver.

Each SS Sturmbann was represented by a Sturmbannfahne or battalion flag, which took the form of a brilliant red ground with a large black mobile swastika on a white circular field, with black and silver twisted cord edging. In the upper left corner or canton, a black Fahnenspiegel was embroidered in silver thread with the Sturmbann and Standarte numbers in Roman and Arabic numerals respectively.

The foremost manufacturer of SS flags and standards was the well-known firm of Fahnen-Hoffmann, Berlin.

Fig 9 *Allgemeine-SS Standards*
Top: The 'Deutschland Erwache' Standard, or
Feldzeichen, of the 1st SS Fuss-Standarte 'Julius
Schreck';
Bottom Left: Battalion Flag of Sturmbann III of the 1st
SS Fuss-Standarte;
Bottom Right: Cavalry Standard of the 15th SS
Reiterstandarte.
Reproduced from the Organisationsbuch der NSDAP,
1943 edition

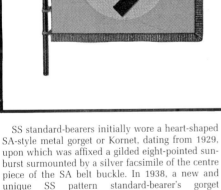

SS standard-bearers initially wore a heart-shaped SA-style metal gorget or Kornet, dating from 1929, upon which was affixed a gilded eight-pointed sunburst surmounted by a silver facsimile of the centre piece of the SA belt buckle. In 1938, a new and unique SS pattern standard-bearer's gorget appeared, crescent-shaped and featuring a large eagle and swastika and a suspension chain embossed with runes and death's heads. SS flag-bearers also wore a massive bandolier in black, with silver brocade edging.

Command flags or Kommandoflaggen, in the shape of rigid pennants on flag poles, were carried as unit markers at large parades or, in smaller versions, were flown from the front nearside mudwing of staff cars. They were square, rectangular or triangular in form depending upon designation, and were made of black and white waterproof cloth with rustproof silver thread. Command flags were usually covered in a transparent celluloid casing during inclement weather.

Overleaf:
Fig 10 *Allgemeine-SS Command Flags*
These were generally displayed on vehicles when carrying the high-ranking personnel concerned. This representative selection includes the flags used by the Reichsführer-SS, Chiefs of the Hauptämter, Oberabschnitte and Abschnitte Commanders, and leaders of Fuss-Standarten, Reiterstandarten, and various Sturmbanne. *Reproduced from the* Organisationsbuch der NSDAP, *1938 edition*

Stand. 1938	*Kommandoflaggen*

Reichsführer ⁴⁴

Hauptamtschefs

Amtschefs

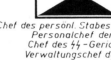

Chef des persönl. Stabes des RF ⁴⁴
Personalchef der ⁴⁴
Chef des ⁴⁴-Gerichts
Verwaltungschef der ⁴⁴
Reichsarzt der ⁴⁴

Führer der ⁴⁴-Sammelstelle

Inspekteur der ⁴⁴-Reitschulen

⁴⁴-Standortführer Berlin

Führer der ⁴⁴-Oberabschnitte
(⁴⁴-Oberabschnitt Süd)

Kdt. d. ⁴⁴-Übungslagers Dachau

(14. ⁴⁴- Standarte)

Führer der ⁴⁴-Abschnitte
(⁴⁴-Abschnitt II)

Führer der ⁴⁴-Standarten

(15. ⁴⁴-Reiterstandarte)

(⁴⁴-Sturmbann I d. 3. ⁴⁴-Std.)

Führer der ⁴⁴-Sturmbanne
(⁴⁴-Pioniersturmbann 3)

(⁴⁴-Nachrichtensturmbann 3)

5 The SS and the Police

THE 'STAATSSCHUTZKORPS' IDEA

The failure of the Munich Putsch in 1923, which was smashed by the police rather than the army, brought home to Hitler the fact that unrestricted control of the police would be an essential element in the successful foundation of a long-term Nazi State. Consequently, the period immediately following the assumption of power on 30 January 1933 witnessed a concerted effort by the Führer to have his most trusted lieutenants nominated to senior police positions in the governments of the various provinces, or Länder, which existed under the Weimar Republic. Foremost amongst these men was Hermann Göring, one of the first Nazis elected to the Reichstag and its President since 30 August 1932, who received ministerial duties in both the national and Prussian governments. As Prussian Minister of the Interior, he became responsible for policing the Reich capital and two-thirds of the land area of Germany. Göring appointed Kurt Daluege, head of the Berlin SS, as his Chief of Prussian Police and Rudolf Diels, his cousin's husband, as Deputy Chief. He then moved swiftly to separate the Prussian Political Police, which dealt with subversives, from the rest of the organisation. On 27 April he created a new political department staffed by 35 men, to be called the Secret State Police or Geheime Staatspolizei (Gestapo), and assigned Diels to head it. The Gestapo was instructed that it could disregard the restrictions imposed by Prussian state law, and it was removed from the control of the Prussian Ministry of the Interior to new offices at 8 Prinz-Albrecht-Strasse, Berlin, and made an independent force responsible to Göring personally. By mid 1933, therefore, Göring had a firm grip on the largest provincial police force in Germany and launched it and the SA against the Communists and other opponents of the new order.

Diels, however, soon became a problem. He was a professional policeman, not a Nazi, and at once went to war against all extremists and lawbreakers, regardless of political persuasion. His fledgling Gestapo, armed with machine-guns, regularly surrounded ad hoc SA and SS detention centres in Berlin and forced the Brownshirts to surrender and release their badly beaten political prisoners. Daluege and some SS men who worked their way into the Gestapo began to campaign viciously for the downfall of Diels and his faction, and such infighting developed that it eventually became commonplace for members of the Gestapo to arrest one another. Daluege even plotted to invite Diels to a meeting and then throw him out of an upper-storey window! But Diels continued to enjoy Göring's patronage and friendship, and retained his command of the Gestapo.

While Göring was the first official of the Third Reich to assert a measure of personal authority over the regular provincial police, it remained for Himmler to realise that ambition on a national scale. When the Gauleiter of Munich-Upper Bavaria, Adolf Wagner, became Bavarian Minister of the Interior at the beginning of March 1933, his natural choice as Police President of Munich was Himmler, who had been Head of Security at the NSDAP headquarters in the city for over a year. On 1 April, Himmler was appointed Commander of the Political Police for the whole of Bavaria, a position which gave him the power to challenge Göring's Prussian supremacy. He found an ally in the Reich Minister of the Interior, Dr Wilhelm Frick, a former Munich policeman who was a confirmed opponent of the autonomy of the Länder and an old enemy of Göring. With Frick's support, Himmler was nominated Chief of Police in province after province until only Prussia remained out of his reach.

In January 1934, Frick laid before Hitler a Bill for the Administrative Reorganisation of the Reich. As a result of its acceptance, all the provincial police forces were to be amalgamated to form the first national German Police Force, officially termed 'die Deutsche Polizei', under the Reich Minister of the Interior. Swift changes were made, including the incorporation of the eagle and swastika on to existing police uniforms. Göring stood fast for a time in Prussia, and he might have frustrated the unification process entirely were it not for the growing dread of Röhm and the SA. The Stabschef was hungry for power and eager to trample on anyone who stood in his way. The menacing presence of the SA, and the fact that the SS was the only reliable body which could capably oppose it, finally persuaded Göring to compromise. He ousted his beleaguered protégé Diels on 20 April 1934 and appointed Himmler as Chief of the Prussian Gestapo, with SS-Brigadeführer Reinhard Heydrich as his Deputy. Only two months later, the Göring/Himmler/Heydrich triumvirate successfully decapitated the SA in the Night of the Long Knives.

During 1935, the intrigues continued and Himmler took his turn of coming into conflict with Frick. The latter was anxious to pursue his aim that all German police forces should ultimately be subordinated to him alone, as Reich Minister of the Interior. To that end he sought the support of Daluege, still head of the uniformed police in Prussia, against Himmler. Frick proposed that Daluege should be nominated Chief of the German Police on the understanding that he would take his instructions only from the Ministry of the Interior. Not surprisingly, Daluege expressed interest, but both he and Frick were outmanoeuvred by Himmler and Heydrich who had got wind of the plot to undermine them. On 9 June 1936, Heydrich approached Hitler direct and presented a strong case for giving Himmler the rank of Minister and title Chief of the German Police. The crux of Heydrich's argument was that Himmler's efficiency and personal loyalty to the Führer were beyond question, and he would cut out the 'middle man', Frick. Frick retaliated, but was successful only in his objection that Himmler should not be given Ministerial rank. On 17 June 1936, the Reichsführer-SS was appointed to the newly created government post of Chief of the German Police in the Reich Ministry of the Interior (Chef der Deutschen Polizei im Reichsministerium des Innern), answerable only to Hitler. Heydrich was rewarded for his efforts by being put in charge of the security police and Daluege accepted command of the uniformed police. The entire system was reorganised around these two major divisions and, with the introduction of a series of new police uniforms, all vestiges of the old Länder forces finally disappeared.

Himmler was now the undisputed head of two important but separate organisations, the SS and the national police. The police, however, by far the more powerful and intrusive agency, affecting the daily lives of the entire German population, consisted of individuals who were not racially screened and, more importantly, not always politically reliable. Consequently, one of Himmler's first actions on assuming command was to expel 22 police Colonels, hundreds of junior officers and thousands of NCOs who were considered to have Socialist sympathies. The end result, in terms of lost expertise, was catastrophic. Those dismissed had been professionals, and totally outclassed the SS men brought in to replace them. Many had to be reinstated after a hastily arranged programme of Nazi indoctrination.

The Nazification of the existing police membership was a short-term expedient, however. Himmler now began to formulate his greatest project, the merger of the SS and police into a single 'Staatsschutzkorps' or State Protection Corps, so that the conventional police forces could be done away with altogether. This was to be achieved first by reorganisation and then by the absorption of police personnel into the SS. Acceptable members of the uniformed police would join the Allgemeine-SS, forming interim combined SS-Police units in the major cities, while security policemen who fulfilled the various racial and ideological requirements of the SS would enrol in the SD. In Autumn 1936, as the first stage in this process, various SD leaders were appointed Inspectors of Security Police and charged with promoting the gradual fusion of the Gestapo, Kripo and SD. A year later the SS Oberabschnitte commanders became the first Höhere SS-und Polizeiführer, assuming responsibility for all SS and police formations in their regions. Most important of all, a great recruiting drive was set in motion at the beginning of 1938 to encourage young members of the Allgemeine-SS to join the police as a full-time career. The ultimate intention was to replace the older and retiring police officers with 'new blood' so that, through a progression of selective recruitment, accelerated promotion and natural wastage, the Staatsschutzkorps would be in full operation and the police disbanded by 1955.

With the object of picking only the most reliable serving members of the police for acceptance into the SS, Himmler issued a Rank Parity Decree on 26 June 1938 which laid down the following provisions:

(i)   Members of the police could, on application, be accepted into the SS provided that:
        (a) They fulfilled general SS recruiting conditions, and
        (b) They had been members of the NSDAP or any of its organisations before 30 January 1933, or they had been Patron Members (FM) of the SS before 30 January 1933, or they had served for at least three years in the police under RfSS command and had proved themselves satisfactory.
(ii)   The Reichsführer-SS reserved to himself the right to authorise the acceptance of any further categories of persons, including most police Generals who would normally have been rejected by the SS on account of their age.
(iii)   Acceptance into the SS would take place according to the police rank held.
(iv)   Police civilian employees could be incorporated into the SS with SS rank corresponding to their Civil Service grade.
(v)   Rank parity promotions would take place from case to case.

The effect of provision (i) of the decree was that only racially and physically suitable and politically reliable members of the police would be accepted into the SS and, thereafter, into the proposed Staatsschutzkorps. However, provisions (ii) to (v) threatened to swamp the Allgemeine-SS with police officials who were to be automatically given SS ranks corresponding to their status in the police, although they had never held any junior SS position before. For instance, a police Oberwachtmeister would enter the SS straightaway as a Hauptscharführer, a Major as a Sturmbannführer, an Oberst as a Standartenführer, and so on. Consequently, a practical ceiling had to be put on the number of policemen who could be incorporated into the SS each year, and competition for places became fierce. Successful applicants were normally taken into the SS Stammabteilungen and were permitted to wear the SS runes embroidered on a patch below the left breast pocket of the police tunic.

The outbreak of war in 1939 dealt a mortal blow to the steady progression towards a Staatsschutzkorps, for the majority of the finest potential police recruits from the Allgemeine-SS were suddenly swallowed up by the Wehrmacht. Nev-

Plate 52   Portrait photograph of Heinrich Himmler, circulated to all police stations in 1936 after his appointment as Chef der Deutschen Polizei.

Plate 53   A jovial Himmler broadcasts to the nation on 'German Police Day', 28 January 1939. *Hoffmann*

Plate 54   From 18-22 February 1939, Himmler paid a fact-finding visit to Warsaw as a guest of the Chief of the Polish Police. *IWM*

Plate 55 Unofficial hand-embroidered variant of the cuff title introduced for the SS-Polizei-Division in December 1942.

Plate 56 The Berlin Schutzpolizei parades along the Wilhelmstrasse past Daluege, Himmler and Hitler, 20 April 1939. *Ullstein*

Plate 57 Kurt Daluege in the uniform of SS-Oberst-Gruppenführer und Generaloberst der Polizei, 24 August 1943. From this time on he was continually ill and was, in fact, only semi-conscious when hanged at the end of the war. *Hoffmann*

ertheless, the acceptance of serving policemen into the SS organisation continued apace. During October 1939, no less than 16,000 members of the uniformed police were called up en masse to form the Polizei-Division, a combat unit affiliated to the Waffen-SS, which fought on the Western Front and in Russia. Its soldiers were not obliged to pass the SS racial and physical requirements so were not initially considered to be full SS men. However, the division performed so well around Leningrad at the end of 1941 that the following February it was completely integrated into the Waffen-SS and awarded the title SS-Polizei-Division. Over 30 heavily-armed police regiments also served under SS command as occupation troops throughout Europe, and in February 1945 an SS-Polizei-Grenadier-Division was raised with cadre personnel from the Police School at Dresden.

The Staatsschutzkorps idea was ultimately overtaken by events and never came to fruition. However, while the German police always managed to retain its position as a technically separate State entity, its operational independence was rapidly eroded through continual SS infiltration. By the end of the war, Himmler had inevitably succeeded Frick as Reich Minister of the Interior, and he and his SS Generals completely dominated all branches of both the uniformed and security police forces across the Reich.

THE UNIFORMED POLICE

The Ordnungspolizei or Orpo, the so-called 'Order Police', comprised all uniformed civil police personnel and was by far the larger of the two main divisions of the German police. From its inception in 1936, Orpo was commanded by Kurt Daluege whose powerful position qualified him to become one of the first three SS-Oberst-Gruppenführer in April 1942, the other two being Franz Xaver Schwarz and 'Sepp' Dietrich. The following year he was made Deputy Reichsprotektor of Bohemia and Moravia, and the day-to-day running of Orpo fell to SS-Obergruppenführer Alfred Wünnenberg, formerly commander of the SS-Polizei-Division. By tiat time, the Allgemeine-SS had permeated every aspect of the uniformed police system. SS-pattern rank insignia were sported by police Generals, SS-style swords were worn by police officers and NCOs, and SS-type Feldzeichen standards and battalion flags were carried by police units on ceremonial occasions. A department known as the Hauptstelle der Hauptamt Ordnungspolizei had been set up within the Reichsführung-SS to advise Himmler on all matters concerning the uniformed police and, as Chef der Deutschen Polizei, he made policy decisions regarding its operation and deploy-

ment. In effect, the massive Orpo organisation had become subordinate to, and took its instructions from, the leadership of the Allgemeine-SS.

By 1943 therefore, through his continued absorption of uniformed police responsibilities, Himmler had succeeded in achieving ultimate control of all conventional German police forces, the fire brigade, railway and post office guards, rescue and emergency services, and even night watchmen. Moreover, the corresponding domestic police forces in the conquered territories also came under his authority. The active Allgemeine-SS proper was by that time a relatively small organisation in its own right, and numerically far inferior to the Waffen-SS. However, its leaders directed the operations of hundreds of thousands of uniformed policemen throughout the Greater German Reich, and had access to their intimate local knowledge. In that way, the oft-maligned and faceless bureaucrats of the Allgemeine-SS exercised a power and influence more widespread and effective than anything contemplated by their fighting comrades in the Waffen-SS, who naturally received all the propaganda publicity during the war.

THE SECURITY POLICE

Prior to September 1939, the security police forces of the Third Reich fell into two distinct groups, those of the Nazi Party and those of the German State. The principal Party force was the Sicherheitsdienst des RfSS, or SD, the SS security service, which absorbed all other intelligence services of the NSDAP in June 1934. The State force was known as the Sicherheitspolizei or Sipo (Security Police), a general administrative term used to cover both the traditional Kriminalpolizei or Kripo (Criminal Police) and the more recently formed Geheime Staatspolizei or Gestapo (Political Police). In 1939, all of these groups were united as part of the Staatsschutzkorps programme to become departments of a single newly created SS Hauptamt, the Reichssicherheitshauptamt or RSHA (Reich Central Security Office). These main security police bodies are described in turn below.

● *The SD*

In June 1931, Himmler accepted Reinhard Heydrich, a former Naval communications officer, into the SS as a Sturmführer and set him the task of organising an SS intelligence service to keep watch on the political opposition. Initially known as Department Ic of the SS-Amt, or the Ic-Dienst, then as the Press and Information Service, it was finally renamed the Sicherheitsdienst des Reichsführers-SS (Security Service of the Reichsführer-SS), or SD, in June 1932. By that time, Heydrich had been promoted to SS-Sturmbannführer and with a staff of

Plate 58 SS-Gruppenführer Reinhard Heydrich at his desk in 1937. *Hoffmann*

Plate 59 SD officers who participated in a course at the Italian Colonial Police School in Rome from 9-16 January 1941 are saluted by the Italian Colonial Minister, Teruzzi, *IWM*

Plate 60 Sipo and SD men storming a suspect's house in Warsaw, November 1939. Note the 'Pol', ie. 'Polizei', prefix on the registration plate of their vehicle. *Ullstein*

Plate 61 Hitler pays his last respects to Reinhard Heydrich at the Wagnerian State Funeral service held for him in the Mosaic Chamber of the New Reich Chancellery, 9 June 1942. *IWM*

61

seven civilians established his small SD headquarters in Munich.

When the Nazis came to power at the beginning of 1933, the SD had no more than 200 personnel, most of whom were attached to the various Abschnitte HQs throughout Germany. During the 1933-34 period, however, the service was expanded and many doctors, lawyers and other academics who applied to join the Allgemeine-SS were advised that their best prospects for advancement within the organisation lay with the SD branch. As soon as Himmler took over the Gestapo in April 1934, Heydrich, by then a Brigadeführer, reorganised it and placed as many of his SD men as possible in positions where they could both observe the activities of the political police and gain valuable experience. However, although the SD continued as a separate entity, it had neither the manpower nor the experience to replace the existing political police altogether. Himmler's original plan to incorporate all members of the Sipo into the SD was continually frustrated, and by January 1938 the SD still had only 5,000 full-time and honorary members across the Reich. In fact, with the formation of the RSHA the following year, the SD eventually became superfluous and was itself almost completely absorbed into the security police. Its continued existence as a separate branch of the Allgemeine-SS was due solely to Himmler's desire to retain his SD's unique position as the only intelligence agency of the NSDAP.

The connotations of dread and horror which later attached themselves to the SD in occupied Europe and Russia stemmed from the fact that all members of the security police serving in the conquered territories, whether or not they were members of the SS or SD, were instructed to wear the grey SS uniform with a combination of SD collar and sleeve insignia and police shoulder straps, to give them the protection of military status yet at the same time distinguish them from other uniformed SS, police and Wehrmacht personnel. The atrocities carried out by some of these Sipo men, particularly those attached to extermination squads in the east, reflected directly on the SD proper, the majority of whose members were engaged almost exclusively in academic research, intelligence gathering and policy formulation. In fact, while the death squads which penetrated deep into Soviet territory in 1941 killing Communists, partisans and Jews as they went were entitled 'Einsatzgruppen der Sicherheitspolizei und des SD', only 3% of their members were actually SD men. The greater number were Waffen-SS (34%), army (28%) and uniformed police (22%), assisted by Gestapo (9%) and Kripo (4%).

● The Gestapo

When the Gestapo was established by Göring in 1933, it had 35 members with a budget of 1 million Reichsmarks. Two years later, its membership had risen to over 600 and its budget exceeded 40 million Reichsmarks. As the political police of the Reich, the Gestapo was responsible for gathering information on all subversive individuals and organisations, carrying out plain-clothes surveillance operations and raids, and effecting arrests on a grand scale. It also decided who was to be interned in concentration camps. While the SD simply amassed intelligence, the Gestapo had real power to act on the information contained in its files. Both groups inevitably expended a great deal of energy competing with one another until their amalgamation under the RSHA.

● The Kripo

The Kripo comprised regular police detectives who carried out standard criminal investigation work. Like the Gestapo, they operated in civilian clothes. Their main duties were the investigation of serious statutory offences and common law crimes such as murder, rape, fraud and arson, and the interrogation of suspects. They attended at break-ins, took fingerprints, examined locii for material evidence and prepared relevant reports. The Kripo was the most stable and professional of all the security police forces, and was a favoured recruiting ground for the Reichssicherheitsdienst or RSD, (not to be confused with the SD), an élite force which provided small bodyguard detachments for leading Nazis. Its commander was SS-Brigadeführer Hans Rattenhuber.

● The RSHA

In October 1936, Inspectors of Security Police (Inspekteur der Sicherheitspolizei or IdS) were appointed in each SS Oberabschnitt to improve co-ordination between the Kripo, the Gestapo and the SD. Liaison and interdepartmental co-operation improved thereafter, and on 27 September 1939 the Sipo and SD were brought together to form adjacent departments of the new Reichssicherheitshauptamt or RSHA. Again, a governmental or State office, the Chief of the Security Police, and a Nazi Party office, the Chief of the Security Service, were merged into a single post, Chief of the Security Police and Security Service (Chef der Sicherheitspolizei und des SD, or CSSD). Needless to say, the first CSSD was SS-Gruppenführer Reinhard Heydrich.

The RSHA (often abbreviated 'RSi-H' in SS correspondence to avoid confusion with RuSHA) was divided into seven departments, or ämter, as follows:

Amt I *Personnel.*
This department dealt with all security police and SD personnel matters and was led by SS-Gruppenführer Dr Werner Best, a senior jurist and Heydrich's deputy, until 1940. He was succeeded by Bruno Streckenbach, Erwin Schulz and finally Erich Ehrlinger. Streckenbach went on to command the 19th Division of the Waffen-SS, and Schulz ended the war as security police leader in Salzburg.

Amt II Administration.
It effectively ran the RSHA and was also initially headed by Best, then by Dr Rudolf Siegert, and finally by Josef Spacil, an SS-Standartenführer on the staff of Oberabschnitt Donau.
Amt III SD (Home).
An information service, led by SS-Gruppenführer Otto Ohlendorf, which collated data relating to politics and counter-espionage within Germany. It financed the 'Salon Kitty', a high class brothel in Berlin popular with senior Nazis and wealthy locals. The salon was wired for sound and, depending on what they said during their romps, the clients often found themselves being blackmailed by the SD or arrested by the Sipo shortly thereafter. The prostitutes were in fact female agents of the security police and SD, and went out of their way to entice anti-Nazi remarks from their partners.
Amt IV Gestapo.
Under SS-Gruppenführer Heinrich Müller, the Gestapo continued in its set task of eliminating the enemies of the Nazi regime.
Amt V Kripo.
This active department retained its executive powers in dealing with common crime. Its long-time commander, SS-Gruppenführer Arthur Nebe, was hanged in 1945 for his complicity in the attempt to assassinate Hitler the previous year.
Amt VI SD (Abroad).
An intelligence-gathering service directed against foreign countries, which also organised espionage in enemy territory. It was led first by SS-Brigadeführer Heinz Jost, then by Walter Schellenberg.
Amt VII Ideological Research.
This department was headed by SS-Oberführer Prof Dr Franz Six, and sounded out general public opinion on a range of subjects. Working in conjunction with the Ministry of Propaganda, it monitored the progress of the Nazi indoctrination of the German people. Dr Six was the officer selected to command the security police and SD in occupied Britain, a post which he never took up!

The activities of the RSHA were extremely varied, ranging from the defamation of Tukachevsky and other Soviet Generals, which led to Stalin's purge of the Russian Officer Corps, to the liberation of Mussolini by Skorzeny's commandos. They encompassed anti-terrorist operations, organised assassinations, control of foreigners in Germany, and the collation of political files seized from the police forces of occupied countries. When the Gestapo took over the administration of the Customs Service from the Reich Ministry of Finance, border controls and the combating of smuggling also came under the jurisdiction of the RSHA. As CSSD, Heydrich controlled one of the most complex and all-embracing security police systems the world had ever seen, and in 1940 his standing on an international level was recognised with his nomination to the post of President of Interpol.

A surprisingly high percentage of senior SS officers were attached to the RSHA, since the very nature of its work and the expertise required for many of its operations necessitated that it should be a 'top heavy' organisation so far as rank was concerned. Taking into account every section of the SS, including the vast Waffen-SS, almost a quarter of all officers holding the rank of SS-Sturmbannführer in 1944 (ie 714 out of 3,006 or 23.8%) worked with the RSHA. Corresponding figures for higher ranks were as follows:

- Obersturmbannführer   240 out of 1,199 (20%)
- Standartenführer   95 out of 623 (15.2%)
- Oberführer   41 out of 274 (15%)
- Brigadeführer   31 out of 270 (11.5%)
- Gruppenführer   7 out of 94 (7.4%)
- Obergruppenführer   4 out of 91 (4.4%)
- Oberst-Gruppenführer   0 out of 4 (0%)

These statistics are remarkable, and serve to indicate the size and extent of the security police network in 1944, for they show that no less than one-fifth of all SS Majors and Colonels at that time were Sipo or SD men. Ultimately, there were some 65,000 junior security police officials stationed across Europe and Russia, fed by over 100,000 local informers.

On 27 May 1942, Heydrich, then Deputy Reichsprotektor of Bohemia and Moravia, was blown up by Czech agents in Prague and he died a week later. Upon his death, he was awarded the Blood Order (the last posthumous bestowal of that revered decoration) and he became only the second ever recipient of the highest NSDAP honour, the Deutscher Orden or German Order, a Nazi version of the mediaeval Teutonic Order. Heydrich's assassination stunned Himmler, as it emphasised his own vulnerability to attack. His heavily-armed personal escort battalion, the Begleitbataillon Reichsführer-SS, was immediately doubled in size. On 1 January 1943, after some considerable anxiety and indecision, Himmler finally appointed SS-Obergruppenführer Dr Ernst Kaltenbrunner to fill the combined posts of Chief of the RSHA and CSSD, as Heydrich's successor.

It was inevitable that sooner or later the RSHA would clash with the Abwehr, the Wehrmacht Intelligence Service under Admiral Canaris, but it was not until Canaris was implicated in the 20 July 1944 plot against Hitler that the Abwehr was finally absorbed by Ämter IV and VI of the RSHA, leaving the German armed forces as the only major European military organisation without its own intelligence network. As the war drew to a close, Sipo and SD men furnished themselves with false papers and scurried underground, only to be rooted out again to face trial for their wartime activities or, more often, to continue in their old specialist roles as East and West prepared for what seemed then an almost unavoidable confrontation.

SS-POLICE REGIMENTS AND FOREIGN AUXILIARIES

During the period 1940-42, a large number of younger members of the Ordnungspolizei, supplemented by Allgemeine-SS conscripts, were transferred to 30 newly created independent Police Regiments comprising around 100 battalions, each of 500 men. They were organised and equipped on a military basis and served as security troops in all occupied countries. In February 1943 these German formations were officially designated SS-Police Regiments, to distinguish them from the recently raised native 'Police Rifle' units, and they subsequently gained a reputation for extreme brutality and fanatical loyalty to Himmler and the Nazi regime.

The vast majority of SS-Police Regiments were posted to Russia, eastern Europe and the Balkans, to deal with the roaming partisan bands of Brigade strength or even larger that were causing constant havoc behind the German lines. In 1942, Himmler was made responsible for all counterguerrilla operations, and he appointed SS-Obergruppenführer Erich von dem Bach, formerly head of Oberabschnitt Nordost, as his Chief of Anti-Partisan Units (Chef der Bandenkampfverbände). It quickly became apparent that the territories to be controlled, particularly in Russia, were so vast that the SS-Police needed additional support. Consequently, various pro-German local militias and home guard units composed mainly of Balts, Cossacks and Ukrainians were consolidated into an auxiliary police force known as the Schutzmannschaft der Ordnungspolizei, or Schuma, later expanded to include a Schutzmannschaft der Sicherheitspolizei. Members of the Schuma were generally nationalists at heart,

and they viewed the German forces as liberators. Moreover, on a practical level, their service in the Schuma ensured that they and their families received favourable treatment from the Nazis. Schuma units often committed terrible atrocities against their own countrymen, in an effort to prove that their loyalty to the Reich was beyond question and that they were 'more German than the Germans'.

In Poland, 12 SS-Police Regiments supported the Wehrmacht in maintaining order, backed up by the Polish Police and 12 Schuma battalions. Fourteen SS-Police Regiments served in Byelorussia, as did seven Police Rifle Regiments, which were mixed German-Russian units, and a vast number of Schuma battalions. In Estonia, 26 Schuma battalions were formed, being redesignated 'Estonian Police Battalions' in May 1943 and issued with German police uniforms on account of their reliable record. An estimated 15,000 Latvians and 13,000 Lithuanians served in 64 other Schuma battalions which were deployed right across the Eastern Front, from the Ostland

to Yugoslavia, while the Ukraine alone supplied 70,000 volunteers to staff a further 71 Schuma battalions. In Croatia, pro-Nazis set up a regimental-sized 'Einsatzstaffel', based on the Allgemeine-SS and dressed in quasi-SS uniform, and 15,000 more went into a multi-national 'German-Croatian Gendarmerie' of 30 battalions. On a smaller scale, the Serbians produced 10 auxiliary police battalions, and the Albanians two Police Rifle Regiments.

All of these native auxiliary formations (and there were many more than those mentioned briefly here) were completely separate from the foreign legions of the Wehrmacht. They were police organisations directly subordinate to the local Orpo or Sipo commanders and, ultimately, took their orders from Himmler through his HSSPfs. In effect, they were remote extensions of the Allgemeine-SS, operating in the occupied territories.

In 1944, the German SS-Police Regiments and Waffen-SS were given their own decoration, the Guerrilla Warfare Badge, which was the only combat award officially designated as a 'War Badge of the Waffen-SS and Police'. While it was also open to all members of the Wehrmacht engaged in anti-partisan operations, the SS and police regarded it as being created specifically for them, and holders wore it proudly on every possible occasion, as it represented participation in one of the most ferocious campaigns of the war, where no quarter was asked for or given.

SENIOR SS AND POLICE COMMANDERS

From 1937, each Oberabschnitt commander normally held the post of Höhere SS- und Polizeiführer or HSSPf, the Senior SS and Police Commander in the Region. He acted as Himmler's representative and had technical jurisdiction over all SS and police formations based in his Oberabschnitt. The close relationship between the SS and police subsequently resulted in a joint administration at Regional level, and this amalgamation was particularly convenient in newly occupied territories where it was necessary to rapidly set up tried and tested administrative structures for both the SS and the police. In the conquered countries therefore, as in Germany itself, SS headquarters and police command posts were often established in the same building, with frequent interdepartmental transfers of staff. The Chief of the Hauptamt Persönlicher Stab RfSS, SS-Obergruppenführer Karl Wolff, was appointed to the unique post of Höchste SS- und Polizeiführer (Supreme SS and Police Commander) in 1943 and was, in name at least, the highest ranking of all the HSSPfs. However, he was permanently based in Italy and had little influence on other areas.

In November 1944, the list of HSSPfs based within the Reich proper read as follows:

Oberabschnitt	HSSPf
Alpenland	SS-Ogruf Erwin Rösener
Böhmen-Mähren	SS-Ogruf Karl Hermann Frank
Donau	SS-Gruf Walter Schimana
Elbe	SS-Gruf Ludolf von Alvensleben
Fulda-Werra	SS-Ogruf Josias Erbprinz zu Waldeck und Pyrmont
Main	SS-Ogruf Dr Benno Martin
Mitte	SS-Ogruf Rudolf Querner
Nordost	SS-Ogruf Hans Prützmann
Nordsee	SS-Gruf Georg-Henning Graf Bassewitz-Behr
Ost	SS-Ogruf Wilhelm Koppe
Ostsee	SS-Ogruf Emil Mazuw
Rhein-Westmark	SS-Gruf Jürgen Stroop
Spree	SS-Ogruf August Heissmeyer
Süd	SS-Ogruf Karl Freiherr von Eberstein
Südost	SS-Ogruf Heinrich Schmauser
Südwest	SS-Ogruf Otto Hofmann
Warthe	SS-Gruf Heinz Reinefarth
Weichsel	SS-Gruf Fritz Katzmann
West	SS Ogruf Karl Gutenberger

The SS and police forces working outside Germany, in the occupied territories, were controlled by the undermentioned HSSPfs at that time:

Territory	HSSPf
Adriatic Coast	SS-Gruf Odilo Globocnik
Albania	SS-Gruf Josef Fitzthum
Baltic States (Oa. Ostland)	SS-Ogruf Friedrich Jeckeln
Croatia	SS-Gruf Konstantin Kammerhofer
Denmark	SS-Ogruf Günther Pancke
Hungary	SS-Ogruf Otto Winkelmann
Italy	SS-Ogruf Karl Wolff (Höchst. SS-u.Pol. F.)
Netherlands (Oa.Nordwest)	SS-Ogruf Hanns Rauter
Norway (Oa.Nord)	SS-Ogruf Wilhelm Rediess
Serbia	SS-Gruf Dr Hermann Behrends
Slovakia	SS-Ogruf Hermann Höfle

Subordinate to the HSSPfs, a number of local SS- und Polizeiführer and Polizeigebietsführer directed SS and police operations in areas particularly troubled by partisans and other civil insurgents. At the end of 1944, they were listed as follows:

Locality	SS-u.Pol.F.
Banja Luca	SS-Staf Paul Dahm
Bosnia	SS-Brigf Karl Brunner
Italy (Central)	SS-Oberf Karl Bürger
Italy (Central Highlands)	SS-Oberf Ernst Hildebrandt
Italy (West Highlands)	SS-Brigf Willy Tensfeld
Krakow	SS-Brigf Theobald Thier
Metz	SS-Brigf Anton Dunckern
Montenegro	SS-Brigf Richard Fiedler
Radom	SS-Brigf Dr Herbert Böttcher
Sarajevo	SS-Oberf Werner Fromm
Warsaw	SS-Brigf Otto Paul Geibel
Zagreb	SS-Brigf Willi Brandner

Finally, each major city across Germany and the occupied territories had its Befehlshaber der Ordnungspolizei (BdO) and its Befehlshaber der Sicherheitspolizei und des SD (BdS), whose authorities were restricted to their local uniformed police and security police forces respectively.

62

Plate 62 Himmler's Chief of Anti-Partisan units, SS-Obergruppenführer Erich von dem Bach, accepting the surrender of the Polish Home Army General Bor-Komorowski after the Warsaw Uprising, Ozarow, 2 October 1944. Von dem Bach is wearing the Guerrilla Warfare Badge, and the police officer in the background has Sig-Runes on his left breast pocket, denoting his membership of the SS. *IWM*

6 The Racial Concept

HERRENVOLK AND UNTERMENSCHEN

The notion that the Germanic master race or Herrenvolk had somehow been endowed with an inherent superiority, contrasting particularly sharply with the corrupt characteristics of Slavs, Latins and Jews, enjoyed widespread support in Germany from the mid-19th Century. Theories were propounded that stronger peoples had a natural right to dominate or even exterminate weaker nations in the general struggle for survival, and various versions of the message, often supported by claims of scientific research, appeared in journals over the years.

One of the latter-day proponents of racial ideology was Alfred Rosenberg, born the son of an Estonian shoemaker in 1893. Rosenberg studied in Russia and received a degree in architecture from the University of Moscow. Having fled to Germany after the Russian Revolution, he settled in Munich and joined the Thule Society whose members specialised in anti-Bolshevik and anti-Semitic philosophy. In 1920 he enrolled in the Nazi Party with membership No 18, and immediately won Hitler's attention with the publication of the first of his many books attacking Judaism. In 1923, Rosenberg was nominated by the Führer as editor of the NSDAP newspaper, the *Völkischer Beobachter*, which thereafter vigorously denounced Communists, Jews, Freemasons and Christians. Rosenberg ultimately proposed a new religion which would counter the weak doctrine of Christian love with a strong ideal of racial superiority. In 1930 he produced his masterpiece, *The Myth of the Twentieth Century*, a massive tome which concluded that any given culture would always decay when humanitarian ideals obstructed the right of the dominant race to rule those it had subjugated. The latter were degraded in the book to the level of Untermenschen, or sub-humans. According to Rosenberg the mixture of blood, and the sinking of the racial standard contingent upon it, was the primary cause for the demise of all cultures. Although over 20 million copies of *The Myth of the Twentieth Century* were eventually sold, few people could later be found who had actually had the stamina to wade through it from cover to cover.

One who did read and admire Rosenberg's theories, however, was Richard Walther Darré, a World War 1 artillery officer who turned to agriculture after 1918 and whose consuming enthusiasm was the peasantry. In 1929 he wrote a book entitled *Blood and Soil – The Peasantry as the Life Source of the Nordic Race*, which called for an energetic programme of selective breeding to ensure the increase of Nordic peasant stock and their gradual domination of the Jews and Slavs. In Darré's view, blood alone determined history, ethics, law and economics, and the blood of the German farmer was related to the ground he worked. The farmer who toiled the land would be buried in the same soil, therefore the farmer's daily bread was, in fact, the

blood of his forefathers, which fertilised the earth. German blood would be passed on from generation to generation by means of the soil. Himmler loved the book, befriended its author, and took him into the SS to pursue his research with official sanction. At Hitler's request, Darré later prepared an agricultural policy for the NSDAP which favoured Aryan farmers and re-established the mediaeval hereditary system by which no farm land could ever be sold or mortgaged.

Heavily influenced by Darré, Himmler now began to use agricultural metaphors to justify his new SS recruitment policy of racial selection. In 1931 he wrote, 'We are like a plant-breeding specialist who, when he wants to breed a pure new strain, first goes over the field to cull the unwanted plants. We, too, shall begin by weeding out people who are not suitable SS material'. Applicants for the SS were soon being categorised according to their racial characteristics, from I-a-M/1 (racially very suitable) to IV-3-c (racial reject). Himmler's rapidly increasing obsession with racial purity began to motivate more and more of his schemes during the 1930s. At his behest, the SS kept a genealogical register of its members, and the Reichsführer often pored over it like a horse breeder examining a stud book. He ordered elaborate investigations into his own ancestry and that of his wife, to gather irrefutable evidence of their pure German lineage, and dreamed of a new feudal Europe, cleared of Untermenschen, in which model farms would be operated by a racial élite. The spearhead of that élite was to be the SS, an Orden nordischer Rasse or Order of Nordic Men of the purest selection, acting as guardians of the German people. To paraphrase Himmler, they would 'march onward into a distant future, imbued with the hope and faith not only that they might put up a better fight than their forefathers but that they might themselves be the forefathers of generations to come, generations which would be necessary for the eternal life of the Teutonic German nation'.

As foretold in *Mein Kampf*, Hitler's Nürnberg Laws of 1935 deprived Germany's Jews of Reich citizenship, the vote and eligibility for appointment to State offices. Marriage or extra-marital relations between Jews and Germans was forbidden, and Jewish businesses closed down. By 1938, the Nazis were raising an international loan to finance the emigration of all German Jews and their resettlement on some of Germany's former overseas colonies. When war broke out, however, Jews began to be moved instead to Ghettos in occupied Poland, which was a cheaper and more expedient alternative. This racial fanaticism reached its ultimate and infamous conclusion at the end of 1941 when it became clear that an easy victory would not be won and that World War 2 might drag on for years. The complex prewar plans for the peaceful removal of Jews and Slavs from Reich territory were now shelved. Einsatzgruppen in the east had been executing Jews and suspected partisans on an ad hoc basis since the invasion of Russia, but the actual

Die Bildermappe Willrichs zeigt uns Köpfe von SS-Männern aus allen Gegenden Deutschlands. Sie soll dem Beschauer vor Augen führen, daß dieses nordische Blut, das diese Gesichter geformt und geprägt hat, dem ganzen deutschen Volk eigen ist und niemals der das deutsche Volk trennende, sondern stets nur der das deutsche Volk verbindende Blutsteil ist.

Je länger man diese Gesichter ansieht, desto bekannter kommen sie einem vor. Wir treffen sie nicht nur in der heutigen Zeit in allen Gegenden unseres Vaterlandes, sondern finden sie wieder, wenn wir uns die Bilder der Ahnen unseres Volkes aller Zeiten vergegenwärtigen.

Mögen die Arbeiten Willrichs, von denen ich wünschen möchte, daß möglichst viele deutsche Menschen — besonders junge — sie zu sehen bekommen, dazu beitragen, das ewige Gesicht germanisch-deutschen Blutes ins Gedächtnis zu rufen und damit die große Verpflichtung, dieses Blut rein zu erhalten und zu mehren.

Der Reichsführer-SS

H. Himmler

Plate 63   Introductory page to a series of prints by the renowned German artist Wolfgang Willrich, commissioned by Himmler in 1936 to illustrate the racial purity of the SS.

Plate 64   Willrich print depicting an Unterscharführer on the staff of the SS Officers School at Braunschweig as the paragon of Nordic manhood.

Plate 65   Security Policemen searching Jews in the Warsaw Ghetto, November 1939. *Ullstein*

Plate 66 An SS medical officer, from Mengele's staff, examining a newly-arrived consignment of Jews at the railway sidings at Auschwitz-Birkenau in 1944. Those deemed unfit for work were dispatched for immediate extermination. *Ullstein*

Plate 67 SS men guarding Hungarian Jews at Auschwitz railway terminal, summer 1944. This candid photograph was found in Czechoslovakia at the end of the war, among the possessions of a dead Waffen-SS soldier who had previously served at the camp. *Ullstein*

Plate 68 Oak casket carved with Sig-Runes, a swastika, a Hagall-Rune, oakleaves and acorns. It was used at SS wedding ceremonies as a container for presentation copies of *Mein Kampf*

process of killing was random, and had to be accelerated. On 20 January 1942, Heydrich convened a meeting of representatives of the various government ministries at the pleasant Berlin suburb of Wannsee, and they decided upon a much simpler and irrevocable 'Final Solution' to the problem. All the Jews and Slavs of Europe and western Russia were to be rounded up and transported to specified locations to be worked to death, then cremated. Those who were unfit for work would be killed on arrival by gassing. To that end, large Vernichtungslager or extermination camps were established at Auschwitz, Belzec, Chelmno, Majdanek, Sobibor and Treblinka, all in Poland, and there were minor ones set up at Kaunas, Lwow, Minsk, Riga and Vilna. Naturally, all were placed under the control of the Reich's racial warriors, the SS. Their history is well known. In 1946, the Nürnberg indictment concluded that these camps witnessed the deaths of 5,700,000 Jews, Slavs and Gypsies between 1942 and 1945, in the Nazi drive towards the 'racial purification of Europe'.

At Auschwitz, the main extermination camp, racial experiments were carried out in the same way as Rascher engaged upon medical experiments at Dachau. Skeletons of victims were collected for racially-based 'scientific measurements'. Skulls and skin types were compared, eyes and noses categorised, brains weighed and hair graded. An assortment of SS eugenists from Ahnenerbe strove to prove by their research that humans could be bred exactly like animals, with full pedigrees. The most infamous of them all was Josef Mengele, a Doctor of Philosophy (Munich) and Doctor of Medicine (Frankfurt/Main), who was rabidly inspired by the hope of eliminating all racial impurities and physical abnormalities from the German people. He served as a medical officer with the Waffen-SS in France and Russia, and in 1943 was appointed Chief Doctor at Auschwitz, with an unlimited supply of human guinea-pigs at his disposal. At once, he began a study of deformities. All prisoners who were in any way malformed were immediately butchered upon their arrival at Auschwitz so that Mengele and his assistants could examine the bodies in a special dissection ward. No twins, dwarves or hunchbacks escaped his scalpel. He even sewed normal twins together to create artificial Siamese twins, and injected the brown eyes of living patients in an effort to turn them blue. These racial experiments caused untold agonies and had little or no practical benefits, unlike some of the purely medical experiments carried out in other camps.

Modern apologists for the Waffen-SS have consistently put forward the argument that the horrors which took place in concentration and extermination camps during the war must have been unknown to ordinary SS soldiers fighting at the battlefront, on the basis that the camps had nothing at all to do with the Waffen-SS. In fact, that whole hypothesis is fatally flawed, for the camps were reclassified by Himmler in April 1941 and actually became an integral part of the Waffen-SS! From that time on, during the worst atrocities, camp officers and guards wore Waffen-SS uniforms with distinctive brown piping, and carried Waffen-SS paybooks. The permanent camp administrative staffs of older Totenkopf NCOs were reinforced by substantial numbers of wounded and recuperating officers and guards transferred in on a temporary rota basis from various battlefield SS units, of which the Totenkopf-Division was only one. For example, Feldgendarmerie elements of the Leibstandarte and men from the 13th SS-Division were stationed at Buchenwald and Gross-Rosen camps in 1943, while 'Wiking' Division personnel found themselves in the unfortunate position of manning Belsen when it was liberated by the British. Karl Gebhardt, supervisor of medical and racial experiments at the camps, had formerly been a front-line surgeon with SS-Division 'Das Reich', and Richard Glücks, the man in daily operational charge of the whole concentration camp system, was a Waffen-SS General as well as being Inspekteur der Konzentrationslager. The Waffen-SS men who transiently staffed the camps took their directions from the permanent cadres of Totenkopfverbände veterans, and were assisted by foreign auxiliaries, selected prisoners, and even a few factory guards, SA and Wehrmacht personnel in 1944-45. So while the WVHA administered the camps and the RSHA decided who was to be incarcerated in them, members of the Waffen-SS effectively ran them and were certainly not exempt from practising the 'Final Solution' at grass roots level.

MARRIAGE IN THE SS

Under Himmler, the SS came to regard itself not merely as a temporary political association but as a 'Sippe', ie a tribe or clan. The same racial qualities looked for in the SS man were therefore also required of his wife.

The Engagement and Marriage Order of the SS, one of the oldest fundamental laws of the organisation, was issued by Himmler on 31 December 1931, and read as follows:

'(i)   The SS is an association of German men, defined according to their Nordic blood and specially selected.

(ii)   In conformity with the National Socialist conception of the world, and recognising that the future of our people is founded on selection and the preservation of good German blood, free from all taint of hereditary disease, I now require all members of the SS to obtain the authorisation of the Reichsführer-SS before marriage.

(iii)   Consent to marry will be given or refused solely on the grounds of racial or physical considerations, and with a view to congenital health.

(iv) Any SS man who marries without seeking the prior authorisation of the Reichsführer-SS, or who marries in spite of being refused such authorisation, will be dismissed from the SS.

H. HIMMLER

To administer the new racial and marriage procedures, Himmler created the SS Race and Settlement Office on the same day the order was issued, and placed it under Darré, his racial Guru.

The main objects looked for in adjudging the marriage applications of SS men were, firstly, racial purity and, secondly, physical compatibility between the two partners likely to result in a fertile union. Thus an application to marry an elderly woman, or a woman markedly bigger or smaller than the intended husband, was likely to be rejected. The prospective bride and her family had to prove their Aryan ancestry back to the mid-18th Century, uncontaminated by the presence of Jewish or Slavonic ancestors. She further had to demonstrate that she was free from all mental and physical disease and had to submit to an exhaustive medical examination, including fertility testing by SS doctors. Only after a couple had successfully completed all these tests could an SS marriage take place. More than a few members found the marriage regulations impossible to live with, and in 1937 alone 300 men were expelled from the SS for marrying without approval.

Christian weddings were replaced in the Allgemeine-SS by pseudo-pagan rites presided over by the bridegroom's commander. Marriages no longer took place in churches but in the open air under lime trees, or in SS buildings decorated with life runes, sunflowers and fir twigs. An eternal flame burned in an urn in front of which the couple swore oaths of loyalty, exchanged rings and received the official SS gift of bread and salt, symbols of the earth's fruitfulness and purity. A presentation copy of *Mein Kampf* was then taken from a heavy oak casket carved with runes, and handed over to the groom. Finally, as the couple departed from the ceremony, they invariably passed through a sombre arcade of saluting brethren.

It is interesting to note that the marriage rules applied not only to male members of the SS but also to female employees and auxiliaries. In the case of the latter, if they were already married when they applied for appointment with the SS, they were obliged to produce on behalf of their husbands records and genealogical charts going back to the grandparents for examination by RuSHA.

THE CHILDREN OF THE SS

Throughout the 1920s, Germany was reeling from the catastrophic losses of manpower suffered between 1914 and 1918. The SS therefore demanded that its racial élite should quickly breed and multiply and in 1931 Himmler announced that it was the patriotic mission of every SS couple to produce at least four children. Where that was not possible, the SS pair were expected to adopt racially suitable orphans and bring them up on National Socialist lines.

To show the interest the SS had in its children, the organisation created a range of official gifts for them. At the birth of their first child, Himmler sent each set of SS parents a ribbon and bib of blue silk, symbolising the unity of birth, marriage, life and death, and a silver beaker and spoon representing eternal nourishment. During the subsequent pagan naming ceremony, which replaced the traditional Christening in SS circles, the child would be wrapped in a shawl of undyed wool embroidered with oak leaves, runes and swastikas, while both parents placed their hands on the baby's head and pronounced names like Karl or Siegfried, Gudrun or Helga, and, of course, Adolf or Heinrich. The Reichsführer served as nominal godfather to all SS children born each year on the anniversary of his birthday, 7 October, and on the birth of a fourth child he sent the happy parents a letter of congratulations and a Lebenleuchter, a silver candlestick engraved with the words, 'You are a link in the eternal racial chain'.

However, despite Himmler's exhortations, the SS birthrate during the 1930s remained average for the country as a whole. Wages were low, and children were expensive. On 13 September 1936, in a further desperate attempt to encourage SS families to have more offspring, the Reichsführer established a registered Society known as Lebensborn or the Fountain of Life. Senior full-time SS leaders were expected to make financial contributions so that the Society could provide maternity homes to which both married and unmarried mothers of SS children could be admitted free of charge. Although affiliated to RuSHA, Lebensborn was directly subordinated to SS-Standartenführer Max Sollmann of the Hauptamt Persönlicher Stab RfSS. Its stated objectives were:

(i) To assist in sustaining large racially valuable families;

(ii) To look after pregnant mothers of good race; and

(iii) To care for the children of racially suitable unions.

Maternity homes were quickly set up at Hohehorst, Klosterheide, Polzin, Steinhöring and Wienerwald, and Himmler took an intense personal interest in them. Every detail fascinated him, from the shapes of the noses of newly-born infants to the volume of milk produced by nursing mothers, the most prolific of whom received Mothers' Crosses and other special recognitions. Any babies appearing with mental or physical handicaps were smothered

92

at birth and, so far as the mothers were concerned, were said to be 'still-born'. Despite the contemporary salacious rumours about brothels and 'SS stud farms', only a small percentage of children appearing from the Society's homes in peacetime were illegitimate. The establishment of the Lebensborn homes was a genuine attempt by Himmler to provide free but high quality maternity care for the poorer SS families.

The outbreak of war in 1939 stimulated the Reichsführer to remind all members of the SS that it was now their most urgent duty to become fathers. On 28 November, he issued the following instruction:

'Order to the SS and Police.
Every war involves a shedding of the purest blood. A multitude of victories will mean a great loss of it, but the death of our best men will not in itself be the ultimate consequence. What will be worse will be the absence of children who have not been procreated by the living during the war, and who cannot be procreated by the dead after the war.

Regardless of the civil law and normal bourgeois customs, it must now be the duty of all German women and girls of good blood to become mothers of the children of SS soldiers going to the Front, not frivolously but in all moral seriousness.

The future of these children will be ensured as follows:
(i)   Official guardians will take over the wardship, in the name of the Reichsführer-SS, of all legitimate or illegitimate children of good blood whose fathers have fallen in the war.
(ii) The Chief of the Rasse- und Siedlungshauptamt and his staff will observe discretion in the keeping of documentation relating to the parentage of such children.
SS men must see clearly that, in complying with this order, they will perform an act of great importance. Mockery, disdain and non-comprehension will not affect us, for the future belongs to us!
H. HIMMLER'

It was the same concern to ensure the future of the race which was behind Himmler's subsequent 'Special Order' of 15 August 1942. It indicated that when an SS family had only one son left, and he was of military age, he would be withdrawn from the battlefield and sent home for a year in order to have children and preserve his lineage. Therefore, no justification could exist for SS men to fall short in their biological duty. In fact, failure to carry it out hampered their careers. By virtue of a Himmler memorandum issued in February 1944, all recommendations for the promotion of married SS officers had henceforth to include details of their date of marriage, age of wife, number of children and date of birth of the last child. Where the last child was

born more than two years previously, and where the wife was not over 40 years of age, an explanation had to be added as to why no more children had been conceived. If there was no sufficient explanation, the application for promotion would be rejected. In a similar vein, a 44-year-old bachelor, SS-Hauptsturmführer Franz Schwarz, was threatened in 1943 that if he had not married within the year he would be dismissed from the SS!

The Lebensborn Society continued to operate until the end of the war, and new SS maternity homes were opened up in Oslo, Schwarzwald, Schloss Wegimont in Belgium, and Taunus. Suitable foreign children, usually orphans, and even infants who had been torn from their Polish, Czech or Russian families by VOMI officials because they were recognised as being of Nordic descent, were accepted into Lebensborn homes to be adopted by childless SS couples. Ultimately, more than 80,000 non-German children were thus 'Germanised' by the SS.

RUSHA

The SS Race and Settlement Office, created on 31 December 1931 under Darré, achieved Hauptamt status on 30 January 1935 and was renamed the SS Rasse- und Siedlungshauptamt or RuSHA, the SS Race and Settlement Department. It was therefore one of the three oldest Hauptämter in the Reichsführung-SS, and in 1937 consisted of the following seven ämter:

I   – Organisation & Verwaltungsamt (Organisation & Administration)
II   – Rassenamt (Race)
III – Schulungsamt (Education)
IV   – Sippen- und Heiratsamt (Family & Marriage)
V   – Siedlungsamt (Settlement)
VI   – Amt für Archiv und Zeitungswesen (Records & Press)
VII – Amt für Bevölkerungspolitik (Population Policy)

In the general reorganisation of SS administration which took place in 1940, RuSHA, like the SS Hauptamt, lost some of its functions and retained only the Rassenamt, Sippen- und Heiratsamt, Siedlungsamt and Verwaltungsamt. It was thus stripped down to the bare essentials for continuing the work indicated by its title. Nevertheless, in spite of this restriction in its field of activity, the volume of work undertaken by RuSHA necessarily increased with the progress of the war. That was due partly to the physical expansion of the SS, and partly to the repatriation of racial Germans from Russia and the Balkans and their resettlement in Germany and the occupied areas of Poland.

The main duty of RuSHA was to translate into practice the general racial theories of SS ideology. To assist in the execution of its policy it had a special officer (Führer im Rasse- und Siedlungswesen) on the staff of each Oberabschnitt, and Family Welfare Offices (Sippenpflegestellen) set up in the larger towns of Germany and the occupied countries. With the racial laws of the SS as a basis, it was the task of RuSHA and its agencies to supervise the selection and breeding of SS men and to foster the general well-being of the SS in accordance with its code of 'tribal solidarity'.

In theory, as already discussed, every candidate for entry into the SS had to furnish documentary proof of Aryan descent. In all cases, RuSHA was the only competent authority for checking racial and genealogical records and deciding on the racial suitability of the person concerned. In peacetime, and in wartime so far as the Allgemeine-SS was concerned, this procedure was strictly adhered to. With the rapid expansion of the Waffen-SS after 1940, however, the racial rule became something of a dead letter for its 750,000 rank and file. During the war, the hard-pressed RuSHA authorities were content to accept a signed declaration of Aryan descent from enlisted German and West European Waffen-SS men, which could be investigated later when necessity demanded or when the opportunity presented itself. Needless to say, the Armenians, Turkestanis and other non-Germanic volunteers who fought alongside the Waffen-SS at the end of the war were never considered for SS membership proper, but were looked upon simply as auxiliary troops who wore a sort of diluted SS uniform for convenience sake. They were prohibited from sporting the SS Runes, and all had their own distinctive badges so that there would be absolutely no possibility of their being mistaken for 'real' SS men.

VOMI

When the Nazis came to power, millions of racial Germans, or Volksdeutsche, were living in central and eastern Europe. Ever since the Middle Ages, their ancestors had moved eastwards from their original German territories to find new lands and livelihoods. Settling in an enormous region stretching from the Baltic States in the north to the Volga and the Caucasus in the south, these migrants formed closely knit communities that remained independent of their neighbours and retained strong ties of kinship with the old 'heimat'. They had their own association, the League for Germans Abroad or Volksbund für das Deutschtum in Ausland (VDA), which was taken over by the NSDAP in 1930 and put under the direction of Werner Lorenz, a former World War I pilot who owned a vast estate near Danzig and had the reputation of being something of a bon vivant. Lorenz joined the SS in 1931, and

his sophisticated lifestyle, combined with his unique ability to be equally at ease with both diplomats and peasant farmers alike, soon brought him to Himmler's attention.

From the outset, the Nazis were counting on ethnic Germans to augment their new Reich's depleted population and help in its ultimate expansion eastwards. Himmler in particular vowed to take German blood from wherever it could be found in the world, and to 'rob and steal it' whenever he could. To that end, an agency of the NSDAP known as the Büro von Kursell was formed in March 1936 to co-ordinate attempts to encourage the return of Volksdeutsche to the homeland. In 1937 it was renamed the Volksdeutsche Mittelstelle or VOMI, the Department for the Repatriation of Racial Germans, and put under the direction of Lorenz, now an SS-Obergruppenführer. Under Lorenz, VOMI performed so efficiently that in July 1938 Hitler increased its power. It absorbed the VDA and other similar agencies, brought together rival factions in the ethnic German communities, and funnelled in money to build recreation facilities and hospitals and spread Nazi propaganda. VOMI also investigated the politics of individual ethnic Germans, and began compiling files on those suspected of opposition to the Führer.

Although VOMI was not formally incorporated into the Allgemeine-SS until 1941, Himmler quickly made it his own instrument. He infiltrated SS men into the department and persuaded its existing staff to join the SS. The Reichsführer also installed as Lorenz's deputy an SS colleague, Gruppenführer Dr Hermann Behrends of the SD, by which means Heydrich was soon using VOMI to plant SD officials in far-flung communities of racial Germans in eastern Europe.

Himmler first exercised his new-found authority in foreign affairs in Czechoslovakia. Created after the old Austro-Hungarian Empire was carved up in 1919, Czechoslovakia was home to more than 3 million people of German descent. Most of these Volksdeutsche lived in the country's western part, the Sudetenland, and their presence became a wedge by which Hitler began to splinter the Czech republic in 1938. He used VOMI and the SS to continuously penetrate Sudeten communities. SD agents provocateur played upon the grievances of the Sudeten Germans, who had been hit hard by the depression and felt mistreated by the Czech government, and SS funds subsidised the pro-Nazi Sudeten German Party under Dr Konrad Henlein. Heydrich won the allegiance of Henlein's deputy, Karl Hermann Frank, and VOMI helped form a secret fifth column to subvert the Czech government in the event of a German invasion. However, the mere threat of armed conflict was sufficient for the Czechs to cede the Sudetenland to Germany as of 1 October 1938. Henlein became Gauleiter of the area, and both he and Frank were rewarded by Himmler with the rank of SS-Gruppenführer.

The emergence of the SS as a force in foreign policy had relegated von Ribbentrop's diplomats to a back seat during the Sudeten Crisis, and Hitler again looked to VOMI and the SS as he plotted to take over the rest of Czechoslovakia. Late in January 1939, the Führer assigned Heydrich and other leading members of the SD key roles in the final dismemberment of the country. Hitler's plan hinged upon provoking trouble in the eastern province of Slovakia, where nationalist feelings had been stirred by the events in the Sudetenland. A team of SS men led by Gruppenführer Wilhelm Keppler set off bombs in Bratislava and put the blame on the Slovaks. VOMI organised street demonstrations and SD groups led by Heydrich's troubleshooter, Alfred Naujocks, carried out further acts of provocation. On 15 March, rather than risk war, the Czechoslovakian President agreed to German 'protection' of the provinces of Bohemia and Moravia, while Hungary grabbed the easternmost and last remaining province, Ruthenia.

Late in August 1939, Hitler turned once more to the SS to provide his excuse for invading Poland. Heydrich dreamed up scores of incidents which could be attributed to Polish extremists and thus justify a German attack. These were played out by a dozen teams of SD men and police officers under the Gestapo chief Heinrich Müller. The most important of the bogus raids, codenamed Operation 'Himmler', was launched by Alfred Naujocks against a German radio station at the border town of Gleiwitz on 31 August. The following day, citing the attack, Hitler announced his declaration of war against Poland.

During September 1939, the advances of the Red Army into eastern Poland in accordance with the Nazi-Soviet Pact brought some 136,000 Volksdeutsche under Russian occupation. In discussions with Berlin, however, the Soviets agreed to let these people leave. Moreover, the Reich also negotiated for the transfer of another 120,000 ethnic Germans living in the Baltic States. Throughout the winter of 1939-40, the first 35,000 east European Volksdeutsche were evacuated from Wolhynia. The provisions of the Russo-German Resettlement Treaty had to be completed by November 1940, and during October alone some 45,000 rapidly uprooted men, women and children made the long and so-called 'final trek' from Bessarabia and northern Bukovina to VOMI reception camps in Pomerania, East Prussia and the Warthegau before leaving for permanent settlement in the incorporated Polish territory. By mid-1941, 200,000 racial German repatriates had been given possession of 47,000 confiscated Polish farms comprising a total of 23 million acres.

As the Reich expanded further eastwards into the Ukraine after 1941, masses of Volksdeutsche were moved out from Rumania, Hungary, Albania and Yugoslavia for resettlement in the newly occupied lands under the Eastern Ministry of Alfred Rosenberg. Each family was permitted only 50 kg of personal possessions or two horse-drawn wagon loads, and some wagon trains travelled as many as 2,000

miles in scenes reminiscent of the American frontier era. All arrivals were probed by SS doctors and racial examiners from RuSHA to confirm that they were suitable to be reclassified as Reichsdeutsche and given German citizenship, but long stays in VOMI's 1,500 resettlement and transit camps left many Volksdeutsche feeling disappointed, embittered and hopeless. By 1945, VOMI had forcibly moved as many as 1,200,000 ethnic Germans, the bulk of whom became displaced persons at the end of the war.

THE RKFDV

While VOMI dealt with the transportation of Volksdeutsche repatriates and RuSHA supervised their racial purity, their actual resettlement was the responsibility of a third SS organisation, the Reichskommissariat für die Festigung des deutschen Volkstums in Ausland or RKFDV, the Reich Commission for the Consolidation of Germanism Abroad. It was created on 7 October 1939, with Himmler as its Reichskommissar, and he immediately established a Berlin staff HQ, the Hauptamt RKF, directed by SS-Obergruppenführer Ulrich Greifelt. To administer the financing of its operations, a Land Bank Company was set up under SS-Obersturmbannführer Ferdinand Hiege and money poured in from the sales of confiscated Jewish and Polish property.

Himmler intended that not only repatriated racial Germans but also crippled SS ex-servicemen and returned veterans should eventually be settled in the eastern territories as 'Wehrbauern' or 'Peasant Guards', to provide a buffer between the Reich proper and the unconquered wilderness beyond the Urals. From 1940, SS recruiting propaganda laid considerable stress on the opportunities which would be open to all SS men after the war, with the promise of free land in the east, and a number of SS soldiers invalided out from the services were employed on preparatory settlement work with the so-called 'SS-Baueinsatz-Ost'. In the words of SS-Obergruppenführer Otto Hofmann of RuSHA, 'the east would belong to the SS'.

In May 1942, SS-Oberführer Prof Dr Konrad Meyer of the Hauptamt RKF finished drawing up the great resettlement plan on behalf of Himmler. Under its terms, the Baltic States and Poland were to be fully Germanised. The occupied east would be carved up into three huge provinces or Marks (Ingermanland, Narev and Gotengau) under the supreme authority of the Reichsführer-SS, who was to be their new liege lord. He would direct the settlers to the areas provided for them and grant them lands of varying types, 'life fiefs', 'hereditary fiefs' and 'special status properties'. Provincial headmen appointed by Himmler were to supervise the Marches of the new SS Empire. After a 25-year period of racial purification, it was calculated, their population would be 50% Germanic. There would be a system of 26 eastern strongpoints consisting of small towns of about 20,000 inhabitants, each surrounded by a ring of German villages at a distance of about three miles, to guard the intersections of German communications arteries. The villages themselves were to comprise 30 to 40 farmhouses and have their own SS 'Warrior Stürme' to which all male inhabitants would belong. Working along Viking lines, it was to be the greatest piece of continental colonisation the world had ever seen, designed to protect western civilisation from the threat of Asiatic invasion.

From the beginning, however, Himmler and the RKFDV encountered insurmountable obstacles set up by competing Nazi satraps in the occupied lands, each intent upon securing his own niche of influence in the new Empire. Neither Hans Frank, Governor-General of Poland, nor Alfred Rosenberg, Minister for the Occupied Eastern Territories, were SS men and they owed no allegiance to the Reichsführer. Several Gauleiters, particularly Erich Koch, Reichskommissar in the Ukraine, and Wilhelm Kube, Reichskommissar in Byelorussia, fought consistently to hinder the resettlement programme in

Plate 69 Young German girls from a Lebensborn home, their heads garlanded with flowers in pagan style, give the Nazi salute at Nürnberg in 1938. *IWM.*

their areas, which they saw as an SS impingement on NSDAP authority. Even Albert Forster, the Gauleiter of Danzig-West Prussia, who was an SS-Obergruppenführer and had been a member of the SS before Himmler himself, was so antagonistic to the prospect of taking Volksdeutsche settlers into his domain that ships carrying repatriates from Estonia to Danzig had to be re-routed.

In the end, the practicalities consequent upon the turn of the tide of war smashed Himmler's dream of an eastern Germanic Empire run by the SS. From 1943, Hitler felt that repatriated ethnic Germans could better be used in solving Germany's pressing domestic labour shortage, and Himmler had little choice but to listen and agree. Thereafter, Volksdeutsche were brought 'home to the Reich' only to work in the thriving armaments industry and staff the factories and farms that had been depleted by Wehrmacht recruitment. In so doing, they toiled alongside the Poles, Russians and other imported slave labourers whom they were meant to have replaced in the east. Ironically, huge numbers of anti-Communist Slav volunteers in the Schutzmannschaft and Wehrmacht, technically Untermenschen by SS standards, were by that time being relied upon to bolster the Nazi régime in the occupied territories. Himmler had attempted to do too much too quickly, to reverse the developments of a thousand years in a single decade, and the whole racial concept had come crashing down about his head.

96

7 The SS and History

GERMANIC LORE AND PAGANISM

During the 19th Century, Germany witnessed a resurgence of nationalism and in the progression towards a unified Reich there grew a tremendous interest in Mediaeval history and the mysteries of ancient Germanic legend. This fascination was fired by the operatic works of Richard Wagner (1813-83), a rabid anti-Semite whose early romantic heroes such as Parsifal and Lohengrin were the epitomes of knightly chivalry, continually battling against the forces of evil. Wagner's last and epic work, however, 'Der Ring des Nibelungen' or 'The Ring of the Nibelung' was set in the murky world of Dark Age fables. Its four great interconnecting operas, viz 'Rheingold', 'Die Walküre' (which included a Valkyrie named Siegrune!), 'Siegfried' and 'Götterdämmerung', were acted out in a land of Gods, giants, dragons, supermen and slavish sub-human dwarves, where a magical ring and enchanted sword bestowed limitless power and invincibility upon their owners. The Ring Cycle had a timeless message about the human desire for influence and wealth at the expense of all other things, but the moral of the tale was soon lost in its telling, as the operas with their sublime music captivated and bewitched those who attended them, and instilled in the audiences a feeling of racial unity and national identity which seemed to extend back to the beginning of mankind. Hitler himself was to be inspired in his youth by Wagner's music, and it was while he was entranced by it that he conceived his great plans for the future of Germany. He said years later, 'For me, Wagner was someone godly and his music is my religion. I go to his concerts as others go to church.'

Exalted by the works of Wagner and by the writings of the philosopher Friedrich Nietzsche (1844-1900), whose book *Man and Superman* divided the world into masters and slaves and foresaw the coming of a great leader who would build a new order of 'Übermenschen', a number of German nationalists founded the Thule Society in Berlin in 1912. The Society took its name from the legendary 'Ultima Thule' or 'Land at the End of the World', supposedly the birthplace of the Germanic race, and its primary purpose was to serve as a literary circle for the study of ancient German history and customs. After 1918, it became fanatically anti-Bolshevik and anti-Semitic, and eventually propounded the aim of unifying Europe under the leadership of a Great Germanic Reich. Significantly, the symbol of the Thule Society was a sunwheel swastika.

The Bavarian branch of the Society was small, but its membership was hand-picked and included Himmler, Hess and Röhm. The nobility, the judiciary, higher academics, leading industrialists, and army and police officers were all represented to the virtual exclusion of the lower classes. Thule conducted open nationalistic propaganda through its own newspaper, the Munich *Völkischer Beobachter*

edited by Dietrich Eckart (who later coined the Nazi battle-cry 'Deutschland Erwache!' or 'Germany Awake!'), and set up a secret intelligence service which infiltrated Communist groups. It maintained and financed three Freikorps units, ie Oberland, Reichskriegsflagge and Wiking, and to win popular support to its cause promoted the German Workers' Party under 'front-man' Anton Drexler in 1919. When Drexler's Party was taken over by Hitler and expanded under its new name as the NSDAP, it completely absorbed the Thule Society together with its newspaper, nationalist programme and racist policies.

Through his association with Thule, Himmler became obsessed with pagan Germanic culture, an obsession which grew ever stronger as the years went by and one which came to influence his entire way of life and that of the SS. During the early 1930s, the Reichsführer established an SS-sponsored Society for the Care of German Historic Monuments and acquired a publishing house, Nordland-Verlag, to spread his ideas to the general public. Plans for the systematic creation of a cultural framework to replace Christianity, referred to as the Development of the German Heritage, were worked

Fig 11 *Advertising Poster for the Thule Society, 1919* Note use of the sunwheel swastika.

98

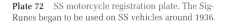

Plate 70 Over 120,000 Germans enjoyed an impressive neo-pagan summer solstice celebration in the Berlin Olympic Stadium on 21 June 1939. The event was organised jointly by the SS and the Ministry of Propaganda. *IWM*

Plate 71 Sig-Runes decal introduced on 12 August 1935 for wear on SS steel helmets. It was initially restricted to the Leibstandarte, SS-VT and SS-TV, but was later authorised for all members of the SS organisation, including non-Germanics in the Waffen-SS.

Plate 72 SS motorcycle registration plate. The Sig-Runes began to be used on SS vehicles around 1936.

out between Himmler's Personal Staff and selected academics in 1937. A new moral philosophy based on the supposed beliefs of the old Germanic tribes was formulated and two pagan rites, the summer and winter solstices, revived to replace Christian festivals. The summer event centred around sporting activities and the winter one, the Yule, was a time devoted to the honouring of ancestors. God became 'Got' in SS circles (allegedly the old Germanic spelling), to distinguish the pagan SS God from the conventional Christian 'Gott', the suggestion to use the word having emanated from Karl Diebitsch during his preparation of new SS wedding and child-naming ceremonies.

It is evident that Himmler truly saw himself as founder of a new Pagan Order which would eventually spread across Europe and last at least as long as the German millennium ushered in by Adolf Hitler. Of course, human nature being what it is, he realised that working towards the accomplishment of his dream was a never-ending task which would still fully occupy 'the tenth or twentieth Reichsführer' after him. In the event, the horrors of World War 2 resulted in more and more SS men returning to the Church of their childhood for comfort and succour until, by 1945, the light of the pagan candle had finally been snuffed out.

THE RUNES

All the uniforms and regalia of Nazi Germany made effective use of symbolism in their designs, but none more so than those of the SS. Alongside the Totenkopf, which has already been discussed in Chapter 4: Uniforms, the SS Runen or SS runes represented the élitism and brotherly comradeship of the organisation, and were consciously elevated to an almost holy status. Indeed, as SS men marched off to war in 1939, they sang their hymn 'We Are All SS' ('SS Wir Alle') which included the line, 'We all stand ready for battle, inspired by runes and death's head' ('Wir alle stehen zum Kampf bereit, wenn Runen und Totenkopf führen').

The word 'rune' derives from the Old Norse 'run', meaning 'secret script'. Runes were characters which formed the alphabets used by the Germanic tribes of pre-Christian Europe for both magical and ordinary writing. There were three major branches of the runic alphabet and a number of minor variants, and some runes doubled as symbols representative of human traits or ideals much as the Romans used oak and laurel leaves to denote strength and victory. In 98 AD, in his work *Germania*, the historian Cornelius Tacitus described in detail how the Germans engaged in divination by runes.

In the 19th and early 20th Centuries, runes began to be re-examined by the fashionable 'Völkisch' or 'folk' movements of northern Europe, which promoted interest in traditional stories, beliefs and fes-

tivals. Among these groups was the Thule Society, and through his association with its activities Himmler began to look back to the mystical dark age Germanic period for much of his inspiration. He had always had a fascination for cryptic codes and hidden messages, so it was doubly appropriate that he should tap many of the ideas in pagan symbolism and adopt, or adapt, certain runes for use by his SS.

All pre-1939 Allgemeine-SS Anwärter were instructed in runic symbolism as part of their probationary training. By 1945, 14 main varieties of rune were in use by the SS, and these are described below and shown in the accompanying illustrations.

● The Hakenkreuz
The Hakenkreuz or Swastika was the pagan Germanic sign of Donner (or Thor), the God of Adventurers. During the 19th Century it came to be regarded as symbolic of nationalism and racial struggle, and in the post-1918 period was adopted by several Freikorps units, primarily the Ehrhardt Brigade. As the senior badge of the Nazi Party and State, it inevitably featured on many SS accoutrements, either static (ie standing flat) or mobile (ie standing on one point to give the appearance of an advancing movement). An elongated version of the mobile swastika was used by the Germanic-SS in Flanders.

● The Sonnenrad
The Sonnenrad or Sunwheel Swastika was the Old Norse representation of the sun, and was taken up as an emblem by the Thule Society. It was later used as a sign by the Waffen-SS divisions 'Wiking' and 'Nordland', many of whose members were Scandinavian nationals, and also by the Schalburg Corps, which was in effect the Danish branch of the Germanic-SS.

● The Sig-Rune
The Sig-Rune (also known as the Siegrune) was symbolic of victory. In 1933, SS-Sturmhauptführer

Fig 12   *Runic Symbols used by the SS*
A.   Hakenkreuz
B.   Sonnenrad
C.   Sig-Rune
D.   Ger-Rune
E.   Wolfsangel
F.   Wolfsangel (Dutch Variant)
G.   Opfer-Rune
H.   Eif-Rune
I.   Leben-Rune
J.   Toten-Rune
K.   Tyr-Rune
L.   Heilszeichen
M.   Hagall-Rune
N.   Odal-Rune

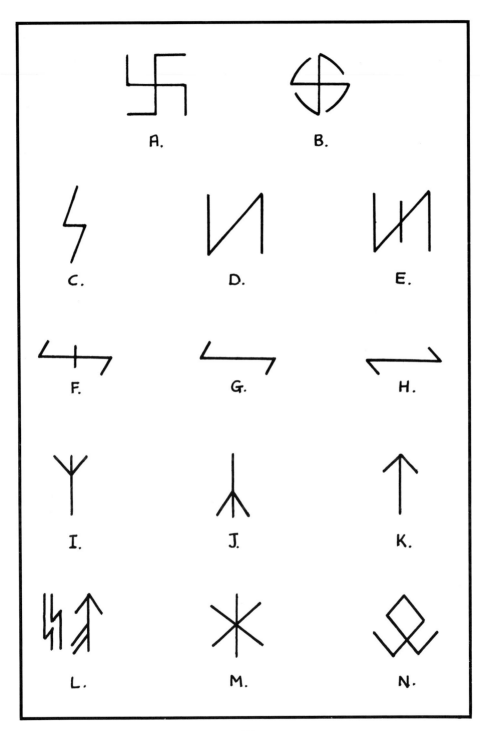

A.

B.

C.

D.

E.

F.

G.

H.

I.

J.

K.

L.

M.

N.

Walter Heck, who was a graphic designer employed by the badge manufacturing firm of Ferdinand Hoffstätter in Bonn, drew two Sig-Runes side by side and thus created the ubiquitous 'SS Runes' insignia used thereafter by all branches of the organisation. The SS paid him 2.50 Reichsmarks for the rights to his design! Heck was likewise responsible for the 'SA Runes' badge, which combined a runic 'S' with a Gothic 'A'.

● The Ger-Rune
The Ger-Rune was symbolic of communal spirit, and featured as a variant divisional sign of the Waffen-SS division 'Nordland'.

● The Wolfsangel
The Wolfsangel or Wolf Hook was originally a pagan device which supposedly possessed the magical power to ward off werewolves. Adopted as an emblem by 15th Century peasants in their revolt against the mercenaries of the German princes, it was thereafter regarded as being symbolic of liberty and independence, although it was also referred to as the 'Zeichen der Willkür' or 'Badge of Wanton Tyranny' during the Thirty Years War. The Wolfsangel was an early emblem of the Nazi Party, and was later used as a sign by the Waffen-SS division 'Das Reich'.

● The Wolfsangel (Dutch Variant)
A squat version of the Wolfsangel with hooked arms was the badge of the WA (Weer Afdeelingen), the Dutch Nazi Party's equivalent of the German SA, and was also the emblem of the Germanic-SS in the Netherlands. It was later adopted by the Waffen-SS division 'Landstorm Nederland', which comprised Dutch volunteers.

● The Opfer-Rune
The Opfer-Rune symbolised self-sacrifice. It was used after 1918 by the Stahlhelm war veterans' association and was later the badge which commemorated the Nazi martyrs of the 1923 Munich Putsch. It also formed part of the design of the SA Sports Badge for War Wounded, which could be won by disabled SS ex-servicemen.

● The Eif-Rune
The Eif-Rune represented zeal and enthusiasm. It was the early insignia of specially selected SS adjutants assigned personally to Hitler and, as such, was worn by Rudolf Hess in 1929.

● The Leben-Rune
The Leben-Rune or Life Rune symbolised life and was adopted by the SS Lebensborn Society and Ahnenerbe. It likewise featured on SS documents and grave markers to show date of birth.

● The Toten-Rune
The Toten-Rune or Death Rune represented death, and was used on documents and grave markers to show date of death.

● The Tyr-Rune
The Tyr-Rune, also known as the Kampf-Rune or Battle Rune, was the pagan Germanic sign of Tyr, the God of War, and was symbolic of leadership in battle. It was commonly used by the SS as a grave marker, replacing the Christian cross, and a Tyr-Rune worn on the upper left arm indicated graduation from the SA Reichsführerschule, which trained SS officers until 1934. It was later the specialist badge of the SS Recruiting and Training Department, and an emblem of the Waffen-SS division '30 Januar' which comprised staff and pupils from various SS training schools.

● The Heilszeichen
The Heilszeichen or Prosperity Symbols represented success and good fortune, and appeared on the SS Death's Head Ring.

● The Hagall-Rune
The Hagall-Rune stood for the unshakable faith (in Nazi philosophy) which was expected of all SS members. It featured on the SS Death's Head Ring as well as on ceremonial accoutrements used at SS weddings. It was also chosen as the sign of the SS-Polizei-Division, since it resembled the traditional 'Police Star' badge.

● The Odal-Rune
The Odal-Rune symbolised kinship and family and the bringing together of people of similar blood. It was the badge of the SS Rasse- und Siedlungshauptamt and emblem of the Waffen-SS division 'Prinz Eugen', which comprised mainly Volksdeutsche from the Balkans.

The finer symbolic points of these runes were never generally appreciated by the majority of Waffen-SS men who wore them during the war, as instruction in their meanings was restricted to the Allgemeine-SS and ceased around 1940.

HIMMLER AND MEDIAEVALISM

As a child, the young Heinrich Himmler followed in his father's footsteps by collecting small and inexpensive mediaeval artifacts. At school, he read avidly about the arrival of Vikings in the Lake Ladoga area around the year 700, their adoption of the name Rus, and how their descendants, the Norse tribe known as Russians, repelled the Mongols and settled all across the east from the Baltic to the Black Sea. He was also fascinated by the tale of Rurik the Dane, founder of Novgorod and Kiev around 856, and the story of the Saxon King Heinrich I, 'The Fowler', elected King of All Germany in 919, who had checked the incursions of Bohemians and Magyars from the east and laid the basis of the German Confederation of Princes which became, under his son Otto, the Holy Roman Empire.

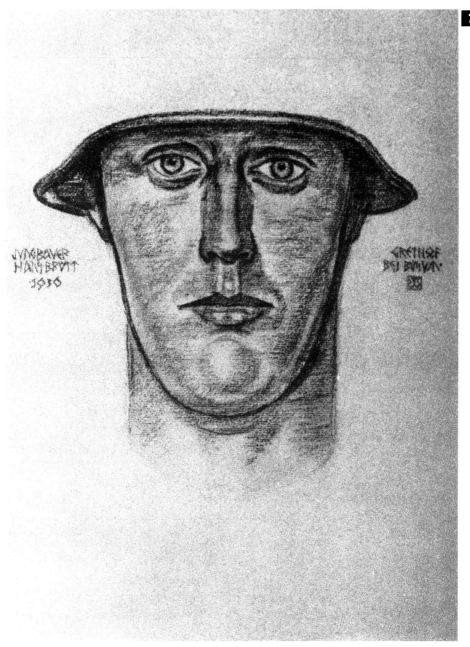

Plate 73 Willrich print showing SS-Mann Hans Brütt, a peasant farmer from Grethof. The frontal style of this drawing is intentionally reminiscent of Mediaeval Viking and Norman sculpture. Note also the pseudo-runic caption to the portrait.

Plate 74 Oak carving featuring a sword, shield, steel helmet and runes, typical of the pseudo-mediaeval wall decorations which adorned Himmler's castle at Wewelsburg.

Plate 75 Himmler delivering a eulogy on Heinrich I in Quedlinburg Cathedral, 2 July 1936. Behind him, from left to right, stand Frick, Daluege, Bouhler, Darré and Heydrich. *Ullstein*

Plate 76 On 23 July 1939, an SS-sponsored parade celebrating '2000 Years of German Culture' was held in Munich. Pseudo-mediaeval and Nazi symbolism mingled on an awesome scale throughout the event. *IWM*

The history which captured Himmler's imagination completely, however, was that of the Order of Teutonic Knights or Deutsche Ritterorden, founded by Heinrich Walpot von Bassenheim in 1198. Like the other hospital Orders of the time, ie the Knights of St John and the Templars, it was established to aid western knights who had been wounded or fallen sick during the Crusades. However, unlike the others, the Teutonic Order was distinguished by the fact that it was exclusively Germanic in its recruitment. In 1211, the Golden Bull of Rimini entrusted to its knights the colonisation of the Slavonic lands to the east of the Elbe. Under its Grand Master, Hermann von Salza, the Order immediately undertook a programme of German expansion, extending domination over Prussia and the Baltic States. It reached its height in the second half of the 14th Century, but was brought to a sudden end in 1410. On 15 July that year, the Teutonic Knights were crushed at Tannenberg by a coalition of Poles, Lithuanians and Mongols. The power of the Order was broken, but the memory of its valorous deeds under the badge of the black cross never ceased to haunt German dreams thereafter.

It seemed to the adolescent Himmler that all of German mediaeval life had centred around the constant struggle between Norseman and Mongol, between Teuton and Slav, and he longed to continue the historic mission of his forefathers. Even as a 19-year-old student, he wrote in his diary that he hoped to live his life in the east and fight his battles 'as a German far from beautiful Germany'. Himmler eventually harnessed this romantic view of history to provide an attractive integrating factor for his SS, recruited as it was from all walks of life. It was not by chance that the SS colours, black and white, were those formerly worn by the Teutonic Knights, who simply handed them down to Prussia. And when Himmler later talked about blood as the symbol of honour and fidelity, he was again appealing to mediaeval tradition. The mysticism of the Blutfahne itself harked back to the chivalric initiation ceremony by which the feudal suzerain was linked to his vassal by sword, fire and blood. For the SS, the Führer was their liege lord, incarnating the eternal principles of life rooted in the sacred and ancestral soil to which the dead would return in order to water and fertilise it with their blood so generously shed.

When his power was consolidated in 1934, Himmler's mediaeval fantasies were given free rein. Obsessed by the old legend that a Westphalian castle would be the sole survivor of the next Slavonic assault from the east, the Reichsführer scoured western Germany until he found the ruined mountain fortress of Wewelsburg near Paderborn, named after the robber knight Wewel von Büren, which had been a focus of Saxon resistance to the Huns and had been rebuilt in triangular form in the 17th Century. Following the example of the Grand Master of the Teutonic Order who built his headquarters at Marienburg, Himmler determined to convert

Wewelsburg into the stronghold of the SS. The castle was duly purchased and the architect Hermann Bartels, a Standartenführer on the Persönlicher Stab RfSS, was given 12 million Reichsmarks and set to work creating a home for his master.

Entering the finished complex in 1935 was like stepping back in time. A grand staircase was bordered by a banister of forged iron, decorated with runic motifs, and the walls of the entrance hall were hung with huge tapestries depicting Germanic and rural scenes. All the woodwork was of oak and everywhere stood marble statues of Heinrich I, Friedrich von Hohenstaufen and other German heroes. Each room was furnished in mediaeval style. The 100ft x 145ft dining room held a massive circular Arthurian oak table around which Himmler and his 12 senior Obergruppenführer (ie Franz Xaver Schwarz, 'Sepp' Dietrich, Fritz Weitzel, Kurt Daluege, Walther Darré, Walter Buch, Udo von Woyrsch, Friedrich-Wilhelm Krüger, Josias Erbprinz zu Waldeck und Pyrmont, Max Amann, Karl Freiherr von Eberstein and Philipp Bouhler) regularly held conferences seated on high-backed pig-skin chairs bearing the names of the owner knights. A fire crackled in the monumental chimney, and behind each General hung his SS coat of arms, specially designed by Karl Diebitsch. The dining room stood above a stone basement with 5ft-thick walls, from which a flight of steps led down to a well-like crypt housing 12 granite columns and known as the 'Realm of the Dead'. The idea was that when each of the 12 SS lords died, his body would be cremated and his ashes entombed in one of these obelisks for all eternity. Himmler's private apartments within the fortress were particularly sumptuous and adjoined a gold and silver strongroom, a hall for his extensive collection of mediaeval weaponry, a library with more than 12,000 books, and an awesome chamber where the Extraordinary SS and Police Court could be convened in special circumstances. There were also magnificent guest rooms set aside for Adolf Hitler, who never appeared at the castle, giving rise to the local village rumour that one day the Führer would be buried there.

Himmler intended that Wewelsburg should ultimately be used as a Reichshaus der SS-Gruppenführer or SS Generals' Residence, but the outbreak of war saw its conversion to SS-Schule Haus Wewelsburg, a staff college for senior SS officers. Its commandant was SS-Obergruppenführer Siegfried Taubert.

A large section of Wewelsburg castle was dedicated to the Saxon ruler Heinrich I 'The Fowler'. The Reichsführer approved that his men nicknamed him 'King Heinrich', and came to see himself as the spiritual reincarnation of The Fowler and the embodiment of his aims to consolidate Germany against the hordes from the east. On 2 July 1936, the thousandth anniversary of the King's death, Himmler inaugurated a solemn remembrance festival at Quedlinburg, once Heinrich's seat, and in 1938 he founded a King Heinrich Memorial Trust to revive the principles and deeds of The Fowler. Numerous SS badges were subsequently struck to commemorate Heinrich as 'Ewig das Reich' or 'The Eternity of the Reich'.

To instil a general feeling of knighthood in all his junior officers and men, the majority of whom never even saw the splendour of Wewelsburg, Himmler rewarded them with the three less grandiose trappings of dagger, sword and ring, already covered in Chapter 4: Uniforms. That mystical combination, harking back to a warrior aristocracy and the legend of the Nibelung, was to symbolise the Ritterschaft of the new SS Order, at one and the same time both new and yet rooted in the most ancient Germanic past.

THE ACTIVITIES OF AHNENERBE

Himmler's enthusiasm for German history, the ideals of which were to form the basis of the new era, led to his foundation of the Ahnenerbe- Forschungs-und Lehrgemeinschaft, usually abbreviated to Ahnenerbe, the Society for the Research and Teaching of Ancestral Heritage. Its first President was Dr Hermann Wirth, a university lecturer known for his controversial work on the Middle Ages and Germanic antiquity. Wirth had joined the NSDAP in 1925, left in 1926, and re-enrolled in 1933. His book, What is the German Soul?, was dismissed as claptrap by Rosenberg, but he managed to seduce Himmler with the promise that he could study and research Nordic history for the purpose of verifying National Socialist and SS theories by scientific proof. Obergruppenführer Darré of RuSHA also became interested in the scheme, and his assistance was of enormous value since, as Minister of Agriculture, he had huge financial resources at his disposal. It was he who actually paid for the setting up and commissioning of the Society in July 1935, under the auspices of his Ministry.

The following year, however, differences of opinion appeared between Himmler, who saw the German as a nomadic warrior ever in search of new lands, and Darré, who saw him as sedentary and firmly rooted to his own soil. This conceptual argument was to have a profound effect on Ahnenerbe. In November 1936 it was integrated into the Abteilung für Kulturelle Forschung (Section for Cultural Research) of the Persönlicher Stab RfSS, and a few months later, when the split between Himmler and Darré reached the point of no return, the Reichsführer appointed SS-Standartenführer Bruno Galke as a special representative to the Society to undermine Darré's influence. One of Galke's first measures was to totally discredit Wirth, who was Darré's eyes and ears in the Society. Wirth was subsequently dismissed and replaced as President of Ahnenerbe by Prof Dr Walther Wüst, Dean of Munich University, who occupied the Chair of Aryan Culture and Linguistics and who had a much larger audience in academic circles. He was also an SS-Oberführer.

With Wirth gone and Darré's power over Ahnenerbe cancelled out, Himmler proceeded to restructure the Society during the summer of 1937, establishing its new and independent headquarters at 16 Pücklerstrasse, Berlin-Dahlem. He reserved overall control for himself, with the title of Curator, but the day-to-day management was carried out by Wüst, Galke and SS-Standartenführer Wolfram Sievers of the Persönlicher Stab RfSS. Wüst was responsible for the direction of scientific activity, Galke was Treasurer, and Sievers took charge of general organisational matters. The latter was one of the most talented administrators in the Reich, and had many influential contacts among financiers and industrialists as well as access to the Sipo and SD. He soon established a foundation of companies which were prepared to make massive monetary contributions to the Society. Other funds were found from the coffers of the Sicherheitsdienst, thanks to Sievers' friendship with SS-Oberführer Prof Dr Franz Six, who was responsible to the SD for overseeing university policies.

At the end of 1937, Himmler defined the purpose of the reconstituted Ahnenerbe. It was to carry out research into ancient history by studying facts from a scientific and ideological point of view, in an objective manner and without falsification. It was also to be responsible for the setting up in each SS Oberabschnitt of educational and cultural centres devoted to German greatness and the Germanic past. The first such centre was duly established at Sachsenhain, with the reconstruction of a prehistoric Saxon village which included in its display a 5,000-year-old plough and runic inscriptions carved in stone. The whole idea was to show every German that the wealth of his land and culture were the makings of his own ancestors, not things which had been brought in by the Romans or other outsiders.

All of Germany's archaeological excavations were soon put into the hands of the Society. Their overall direction was entrusted first to SS-Obersturmbannführer Dr Rolf Höhne, who was personally responsible for researches at Quedlinburg to find the remains of Heinrich The Fowler, then to Obersturmbannführer Prof Dr Hans Schleif, who organised digs in the Teutoburg Forest where the Germans of Arminius had crushed the Roman legions of Quintus Varus in 9AD. Schleif later teamed up with Obersturmbannführer Prof Dr Herbert Jankuhn to excavate the Viking site of Haithabu in Schleswig, a wall built by King Godfred in the 9th Century to defend the Danes against the incursions of the Carolingians. In time, Ahnenerbe organised similar excavations in Austria, Croatia, Czechoslovakia, Greece, Poland, Serbia and southern Russia, and sponsored associated expeditions to the Near East and Tibet to look for signs of an ancient Nordic presence in these areas.

From 1939, the remit of Ahnenerbe was considerably enlarged. Himmler was no longer content to be restricted to Dark Age history, but now hoped to prove by scientific means the racial hypotheses of National Socialism. In conjunction with the SD, the Society would also look into other matters such as astronomy, control of the weather, the extraction of petrol from coal, the occult, and herbal remedies (Himmler's wife being a qualified homoeopath). Ahnenerbe expanded to include more than 50 departments, employing over 30 university professors. The Reichsführer showed evidence of quite a surprising amount of liberalism in their appointment, and drew a fairly vague line between research ability on the one hand and political reliability on the other. However, the contract he required his academics to sign stipulated that their findings could never be published if they turned out to be contrary to SS ideology.

One of the most controversial figures among the new researchers was SS-Sturmbannführer Dr August Hirt, Professor of Anatomy at the University of Strasbourg, where SS students were particularly numerous. With Himmler's support, it was Hirt who collected thousands of human skulls at Auschwitz for the purpose of making comparative anthropomorphic measurements. He later toured various battlefronts where the Wehrmacht's foreign volunteers were garrisoned, to study the performance and behaviour of combatants as a function of their racial categories. As already covered in Chapter 6: The Racial Concept, other anatomical specialists from Ahnenerbe occupied themselves by examining body parts of different races, while SS-Sturmbannführer Dr Ernst Schäfer was commissioned to develop a special breed of horse on the Russian Steppes for military use in extremely cold temperatures. Little benefit came from any of these activities.

The war's principal sector of scientific research, that of secret weapons, fell under the authority of Ahnenerbe in 1944. Up to the middle of that year, the V1 and V2 rocket development programme at Peenemünde had been directed by Prof Dr Wernher Freiherr von Braun, who was loyal first and foremost to the Wehrmacht even though he was an SS-Sturmbannführer on the staff of Oberabschnitt Ostsee. Himmler knew that the Reich was by then laying all its hopes on secret weapons, and after the army plot to assassinate Hitler on 20 July 1944 he took personal control of the Peenemünde operation from von Braun and placed it under SS-Gruppenführer Dr Hans Kammler. The V1 and V2 programmes fully occupied the best minds of Ahnenerbe for the remainder of the war, but the missiles were ultimately developed too late to avoid Germany's inevitable defeat.

Plate 77 A series of plastic badges sold for the benefit of the annual Nazi Winter Charities Campaign, organised by SS-Gruppenführer Erich Hilgenfeldt. They reproduce finds from SS archaeological digs in Germany, Rome and Greece, to portray the use and development of the swastika in antiquity. Such projects were dear to Himmler's heart.

8 The SS and Education

THE NPEA

While all aspects of educational life in the Third Reich including curriculum, teacher training and staff appointments were controlled by the Nazi Party, the most selective schools and colleges came to be dominated by the SS. Himmler realised only too well that it was essential that the best minds amongst the youth of Germany should be cultivated to ensure a continual pool of talent willing and able to fill the highest positions in the hierarchies of the SS and National Socialist State. University lecturers and school teachers were actively encouraged to join the Allgemeine-SS, and Fritz Wächtler, the head of the NS-Lehrerbund or Nazi Teachers' League, was given the rank of SS-Obergruppenführer.

On 20 April 1933, Dr Bernhard Rust, Reich Minister for Science, Education and Culture, set up the first of a series of special residential schools to train the future Germanic élite. They were termed National Political Educational Institutes or Nationalpolitische Erziehungsanstalten, commonly abbreviated to NPEA or Napolas, although the latter term was unpopular because it sounded too Italian. Three were opened during the course of 1933, at Plön in Schleswig-Holstein, Potsdam in Berlin and Köslin in Pomerania. Five more (Spandau, Naumburg, Ilfeld, Stuhm and Oranienstein) followed in 1934 with a further eight (Bensburg, Ballenstedt, Backnang, Rottweil, Klotzsche, Neuzelle, Schulpforte and Wahlstatt) the next year. Favourite locations were old army cadet schools, requisitioned monasteries or refurbished castles.

From the outset, control of the NPEA schools was hotly contested by various Party bodies. The original mentor of the NPEA system, Joachim Haupt, was an SA officer and he fell from favour after the Night of the Long Knives in June 1934. Dr Robert Ley, head of the Labour Front, then tried openly to attract the Napolas into his sphere of influence, but his project encountered such strong opposition from the Ministry of Education that he relented and set up the rival Adolf Hitler Schools with the support of Baldur von Schirach, leader of the Hitler Youth.

As always, Himmler acted unobtrusively and with the utmost skill. From the time of the first public festivities organised by the NPEA in 1934, he took pains to be invited along and presented as an honoured guest. In July of that year the SS assumed the responsibility of paying for Napola clothing and equipment, and also began to provide scholarships and tuition fees for ethnic German students. On 9 March 1936, SS commitment to the schools was rewarded with the appointment of SS-Obergruppenführer August Heissmeyer as Inspector-General of the NPEA. He set up his own HQ, the Hauptamt Dienststelle Heissmeyer, and subsequently encouraged all NPEA staff to enrol in the Allgemeine-SS. By 1940, the SS had completely taken over the Nap-

olas, with full powers of decision in matters relating to curriculum and personnel appointments. The selection of pupils or Jungmannen was determined by RuSHA, and the NPEA commandants and teachers were subjected to SS discipline.

The rhythm of Napola life was thereafter based on that of the SS. Conventional religion was abolished from the curriculum and replaced by the study of Pagan Germanic rites. The celebration of Julfest, the SS Christmas, brought the pupils together to worship the Child of the Sun, arisen from his ashes at the Winter Solstice. New school songs commemorated the struggle between day and night, and praised the eternal return of life. The night of 21 June became the Night of the Sun, when the boys mounted a 'Joyous Guard' awaiting the sun's triumphal reappearance. Lectures were given on racial superiority and SS ideology, and emphasis was placed on duty, courage and personal obligation.

The SS influence on the NPEA was felt not only in curriculum, but also in dress. Initially, pupils wore Hitler Youth uniforms with the letters 'NPEA' on the shoulder straps. Later, a distinctive olive green, khaki and black uniform with SA/SS-style dagger was devised for the upper age groups and teachers. After 1940, SS cap eagles and arm eagles appeared on NPEA uniform, and a new scheme of ranks which was entirely SS in form was introduced for NPEA staff, as follows:

- NPEA-Untersturmführer — Probationary Teacher
- NPEA-Obersturmführer — Teacher
- NPEA-Hauptsturmführer — Senior Teacher
- NPEA-Sturmbannführer — Deputy Head of Department
- NPEA-Obersturmbannführer — Head of Department
- NPEA-Standartenführer — Deputy Headmaster
- NPEA-Oberführer — Headmaster
- NPEA-Brigadeführer — Local School Inspector
- NPEA-Gruppenführer — National School Inspector

Originally, the Napolas had been conceived as male-only, but with the needs of Lebensborn and similar SS organisations in mind the first all-girls school was opened in 1941 at Achern in Baden, to be followed shortly thereafter by two more. Even some of the previously all-male schools subsequently admitted female pupils and staff.

No less than 27 new Napolas were founded between 1941 and 1942, and with the enormous expansion of the NPEA programme during the war SS influence became paramount. For example, VOMI caused the school at Rufach to include a substantial number of young Volksdeutsche from Bessarabia and Bukovina in the student body. Three schools known as NPEA Reichsschulen were set up in the occupied western territories specifically to take in non-German Nordic pupils, the future leaders of the Germanic-SS. The Reichsschule Flandern at Kwatrecht in Flanders, opened in September 1943, was equipped to accommodate some 800 boys although it never managed to enrol more than 120, all under the age of 14. It was commanded by SS-Obersturmführer Paul Steck. The Reichsschule Nederland für Jungen at Valkenburg in Holland took Dutch boys and was 'twinned' with its nearest German counterpart, the NPEA Bensburg, with regular exchanges of students and staff between the two establishments. The closely associated all-female Reichsschule Nederland für Mädchen was located at nearby Heithuijsen, and was run by a pro-Nazi Dutch baroness.

In December 1944, by virtue of his successes with the NPEA and Reichsschulen, and his position as Commander-in-Chief of the Home Army, Himmler was appointed by Hitler to be supervisor of all schools from which future Wehrmacht and Waffen-SS officers could be recruited. In theory, that put him in charge of almost every educational establishment in the Third Reich!

No official orders were ever issued dissolving the NPEA schools, and the decision to capitulate was usually left to the head of each institution. There was one instance where a school's membership was smartly assembled in ranks as the Allied occupation forces arrived, and another where an NPEA headmaster symbolically surrendered his NPEA and SS daggers to a British Officer. Most pupils were simply too young to offer any effective resistance in defence of their schools.

THE STUDENTS' LEAGUE

Nazi students groups were formed at some German universities as early as 1922, but these were simply gatherings of students who had enrolled in the NSDAP. It was not until February 1926 that a separate student organisation, the National Socialist German Students' League (Nationalsozialistische Deutsche Studentenbund or NSDSt.B), was established at Munich University under Baldur von Schirach. He organised the NSDSt.B into 10 Districts, each under a Kreisführer, and membership was extended to include students at Technical Colleges, Trade Schools and Business Colleges. Ultimately, the proportion of NSDSt.B members at university was lower than that of those attending the other centres of further education. They were encouraged to join the SA and take part in military sports, but less than half did so, many balking at the thought of associating with the Party's rougher elements.

By January 1933 the NSDSt.B still had only 6,300 male and 750 female members. Even after the Nazi assumption of power, enrolment in the organisation was not made obligatory for all students. On the contrary, membership was deliberately selective and restricted to 5% of the student body. As the NPEA accepted only the cream of German school pupils, so the NSDSt.B would take only the best and most reliable students in further education. Each university or institute of higher learning had an NSDSt.B Stamm-Mannschaft or regular company, limited to not more than 60 individuals, all of whom had already to be members of the NSDAP, SA, SS, NSKK or HJ. They signed on for at least a year, and their task was to act as political leaders amongst their fellow students.

Both Himmler, who had a degree in agriculture, and the NSDAP Deputy Führer Rudolf Hess, a history graduate and SS-Obergruppenführer, took a keen interest in NSDSt.B matters. Hess spoke of it as 'a sort of intellectual SS', and Himmler hoped that it would furnish the future élite of the Party. They saw it as a natural extension of the NPEA system, which would continue to oversee those boys and girls from the Napolas who had proved themselves capable of further education. The two were instrumental in the setting up of a new office, the Reich Student Leadership (Reichsstudentenführung or RSF), in November 1936. It had ultimate control over both the NSDSt.B and the ordinary German Student Association (Deutsche Studentenschaft or DSt.) to which all German students automatically belonged. Command of the RSF was given to SS-Obergruppenführer und General der Polizei Dr Gustav-Adolf Scheel, who was nominated Reichsstudentenführer. From that time on, student affairs began to be heavily influenced by the SS. NSDSt.B members were soon kitted out in a dark blue uniform derived from the garb of the Allgemeine-SS and Hitler Youth.

Scheel then set up the NS-Altherrenbund der Deutschen Studenten, a new Nazi alumni organisation, and blackmailed the existing associations of former students into joining it, on pain of being barred from further participation in student life. Only the Catholic alumni bodies refused to capitulate, and they were subsequently outlawed by Himmler. As a result, all financial contributions and legacies from 'old boys' had to be channelled through the Altherrenbund, and so were controlled by the RSF and, ultimately, the SS.

THE HITLER YOUTH

While the majority of ordinary German youngsters never had any associations with the NPEA or the NSDSt.B, most either belonged to or had friends in the Hitler Youth (Hitlerjugend or HJ) and its female equivalent, the League of German Girls (Bund Deutscher Mädel or BDM). After 1933 the HJ was a main source of recruitment for the Allgemeine-SS, and as the power and prestige of the SA declined so those of the SS and HJ increased. In 1936 it was decreed that the whole of German youth was to be

Plate 78 Two schoolboys from NPEA Naumburg taking pictures during the summer solstice celebrations in 1941. Note the SS-inspired Sig-Rune insignia worn on the left arm. *Ullstein*

'educated, outside the parental home and school, in the HJ, physically, intellectually and morally for service to the nation and community'. The HJ initially found it hard to meet the great demands made upon it, and for that reason obligatory membership was delayed for several years. Even so, voluntary enlistment resulted in the number of Hitler Youths reaching 8 million (ie 66% of those eligible to join) at the end of 1938. Compulsory HJ service for all male 17-year-olds was introduced on 25 March 1939, and in September 1941 membership finally became obligatory for both sexes from the age of 10 onwards. Many of the activities, trappings and insignia of the HJ were derived from those of the SS, with much anti-Semitism, neo-Paganism and use of runic symbolism, and co-operation between the SS and HJ became ever closer until by the end of the war the two had merged their interests almost completely. By that time, the ultimate aim of every Hitler Youth was acceptance into the SS.

The élite branch of the Hitler Youth organisation was the HJ-Streifendienst or Patrol Service, created in December 1936. It was in effect an internal police force for the HJ, and kept order at Hitler Youth rallies and camps, controlled transport movements, supervised HJ hostels, and counteracted juvenile crime. Each member was issued with a special pass and an SS-style cuff title and, as needs demanded, a small calibre rifle. In August 1938, under an agreement between Himmler and von Schirach's Reichsjugendführung, the HJ-Streifendienst was reorganised as a sort of preparatory school for the SS. Its training was placed entirely in SS hands and boys were expected to graduate into the SS or police after leaving the service.

Another HJ formation closely associated with the SS was the Landdienst or Land Service, the purpose of which was to provide voluntary agricultural assistance, particularly in the eastern provinces of the Reich. The Landdienst was formed in 1934 and sent urban HJ volunteers on to farms for one year, the so-called Landjahr, to give them agricultural experience. At the outbreak of war, the service had 26,000 members. In February 1940, the Siedlernachwuchsstelle Ost or Eastern Young Settlers Office was created under a joint agreement between the SS and HJ to train youngsters as Wehrbauern, peasant guards who would populate and defend the conquered east. Volunteers were racially scrutinised by RuSHA and had to register with the RKFDV. To further this aim, the Landdienst concept was extended in 1942 to include youths from the Nordic countries of Flanders, Holland, Norway and Denmark who volunteered for employment with the newly-created Germanic Land Service or Germanischer Landdienst. Its badge was the Odal-Rune, and its motto was 'Schwert und Scholle' ('Sword and Soil'). With the turn of the tide of war, however, the Germanic Land Service was officially wound up in March 1944 and many of its male personnel were transferred into the Waffen-SS.

From 1936, the HJ ran weekend courses in field exercises (Geländesport) and rifle shooting. Initially it relied on its own personnel and the Wehrmacht to furnish instructors, but increasingly the SS became involved in Hitler Youth paramilitary training. In 1939 toughening-up camps or Wehrertüchtigungslager (WE-Lager) were established in which boys between the ages of 16 and 18 were put through a three-week course culminating in an award of the K-Schein or War Training Certificate. By 1943 there were around 150 such camps, which included among their trainees and instructors volunteers from Flanders, Holland, Norway, Denmark and Latvia. Their overall commandant was HJ-Oberbannführer Gerhard Hein, who had won the Knight's Cross with Oakleaves while serving with Jäger Regiment 209 in France and Russia.

There was a sound practical reason why the SS took a great interest in the WE-Lager system, for it furnished them with a means of circumventing the Wehrmacht's monopoly on recruitment. The Waffen-SS possessed no powers of direct conscription amongst German nationals, but if a young man could be persuaded to volunteer for the Waffen-SS before reaching his 20th year, the normal age for conscript service, his preference for that branch of the fighting forces was normally respected. The SS therefore strove to persuade WE-Lager boys to volunteer for service in one of its combat divisions after they had obtained their K-Schein.

In February 1943, following the loss of a whole Army at Stalingrad, manpower shortages became so acute that Hitler authorised a programme to encourage voluntary enlistment of 17-year-olds, boys who would not have been subject to conscription until 1946. The SS saw this as a golden opportunity to build up its own forces. Negotiations between Himmler and the Reichsjugendführer, Artur Axmann, began at once, as a result of which it was decided to raise an entirely new Waffen-SS division from Hitler Youths who had completed their courses at the WE-Lager. Recruiting began in the spring and the boys, many of whom came from the Streifendienst and Landdienst, were assembled at the Beverloo military training area in Belgium. By mid-summer, the required number of 10,000 volunteers had been mustered, together with a cadre of 180 officers and 800 experienced NCOs seconded from the Leibstandarte-SS 'Adolf Hitler' and the SS divisions 'Das Reich' and 'Totenkopf', as well as from various army units. In October, the division was officially named 12th SS-Panzer Division 'Hitlerjugend', and command was given to 35-year-old SS-Brigadeführer Fritz Witt, holder of the Knight's Cross with Oakleaves.

The 'Hitlerjugend' division remained in Belgium until April 1944, when it was moved to France and placed on standby in anticipation of the Allied invasion. On 6 June the landings took place, and 'Hitlerjugend' was immediately ordered into action against the British and Canadians at Caen. The fanatical young soldiers, keen to demonstrate their worthiness to wear the honoured SS runes, threw themselves into battle without regard for losses, which were devastating. Over 8,500 of their number were either killed or wounded. Among the fallen was Fritz Witt, killed on 14 June and subsequently replaced as commander by 33-year-old SS-Brigadeführer Kurt Meyer. The division was all but finished off two months later when trapped in the Falaise Pocket. Kurt Meyer was captured, and leadership of what was left of 'Hitlerjugend', about 600 men, passed to 30-year-old SS-Sturmbannführer Hubert Meyer. Towards the end of August, the survivors were transferred hurriedly to Kaiserslautern where the division was brought up to strength again by an infusion of fresh HJ recruits. Under 33-year-old SS-Brigadeführer Hugo Kraas, it went into action once more during the Ardennes Offensive of December 1944. When this attack ground to a halt, the division was moved to Hungary and eventually surrendered to the Americans at Linz in May 1945. A single tank and 455 men were all that remained of one of Germany's foremost armoured divisions.

Late in February 1945, when the advancing Russian Army was closing in on Berlin, special units of saboteurs and partisan guerrillas were formed from

the German populace for the purpose of harassing the approaching enemy. In the event of the capture of the capital, members of these units, known as Werewolves, were to function behind Allied lines in the occupied zones creating what havoc they could. It fell to Himmler, as Commander-in-Chief of the Home Army, to set up the Werewolf organisation and he put it under the command of SS-Obergruppenführer Hans Prützmann, with SS-Brigadeführer Karl Pflaumer as his deputy. However, with all able-bodied personnel already at the frontline or in the Volkssturm, Werewolf had to rely on very young members of the HJ and BDM to make up its numbers.

A variety of duties were entrusted to these boys and girls, including the salvaging and concealment of arms and ammunition, minor acts of sabotage such as puncturing vehicle tyres, and the conveying of messages and distribution of Nazi propaganda throughout the occupied territory of Germany. Older Werewolves seconded from the Allgemeine-SS and Waffen-SS set up secret radio transmitters, took part in assassinations and infiltrated enemy headquarters. Without doubt, the Werewolf organisation inflicted serious damage and, even after the surrender, marauding groups of SS and Hitler Youth participated in acts of sabotage against the American, British, French and Russian occupation authorities.

By its indoctrination of youth through interaction with the NPEA, NSDSt.B, HJ and BDM, the SS ensured that the ideals of Hitler and Himmler survived long after their demise.

Plate 79 Pay book issued in December 1944 to Robert Mlynek, a radio operator in the 4th Company of the 3rd SS Signals Training and Replacement Battalion, attached to 3rd SS-Panzer Division 'Totenkopf'. Mlynek, a former Hitler Youth, was only 17 years old, typical of SS soldiers at the end of the war.

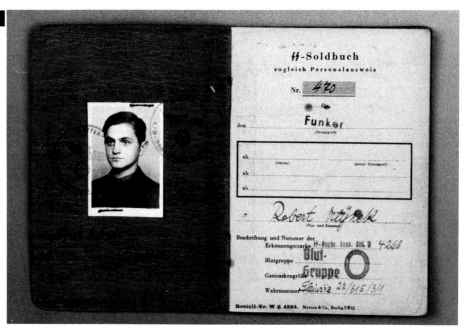

9 The SS Economy

THE WVHA

The SS Wirtschafts-und Verwaltungshauptamt or WVHA, the SS Economic and Administrative Department, received less publicity than any other Hauptamt. In fact, a definite effort was made to keep its sphere of influence from becoming public knowledge. Commanded by SS-Obergruppenführer Oswald Pohl, the WVHA was formed in March 1942 by amalgamating three existing offices, viz:

(i) the old Verwaltungsamt (Administrative Office) of the SS Hauptamt;
(ii) the Hauptamt Haushalt und Bauten (Department of Finance and Building); and
(iii) the office of the Inspekteur der Konzentrationslager (Inspectorate of Concentration Camps).

Its creation solved the problem of conflicting interests and divided authority over such questions as the allocation and control of prison and concentration camp labour leased out to commercial enterprises and employed in SS building operations.

As with the other SS Hauptämter, the province of the WVHA covered the whole SS. The Allgemeine-SS was, for the most part, an unpaid and only lightly equipped organisation, so the administration of both supply and finance for that branch did not require a very extensive or complicated machinery. Nevertheless, the employment of full-time Allgemeine-SS staff, the upkeep of Allgemeine-SS property and the supervision of stocks of weapons, uniforms and equipment at the regional and unit headquarters of the Allgemeine-SS all fell within the scope of the WVHA. The Waffen-SS imposed much larger claims upon it, including the overseeing of administrative units of the Waffen-SS, the provision of Waffen-SS clothing, and the undertaking of engineering and construction work. Moreover, a WVHA Wirtschaftsführer or Economics Official was attached to the HSSPf in each occupied territory to co-ordinate the joint administration of the SS and police. When the National HQ of the Uniformed Police was bombed out in February 1944, it moved most of its departments to the premises of the WVHA, which thereafter carried out services on behalf of the Ordnungspolizei not only in the occupied territories but also in the Reich proper. In addition to these activities the WVHA supervised the whole range of SS economic undertakings, from boot making and horse breeding to the manufacture of soft drinks and the cultivation of rubber plants.

The WVHA was also the supreme financial authority for the whole SS. As far as the Allgemeine-SS was concerned, the WVHA was technically responsible to SS-Oberst-Gruppenführer Franz Xaver Schwarz in his capacity as Treasurer of the NSDAP. However, in view of the dominant position of the SS and the old friendship between Schwarz and Himmler, the Party did not exercise any close practical supervision over Allgemeine-SS funds. The Waffen-SS and police, on the other hand, were officially organs of the State rather than the NSDAP and their cash was administered by the WVHA only under the detailed scrutiny of the Reich Ministry of Finance, which allocated additional State monies as and when required.

As was implicit in its name, the WVHA was responsible for the whole of the administrative side of the SS organisation. To a large extent, the day-to-day work was decentralised and carried out by administrative departments of the various SS Hauptämter, the administrative officers with the HSSPfs, and administrative sections at Oberabschnitt and Abschnitt level. Even so, the WVHA remained in charge of the general supervision and co-ordination of all SS administration, and the appointment of administrative personnel. It had to approve the promotions of administrative officers in the SS and police, and acted in close liaison with the SS Führungshauptamt regarding administrative training courses, for which it maintained two specialist schools at Arolsen and Dachau. The SS Verwaltungsdienst or administrative service included for its enlisted ranks the posts of accountant, baker, billeting official, butcher, clerk, cook, paymaster and storekeeper, while officer grades specialised in agriculture, engineering, forestry and mining, as well as general administrative duties.

The SS maintained its own system of supply distinct from that of the Wehrmacht, for which purpose a large network of depots and stores was built up in Germany and the occupied territories. Operationally, these came under the control of the SS Führungshauptamt, but the actual responsibility for supply was divided between the Führungshauptamt and the WVHA. Broadly speaking, the former dealt with arms, ammunition and the other technical equipment, while the latter was responsible for rations, clothing, wood, coal, fodder and personal items. The WVHA also engaged in the bulk purchase of leather and textiles, although all other raw materials were acquired for the SS by a special Rohstoffamt (Raw Materials Office) attached to the Persönlicher Stab RfSS.

By 1945, the WVHA had developed to incorporate five distinct branches, or Amtsgruppen, with general allocation of functions as follows:

Amtsgruppe A – Finance, Law and Administration (SS-Brigadeführer Heinz Fanslau)
Amtsgruppe B – Supply, Billeting and Equipment (SS-Gruppenführer Georg Lörner)
Amtsgruppe C – Works and Buildings (SS-Gruppenführer Dr Hans Kammler)
Amtsgruppe D – Concentration Camps (SS-Gruppenführer Richard Glücks)
Amtsgruppe W – Economic Enterprises (SS-Gruppenführer August Frank)

Pohl proved to be a very capable administrator of the entire system, and by the end of the war the WVHA had attained a nationwide economic imperium for the SS.

ECONOMIC ENTERPRISES

As well as being a great consumer of goods and materials, the SS was also a large scale producer of them. Before 1939, Himmler indulged in limited productive economic enterprises (SS Wirtschaftsunternehmungen) such as the porcelain factory at Allach and the Apollinaris mineral water works at Bad Neuenahr. The war, however, and the acquisition of large fertile territories, greatly enlarged the scope of these activities. Farming and stockbreeding in Poland, and lumbering, mining and fishing in Russia, all entered the field of SS economics. Ad hoc WVHA Economic Operational Units or SS Wirtschaftskommandos were formed to co-ordinate local entrepreneurial projects, and between 1941 and 1944 the SS exploited the wealth, resources and population of the conquered East on a massive scale.

In wartime Germany itself, an equally great range and even greater ambition of SS economic activity was apparent. Just as the SS achieved a fair measure of independence in the sphere of military supply, so it sought after and received independence in the more general production field. The Concentration Camp system gave the SS a virtually inexhaustible source of cheap expendable labour, and where it was not expedient in any given case to set up an SS enterprise the camp workers could be farmed out to private firms or used on sub-contract work. The projects thus directly or indirectly carried on by the SS ranged from tailoring to armaments and from quarrying to aircraft construction, and nearly 2 million labourers of both sexes were employed by them. By 1944, the SS had developed its own comprehensive and widespread economic system in which was found the raw materials, the factories which processed them, the workers who handled them, and finally the consumers who absorbed them. It ultimately controlled more than 500 manufacturing plants, and produced 75% of Germany's non-alcoholic beverages and practically all of the country's furniture. Moreover, by virtue of this economic activity, the SS maintained influential representatives and contacts at many points throughout normal German industrial life. Indeed, Hitler often joked that Himmler was Germany's biggest industrialist!

For his part, the Reichsführer attached supreme importance to making the best possible use of all available concentration camp labour. It was planned that the building projects of the SS after the war would be on such a large scale that Pohl was ordered as early as 1942 to create a camp reserve of at least 5,000 stonemasons and 10,000 bricklayers before peace was concluded. These workers would be employed to deliver to the State at least 100,000cu m of granite per year, more than was ever produced by all the quarries in the old Reich. Since there were only 4,000 skilled stonemasons in the whole of Germany before the war, an extensive training programme was instigated. Camp commandants were directed to ensure that the efficiency of prisoners selected for training was increased through the provision of suitable food and clothing, and willing trainees were given rewards as an example to the indifferent. One of the biggest incentives was that inmates successfully undergoing training were exempt from transfer to other less humane camps.

Amtsgruppe W of the WVHA, the branch dealing with all SS economic enterprises, was sub-divided into eight distinct departments or Ämter at the end of 1944. These are detailed below, together with the main activities coming under their jurisdiction, to show the immense variety of SS enterprises being undertaken at that time.

Amt I   Deutsche Erd- und Steinwerke GmbH, or D.E.St. (German Clay and Brickworks Co Ltd) under SS-Obersturmbannführer Karl Mummenthey

Section 1: Brickworks
These were located at Sachsenhausen, Neuengamme, Buchenwald and Stutthof concentration camps.

Section 2: Quarries
This section supervised granite quarries at Mauthausen, Gross-Rosen, Flössenburg and Natzweiler; stone quarries at Rotau and Linz; masonry at Oranienburg; gravel dredging at Auschwitz; and an oil shale research distillery at Natzweiler.

Section 3: Pottery and Porcelain Works
These were in operation at Allach, Dachau and also in Bohemia.

Amt II   Baustoffswerke und Zementfabriken (Building Materials and Cement Factories) under SS-Obersturmbannführer Dr Hanns Bobermin

Section 1: Building Materials
These plants made plasterboard, insulation, roofing tiles etc, and were sited in Posen, Bielitz and Zichenau.

Section 2: Cement Factories
The main enterprise under this Section was the Golleschau Cement Works at Auschwitz.

Section 3: Eastern Works
Dealt with the large number of Russian building companies which the SS took over 'lock, stock and barrel' during 1941-42.

117

Amt III   Ernährungs Betriebe (Food Industry)

Section 1: Mineral Water
There were three SS soft drinks factories which went under the trade names of Sudetenquell, Mattoni and Apollinaris, and an associated SS bottling plant, the Rheinglassfabrik.

Section 2: Meat Processing
This was carried out at Auschwitz, Dachau and Sachsenhausen.

Section 3: Bread Making
SS bakeries operated at Auschwitz, Dachau, Sachsenhausen, Herzogenbusch, Lublin and Plaszow.

Amt IV   Deutsche Ausrüstungswerke, or D.A.W. (German Equipment Works)

Section 1: Military Armaments
SS involvement in the armaments and munitions industry increased as the war progressed, not only for the purpose of supplying the Waffen-SS but also to assist conventional arms manufacturers by furnishing them with cheap labour. The SS made many of their own weapons and technical instrumentation at Auschwitz, Neuengamme, Ravensbrück, Sachsenhausen, Stutthof, Lublin and Plaszow, maintained an ordnance testing and repair shop at Stutthof and melted down scrap cable at Dachau. In addition, aircraft parts assembly was carried out at Flössenburg, Mauthausen and Natzweiler on behalf of the Messerschmitt and Junkers companies. Heinkel contracted the SS to produce hangars for them at Sachsenhausen, gun carriages were repaired at Mauthausen, hand grenades assembled at Sachsenhausen, and industrial diamonds cut at Herzogenbusch and Belsen.

Section 2: Carpentry and Cabinet Making
Almost every concentration camp had a furniture workshop, making articles for both military and civilian consumption.

Section 3: Weaving
The vast majority of SS and police uniforms were manufactured at so-called SS-Bekleidungswerke or clothing factories in the concentration camps, with a central store at Dachau. In addition, the SS made webbing and braid for the Wehrmacht on sub-contract to the Schwarz Company of Hamburg.

Amt V   Land-, Forst- und Fischereiwirtschaft (Agriculture, Forestry and Fisheries) under SS-Obersturmbannführer Heinrich Vogel

Section 1: Nutrition and Food Research
This Section purchased both live and dead animals such as guinea-pigs, mice and rats for experimental use in the research institutes of the SS. It also bred Angora rabbits at Auschwitz and maintained medicinal herb and spice gardens in many other camps.

Section 2: Forestry
Administered the economic use of forests situated on SS property.

Section 3: Fisheries
The SS operated a fish processing company under the trade name of Anton Loibl GmbH.

Amt VI   Textil- und Lederverwertung (Reprocessing of Textile and Leather Goods)

There were textile and leather works at Dachau and Ravensbrück which upgraded old uniforms, belts, boots etc, for re-issue to combat units of the Waffen-SS. They also processed clothing confiscated from concentration camp inmates, which was then forwarded to the SS-Bekleidungswerke to be made into uniforms.

Amt VII   Buch und Bild (Books and Pictures) under SS-Sturmbannführer Dr Alfred Mischke

Section 1: Nordland-Verlag
The SS publishing house which produced books and magazines on Germanic history and culture for general public consumption.

Section 2: Bauer & Co
An SS picture restoration company, employed by major European art galleries, which also confiscated valuable paintings for display at Wewelsburg or in the House of German Art.

Amt VIII   Kulturbauten (Cultural Monuments) under SS-Obersturmbannführer Horst Klein

Section 1: Society for the Maintenance of German Monuments
Looked after the upkeep and improvement of historical buildings including the SS castles at Wewelsburg, Kranichfeld and Sudelfeld. Many of the tapestries, wood carvings etc, used to embellish these institutions were manufactured by craftsmen at Buchenwald and other concentration camps. This Section also supervised the SS Damascus School at Dachau.

Section 2: Memorial Foundations
This Section was principally concerned with the King Heinrich Memorial Trust and the Externsteine Foundation, a sanctuary situated amongst a group of rocks in the Teutoburg Forest.

Due to its very nature, Amtsgruppe W was considerably decentralised, with each of its Ämter located away from the WVHA headquarters.

The massive concentration camp industry was supervised on the ground by only a few junior SS officers and NCOs, assisted by a large number of foreign auxiliary troops and senior inmates known as Ältesten. These inmates acted as works foremen or Kapos, and were free from all other camp duties. Political prisoners and hardened habitual criminals were usually entrusted with such jobs since they often wielded great influence over their comrades. Many clerical positions within the camps were also held by selected inmates, and there was a high degree of prisoner self-administration. Employment of inmates on desk work also provided the camp officials with an opportunity to play the prisoners against one another, and make them scapegoats for thefts and other petty crimes committed by the SS men. The permanent SS contingent at each camp was usually fairly small, Dachau, for example, having just 300 Totenkopf veterans, all over 40 years of age, to oversee 17,000 inmates in 1943. However, most camps also had Waffen-SS training grounds situated nearby from which extra men were regularly drafted in on a rota basis, and from which emergency reinforcements could be summoned if required.

During the second half of the war, the working hours of most prisoners were raised considerably. By 1944, an 11hr day had become the rule, even during the winter months, with only Sunday afternoons set aside for rest.

Debility and mortality increased rapidly, and the productivity of inmates remained far below Himmler's and Pohl's high expectations. Consequently, more and more had to be employed to maintain even a static output. Anti-social elements and petty criminals were soon being transferred en masse by the RSHA from conventional German State Prisons to the concentration camps, and according to a WVHA report of 15 January 1945 the number of inmates incarcerated at that time had reached an all-time high of 715,000 including 200,000 women. Probably as many as one-third of those subsequently lost their lives in the exhausting evacuation marches organised in the face of Allied advances on the camps. The total number of prisoners who died during the war from weakness and disease whilst labouring for the SS in the concentration camps and factories of the Reich was estimated by the Nürnberg tribunal at 500,000.

ALLACH PORCELAIN

One of the smallest but best-known of the SS economic enterprises was the making of porcelain and ceramics which, unlike any of the other activities undertaken in the concentration camps, received widespread publicity in the German Press before and during the war.

In Hitler's propaganda scheme, his target was always the broad masses. To that end, the formative years of Nazism witnessed mass-production of cheap music boxes, paperweights, plastic drinking goblets, wall plaques, model soldiers, swastika-embroidered pillows and other household goods which extolled the virtues of the SA and National Socialism. After 1933, however, such worthless items were branded as 'kitsch' or 'trash' and were positively suppressed by the new régime. The Führer now wished to be portrayed as a patron of the arts and antiquity.

Himmler immediately took up the challenge of projecting the Party's new cultural image. He felt that he could influence and better the taste of the German people by the production of beautiful and decorative art pieces, and in 1936 his Persönlicher Stab purchased a small privately-run porcelain plant in the little town of Allach, just outside Munich. The reorganisation of the company was placed in the capable hands of SS-Oberführer Prof Dr Karl Diebitsch, who successfully recruited as his directors and staff the very best artists, designers and potters from the world-famous ceramics factories in Dresden, Meissen, Berlin, Rosenthal and Nymphenburg. A unique concentration of talent was built up including such renowned names as Profs Robert Förster and Theodor Karner, Franz Nagy, Adolf and Richard Röhring, and Detlef Fichter. Artistic advice was also forthcoming from Obergruppenführer Pohl's wife Elenor, who was a qualified designer.

As the enterprise grew the room at Allach was no longer sufficient and the plant transferred to Dachau concentration camp in 1937. By 1940 two separate factories had developed, a ceramics and pottery works at Dachau and a porcelain section back at Allach, which had in the meantime been enlarged. During that period only about 30 highly-skilled craftsmen were employed in the plants, but as selected inmates from Dachau were trained in the work the number grew to over 100 in 1943. There were special showrooms for their products at Berlin, Posen, Warsaw and Lemberg, and turnover reached 800,000 Reichsmarks in 1944.

The Allach project was one of Himmler's favourite concerns, and from the outset he decided that the pieces produced there should reflect the feeling of the new Reich in general, and of the SS in particular. Whereas the Dachau side of the enterprise turned out fairly basic plates, vases, mugs, jars, and other utensils for hospitals, canteens and general public consumption, as well as the pseudo-

Plate 80 'The Allgemeine-SS Cavalry Officer' — one
of the exquisite equestrian subjects produced at Allach.

Pagan earthenware Julleuchter candleholders which adorned SS family tables at Yuletide, the decorative items emanating from Allach were of the very finest quality. About half of them were commissioned by the Persönlicher Stab RfSS for presentation purposes, and the remainder could be bought in the shops. Each piece was marked on the base with two superimposed Sig-runes, the SS quality control symbol.

A great variety of items ultimately came out of the Allach works. Most of the pieces were in classical white porcelain, but a few were hand-coloured. Equestrian subjects included an 18th Century Prussian cavalry officer, a mounted Allgemeine-SS officer, the goddess Diana, hussars and no less than five variants of Frederick the Great. Standing figures such as The SS Standard Bearer, The Police Officer, The RAD Man, The Hitler Youth, The BDM Standard Bearer and The Luftwaffe Officer were presented by Himmler to high-ranking officials of the organisations concerned, while others like The Fencer, The Munich Maid, Til Eulenspiegel, Athena and costumed peasants were popular with contemporary connoisseurs and collectors. A large number of small animal subjects including stags, bears, dogs, elephants and rabbits went on more general sale, and bowls and plates were produced to commemorate SS rallies and to be used as prizes at sporting events, or Yuletide gifts. Many of the products featured in articles appearing in *Das Schwarze Korps*, *FM-Zeitschrift* and the Nazi art magazine *Kunst im Dritten Reich*, and a special exhibition entitled 'Deutsche Künstler und die SS' ('German Artists and the SS') was held in the spring of 1944 to publicise the Allach factory.

The ceramics industry presented one of the more acceptable faces of the SS economy, with workers being very well treated to protect their precious skills. For their part, the captive potters and artists knew it was in their best interest to produce items of the highest quality. The fact that Allach porcelain is still eagerly sought after today is perhaps the finest tribute to their labours.

SWORD MAKING AT DACHAU

While porcelain production was one of the more publicised SS economic activities, one of the least-known was the manufacture of exquisite presentation swords with damascus steel blades. The art of damascus forging was brought to Europe from the Middle East during the Crusades, and involved the continual folding of around 500 white-hot layers of steel and iron which were then immersed in a warm oil. The result was a blade of extreme strength and beauty, with a patterned surface. Damascus swords were popular amongst officers of most western nations during the 18th and 19th Centuries, even though they cost about 30 times as much as their standard issue counterparts. By the early 20th Century, however, far cheaper versions with acid etched blades giving the appearance of damascus steel began to be produced, and the damascus industry was further hit when many of its highly skilled craftsmen perished during World War 1. At the end of 1938 there were only six qualified damascus swordsmiths in the whole of Germany, namely Robert Deus, Paul Dinger, Paul Hillmann, Otto Kössler, Paul Müller and Karl Westler. The majority of these individuals were quite elderly, and there was a real danger of their art dying with them.

Himmler was anxious to preserve the traditions of damascus production, and in December 1938 he ordered the setting up of a Damascus School within the confines of Dachau concentration camp. The theory was that selected members of the Allgemeine-SS, who were cutlers or blacksmiths by profession, would be seconded to Dachau and trained in damascus forging at SS expense. The Reichsführer chose 54-year-old Paul Müller as director of the enterprise, and a contract was drawn up between them. Its terms were as follows:

1. Müller pledged himself to teach designated SS men how to make damascus blades, so that the art would be preserved and carried on by the SS.
2. Müller had to comply with all directions of the Reichsführer-SS, and was responsible to him personally for his actions. He could be recalled from leave should Himmler wish a special presentation sword made urgently.
3. Müller received an initial net monthly salary of 450 Reichsmarks, plus free accommodation.
4. If Müller became unable to work or was restricted in his work because of an industrial injury, he would continue to receive his entire salary.
5. On reaching the age of 65, Müller would receive a life pension of 75% of his salary at retirement.
6. The contract was valid for Müller's lifetime.

Müller had recently fallen on hard times and he jumped at the chance of regular employment which would give him security in his old age. The contract was duly signed, and the SS Damascus School at Dachau went into production.

In 1939 the first 10 students were assigned to the school, and began to forge damascus-bladed 'Geburtstagsdegen' or 'birthday swords' on special commission from Himmler, for presentation to senior Nazi personalities. They also designed one of the three prototype Waffen-SS daggers produced in 1940. As the war dragged on, however, battlefield exigencies inevitably claimed Müller's assistants. By 1943 he had only two apprentices left, Doll and Noth, and one trained damascus craftsman called Flittner. That April all three were drafted into the Waffen-SS, leaving Müller to operate the smithy alone. He objected bitterly to their enforced departure, but the WVHA response to his dilemma was unsympathetic and the situation had to be accepted as a fait accompli.

Paul Müller remained at the Dachau smithy and continued to produce presentation swords for Himmler until the end of 1944. After the war, he returned to his home town of Solingen and practised his craft until six months prior to his death in 1971, at the age of 87. During the 1960s, he was active in the creation of numerous reproduction

Nazi damascus blades including honour daggers, swords and paper knives. His fakes usually bore the raised and gilded inscription "Echt Damast, P. Müller' (Genuine Damascus, P. Müller).

Plate 81 One of the veteran Totenkopf NCOs at Belsen being searched by British soldiers after the liberation of the camp, 17 April 1945. Note the Death's Head collar patch. *IWM*

THE CIRCLE OF FRIENDS OF THE REICHSFÜHRER-SS

The Nazi Party in general, as a nationalist and anti-socialist movement, was always supported even from its infancy by big business, and when the SS attracted a large number of the upper-middle class into its officer corps in the early 1930s, major industrial groupings began to back it in particular. I.G. Farben and the light industrialists who opposed the costly protection of the great Junker landholders, and aimed to promote capital-intensive farming, were natural allies of Himmler. They shared the common goal of building German hegemony in Europe, in a closed economic bloc independent of American capital and the world market. During the spring of 1934, Himmler befriended Wilhelm Keppler, one of I.G. Farben's directors, and bestowed upon him the honorary rank of SS-Gruppenführer. In return, Keppler was instrumental in the creation of the so-called Freundeskreis RfSS or Circle of Friends of the Reichsführer-SS, a group of wealthy industrialists and business advisers. They agreed to make regular financial contributions towards the cultural, social and charitable activities of the SS, in return for Himmler's patronage and protection.

While Keppler was the instigator of the Freundeskreis, its leading member was the renowned financier Kurt Freiherr von Schröder, whose Cologne Bank maintained the special account, code-named 'S', which held Freundeskreis donations. Other prominent members of the Circle included: Dr Rasche, Director of the Dresden Bank; Dr Lippert, Oberbürgermeister of Berlin; Dr Ritter von Halt, Director of the Deutsche Bank; and Gottfried Graf von Bismarck. Heavy industry was represented by, among others, Director-General Röhnert of the Lüdenscheid Metal Works; Steinbrinck of the Flick Steel Consortium; Bingel of the Siemens electrical combine; Bütefisch of I.G. Farben; and Walz of the Bosch chemical concern. After the NSDAP rally in September 1934, the founder-members of the Freundeskreis were invited to Nürnberg and put up in the Grand Hotel as 'guests of the Reichsführer-SS', no doubt in appreciation of the valuable support they gave Himmler at the time of the Röhm Purge.

Throughout the life of the Third Reich, the Freundeskreis deposited vast sums into the coffers of the SS, and a special office was set up under SS-Brigadeführer Fritz Kranefuss to administer donations received from the Circle. For its part, the SS was able to award lucrative contracts in the conquered territories to the companies concerned, and supply them with cheap concentration camp labour. In September 1943 alone, 1,100,000 Reichsmarks went into Account 'S', 200,000 of them from von Schröder personally, who wrote that he was very happy to be able to help Himmler perform his 'special tasks'. Despite their postwar protests, there is no doubt that these pillars of German society played a most important part in oiling the wheels of the SS economic machine.

THE SS INFILTRATION OF GERMAN SOCIETY

Besides the acknowledged and logical development of the SS as regards its fusion with the police and security services, the organisation enlarged its position and range of influence in more insidious ways. By means of an unobtrusive but thorough policy of infiltration, the SS furnished itself with representatives in every branch of official and semi-official German life. It became, in effect, the archetypal 'State Within the State', a closely-knit group of men and women governed by a rigid set of rules, the chief of which was loyalty and unquestioning obedience of orders.

Membership of the SS was always attractive, offering a steady and lucrative job in the agency of the most powerful body in Germany, with the chance of a quick lift on the road to economic, political, professional or even artistic success. Consequently, the SS soon outgrew its origins as a group of guardsmen and came to represent a very carefully organised racial élite composed of intellectuals as well as ex-soldiers, shopkeepers and peasant youths. In May 1944, no less than 300 of the 1,200 leading personalities in Germany, including industrialists, financiers and academics, held SS membership. By that time, SS domination throughout the Reich had become total.

A starting point in the study of SS personalities can be made with the immediate entourage of the Führer. Hitler surrounded himself with SS men, the principal of whom were his secretary, SS-Obergruppenführer Philipp Bouhler, and his personal adjutant, SS-Obergruppenführer Julius Schaub, both constant companions and confidants since the old Stosstrupp days. The Führer's chief medical officer, Prof Dr Karl Brandt, was a Gruppenführer; his personal pilot, Hans Baur, was a Brigadeführer in the RSD; and his chauffeur, Erich Kempka, was a Sturmbannführer. In addition, the majority of Hitler's young valets and aides, including Fritz Darges, Otto Günsche, Wilhelm Krause, Heinz Linge, Hans Pfeiffer, Max Wünsche, and the brothers Hans-Georg and Richard Schulze, were junior SS officers.

As it was with the head of the Party, so it was with the NSDAP itself. One of the key posts at the top of the Nazi hierarchy, that of Party Treasurer, was held by SS-Oberst-Gruppenführer Franz Xaver Schwarz, who controlled the whole financial policy of the NSDAP. Below him were three SS-Obergruppenführer: Walter Buch, the Supreme Party Judge; Max Amann, Chief of the Party Press Office; and Martin Bormann, Head of the Party Chancellery. To

Plate 82 Von Ribbentrop in his uniform as an
honorary SS-Brigadeführer, early 1936. *IWM*

quote only two more examples, SS-Brigadeführer Erich Cassel was Chief of the NSDAP Racial Department, and SS-Brigadeführer Bernhard Ruberg was Deputy Gauleiter of the Foreign Section of the NSDAP, which co-ordinated all Party activities abroad.

Control of access to Hitler and domination of the NSDAP by the SS could perhaps be expected, but the same penetration was also evident in the machinery of the State. Some of the most important posts in the Cabinet were held by SS Generals. Obergruppenführer Dr Hans Lammers was head of the Reich Chancellery, while Constantin Freiherr von Neurath and Joachim von Ribbentrop both served as Foreign Minister. In the various Reich ministries, 39 key positions were occupied by SS men from the ranks of Obergruppenführer down to Obersturmbannführer. In the Foreign Office alone, 10 posts were held by SS officers including Wilhelm Keppler, Walther Hewel, and Prof Dr Werner Gerlach, who were heads of departments. Brigadeführer Kurt Freiherr von Schröder, of the Freundeskreis RfSS, and Dr Alexander Freiherr von Dörnberg, Chief of Protocol, were Ministerial Directors. SS-Oberführer Prof Dr Franz Six, Chief of Amt VII of the RSHA, was also Head of the Foreign Office Cultural Department. Ribbentrop is known to have fought hard to maintain the independence of the Foreign Office and Diplomatic Service against the encroachment of the SD, so it is all the more significant that so many SS men held influential posts in the sphere of activity which he controlled.

In view of Himmler's position after 1943 as Reich Minister of the Interior, it was inevitable that the SS were well represented in that branch of the government. SS-Obergruppenführer Oswald Pohl of the WVHA was a Ministerial Director, and Obergruppenführer Dr Wilhelm Stuckart was a Secretary of State. Moreover, SS-Gruppenführer Prof Dr Friedrich Weber, SS-Brigadeführer Dr Anton Kreissl, and SS-Oberführer Hans Rüdiger were heads of departments. The special significance of the Ministry of the Interior, however, extended beyond the mere list of SS personalities holding office within it. Not only was it the central authoritative ministry in all matters concerning the Home Front, but from it Himmler was able to keep control of the vast German bureaucracy. The power of appointment, promotion and dismissal which he enjoyed as Minister of the Interior was one of the greatest reinforcements to its infiltration policy which the SS achieved.

At Goebbels' Ministry of Propaganda, the Chief of the Reich Press, Dr Otto Dietrich, was an SS-Obergruppenführer. Other SS officers of high rank included: Alfred-Ingemar Berndt, the Controller of Broadcasting; Karl Cerff, a departmental head; Dr Werner Naumann, Secretary of State for Propaganda; and Dr Toni Winkelnkemper, Head of the Foreign Broadcasting Department. As with the Foreign Office, this SS infiltration into the Propaganda Ministry was of particular significance since

Goebbels was no friend of Himmler and can scarcely have welcomed the presence of SS men amongst his subordinates. There is no doubt that this aspect represented a deliberate attempt by the SS to gain control of the German press and the nationwide machinery of propaganda.

At the Ministry of Labour, the Head of the Reich Inspectorate of Manpower was SS-Gruppenführer Prof Rudolf Jung, while SS-Brigadeführer Prof Wilhelm Börger was head of a department and SS-Oberführer Kurt Frey was Reich Inspector of Labour. In the Justice Ministry, SS-Gruppenführer Leo Petri was a member of the People's Court and SS-Oberführer Karl Engert was a Ministerial Director. The Ministry of Agriculture and Food was headed by SS-Obergruppenführer Walther Darré until 1942, when he was succeeded by SS-Obergruppenführer Herbert Backe. SS-Gruppenführer Werner Willikens was a Secretary of State at the Ministry, and SS-Obersturmbannführer Ferdinand Hiege of the Hauptamt RKF was a Departmental Chief. The Minister of Health, Dr Leonardo Conti, was an SS-Obergruppenführer and the Ministries of Economics, Finance and Education all had their share of SS permeation. SS-Gruppenführer Dr Franz Hayler and SS-Gruppenführer Otto Ohlendorff, both important SD officials, were at the first, SS-Brigadeführer Otto Heider at the second, and SS-Standartenführer Prof Dr Albert Holfelder at the last, to name only a sample.

In local government, the tale was the same. Provincial State Ministers and Secretaries, Presidents and Vice-Presidents of State Governments, were but a few of the men whose high SS rank was not always the most publicised feature of their careers. Further down the scale, in municipal affairs, at least six cities had senior SS officers as their Lord Mayors, including the Stosstrupp veteran Karl Fiehler, Oberbürgermeister of Munich.

Turning to industry, Paul Körner, Secretary of State for the Four-Year Plan, and Wilhelm Meinberg, Commissioner for Fuel, were both SS Generals. In other spheres such as armaments, shipping, banking and the motor and textile industries, the SS was again well represented. For instance, SS-Standartenführer Dr August Schwedler was Director of the Reichsbank; SS-Brigadeführer Hans Kehrl was leader of the Textiles Economics Group; SS-Oberführer Jakob Werlin was Reich Inspector of Motor Traffic and Director-General of the Mercedes firm; and SS-Oberführer Rudolf Diels headed the Hermann Göring Shipping Company.

The same was true of the military aristocracy, and some parts of the SS Dienstaltersliste read like a 'Who's Who' of German nobility. In addition to those mentioned elsewhere in this book, aristocratic members of the Allgemeine-SS included General Friedrich Graf von der Schulenburg, Generalmajor Anton Edler Kless von Drauwörth, Kuno Freiherr von Eltz-Rübenach, Oberst Friedrich Freiherr von der Goltz, Oberstleutnant Rolf von Humann-Hainhofen, Carl Reichsritter von Oberkamp, Wilhelm

Plate 83 SS-Obergruppenführer Dr Otto Dietrich, Chief of the Reich Press, addressing the first congress of the Union of National Journalists' Associations at the Doge's Palace in Venice, 9 April 1942. *IWM*

Plate 84 Members of the Reichstag saluting Hitler in 1938. SS uniforms are evident everywhere, and prominent SS personalities in the group include Schaub, von Ribbentrop, Lammers, Otto Dietrich, Darré and Seyss-Inquart. *IWM*

Freiherr von Holzschuher, Rittmeister Erasmus Freiherr von Malsen, Friedrich Erbgrossherzog von Mecklenburg, Carl Graf von Pückler-Burghaus, Friedrich Freiherr von Reitzenstein, Hildolf Reichsfreiherr von Thüngen, Paul Baron von Vietinghoff-Scheel, and Generalmajor Gustav Adolf von Wulffen. The list went on and on. One of the more renowned of their number during World War 2 was Oberst Hyazinth Graf Strachwitz, an SS-Standartenführer on the staff of Oberabschnitt Südost, who won the Knight's Cross of the Iron Cross with Oakleaves, Swords and Diamonds whilst serving as an army Panzer commander on the Eastern Front. He was one of a mere 27 recipients of the coveted decoration, and the only man ever to wear it with the black Allgemeine-SS uniform.

The widespread influence of the SS was not confined to the Reich, for in every occupied country SS men held some of the most important administrative posts. For example, Brigadeführer Dr Wilhelm Kinkelin was leader of the Section for Colonisation Policy in Rosenberg's Eastern Ministry. In Poland, SS-Gruppenführer Dr Otto Wächter was Governor of Galicia and SS-Gruppenführer Dr Richard Wendler Governor of the Lublin District, while two more key positions in Krakow were held by Brigadeführer Prof Dr Heinrich Teitge and Brigadeführer Dr Harry von Craushaar. In Bohemia and Moravia, SS-Obergruppenführer Karl Hermann Frank was Minister of State with Brigadeführer Dr Walther Bertsch as his Minister of Economics and Labour. In the west, Obergruppenführer Dr Werner Best was German Plenipotentiary in Denmark and Obergruppenführer Dr Arthur Seyss-Inquart was Reich Commissioner for the Netherlands. Under them were many SS officers at the head of the civil administration, and all this was in addition to the normal machinery of the SS and police set up in the conquered territories.

The list is by now growing tedious, but one last area of SS infiltration deserves coverage. The realms of education, culture and charitable organisations were no more closed to the ubiquitous figure of the SS than were the high governmental circles or heavy industry. Many university professors were SS officers of high rank and SS-Gruppenführer Johannes Johst was President of both the Reich Chamber of Literature and the German Academy of Poets. SS-Sturmbannführer Hermann Müller-John, bandmaster of the Leibstandarte, was on the Council of the Reich Chamber of Music. Even the German Red Cross Society, under the leadership of SS-Obergruppenführer Prof Dr Ernst-Robert Grawitz, was permeated with SS officials. Similarly, the head of the Nazi People's Welfare Organisation was SS-Gruppenführer Erich Hilgenfeldt, who was also in charge of the annual Winter Charities Campaign. One of his close colleagues, the Reich Women's Leader Gertrud Scholtz-Klink, was the wife of SS-Obergruppenführer August Heissmeyer. The SS likewise dominated the sporting world with, for example, Standartenführer Hans Hieronymus as Secretary of the German Boxing Federation.

This SS penetration into all parts of German life was steadily achieved in two ways. Firstly, in the early days of the Nazi movement, before the SS was in a position to appoint or arrange the appointment of its own men to influential offices, the main method used was the practice of awarding honorary SS rank to important public figures. The new members felt their authority enhanced by the black uniform, while the SS secured well-placed recruits bound to it by the oath of loyalty which could be backed up if necessary by the SS discipline code. Initially there were two categories of honorary officers, the Rangführer and the Ehrenführer. The term Rangführer was used for honorary ranks up to and including Oberstumbannführer, while Ehrenführer covered Standartenführer and above. Both groups wore distinctive ivory-coloured cuff titles. After the separation of the SS from the SA in 1934, the Rangführer grade and the special insignia were abolished, and from that time there was nothing to outwardly distinguish the SS-Ehrenführer from active SS officers.

The second method of SS infiltration reached its full efficiency only after the consolidation of the Nazi regime, and was the direct promotion of SS men to high positions in the State. A marked feature of the German governmental hierarchy was the pluralism of offices held by leading SS figures, which enabled a few men to exercise a disproportionately large influence. The best example was that of Himmler himself, who eventually controlled all military, paramilitary and police forces on the Home Front, as well as two entire Army Groups in the field. He was able to appoint his lieutenants to correspondingly high positions in both the State and, after the July 1944 bomb plot, the Wehrmacht. By the end of 1944, SS-Obergruppenführer Hans Jüttner was Chief of Staff of the Home Army as well as being head of the SS Führungshauptamt, while SS-Gruppenführer August Frank of the WVHA and Verwaltungspolizei had also been appointed Chief of Administration for the Army High Command. That last bastion of the old traditional Germany, the army, had finally fallen to the SS.

The primary function of the SS was to protect Hitler and his régime, and it operated all the more efficiently having placed its representatives and contacts in all sections and at all levels of the society which it guarded. The part it played in preserving the general security of the Third Reich and in strengthening Himmler's position against his rivals from within the NSDAP cannot be over-emphasized. In short, there was nothing in Nazi Germany which was not political, and nothing political with which the SS was not concerned.

11 The Germanic-SS

THE GERMANIC IDEAL

Heinrich Himmler was possessed by the desire to improve the strength and racial composition of the German nation, and saw as the cornerstone of the Greater German Reich an SS organisation with native branches in each of the occupied western territories. The NSDAP hierarchy had long agreed that all the areas which had formerly been part of the German (or Holy Roman) Empire, including Flanders and the Low Countries, should automatically be incorporated into the new Reich, with the mass of their populace eventually attaining full Reich citizenship. Himmler, however, went a step further, demanding that Germany should have the right to bring into its ranks the Germanic peoples of Norway and Denmark, states which had never been part of the Empire. The Reichsführer envisaged the ultimate creation of a new western Germanic state to be called Burgundia, grouping the Netherlands, Belgium and northeast France, which would be policed and governed solely by the SS according to the SS code. Like the proposed Germanised Eastern Marks of Ingermanland, Narev and Gotengau, Burgundia would act as a buffer, protecting Germany proper from invasion. The general aim was to attract all the Nordic blood of Europe into the SS, so that never again would the Germanic peoples come into mutual conflict.

To that end, Himmler established a replica of the German Allgemeine-SS in Flanders in September 1940. This Algemeene-SS Vlaanderen was joined two months later by the Dutch Nederlandsche-SS, and in May 1941 the Norges-SS was formed in Norway. Members of these units retained their own languages and customs, but there was to be no question of a Europe of semi-free pro-German States, each with its own independent SS formation loyal to its own political leader. From the start, Himmler told his western volunteers:

'Be certain of this. There will be in all Europe just one SS – the Germanic-SS under the command of the Reichsführer-SS. You can resist, but that is a matter of indifference to me for we will create it in any case. We do not ask you to turn against your country, nor to do anything repugnant to anyone proud of his country, who loves it and has his self-respect. Neither do we expect you to become Germans out of opportunism. What we do ask is that you subordinate your national ideal to a superior racial and historical ideal, that of the single and all-embracing Germanic Reich.'

Consequently, at the end of 1942, the western formations were removed from the influence of their own national collaborationist political leaders and amalgamated to become the new Germanic-SS under Himmler's direct orders. Their independence gone, they were now merely branches of a single organisation and were retitled Germaansche-SS in

Vlaanderen, Germaansche-SS en Nederland, and Germanske-SS Norge. After the raising in April 1943 of the Danish Germansk Korpset, later called the Schalburg Corps, the Germanic-SS was complete, with a total active membership of almost 9,000 men. Many of them had seen action in Russia, with the foreign volunteer legions of the Waffen-SS. All were duly kitted out with surplus black Allgemeine-SS uniforms imported from Germany, to which suitable national insignia were attached. Their primary wartime task was to support the local police by rooting out partisans, subversives and other anti-Nazi elements.

General responsibility for the supervision of the Germanic-SS and its forerunners rested with the SS Hauptamt, which assisted in the foundation and expansion of the new body. To further this object, a special Germanic Liaison Office or Germanische Leitstelle was set up, with headquarters at 20 Admiral von Schröderstrasse, Berlin, and branches in The Hague, Oslo and Copenhagen. The function of these outposts was to oversee the whole political propaganda and recruiting activity of the SS in the respective areas of western Europe and Scandinavia. It soon became apparent that the Germanic recruits often needed special handling and indoctrination before they could be fully accepted into the SS, and to meet this difficulty a Germanic-SS Training Department was established, with four main training camps at Sennheim in Alsace, Schooten in Belgium, Hovelte in Denmark and Avegoor in Holland. The emphasis in the camps' curriculum was on games, sport and political education. In addition, there was a Germanic-SS Officers' School (Führerschule der Germanischen-SS) at Hildesheim, the purpose of which was to provide general training for future political leaders in the Germanic-SS. Throughout its existence, however, the Germanic-SS was constantly depleted by voluntary enlistments into the Waffen-SS, particularly the 'Wiking' and 'Nordland' divisions.

Each of the four formations which came to make up the Germanic-SS had its own distinct history, and these shall now be covered in turn.

FLANDERS

The Nazis always drew a clear distinction between the two peoples of Belgium, at first favouring the Flemings of Flanders, who were Germanic in language and race, as against the Walloons of Wallonia, who were French-speaking and of Romanic origin. From 1940, Hitler played upon the long-standing resentment felt by Flemings against the Walloon-dominated state of Belgium, which had been created only 110 years before. He encouraged nationalist dissension in the country, supporting the Vlaamsch Nationaal Verbond or VNV (Flemish National Union) of Gustave 'Staf' de Clercq, which saw Flanders as a natural part of the Netherlands rather than of Belgium and which soon absorbed all collaborationist parties in Flanders. The VNV had its own version of the German SA, the Dietsche Militie Zwarte Brigade, and a network of other organisations which paralleled the NSKK, HJ, RAD and NSDAP political leadership.

In September 1940, two pro-German Flemings, Ward Hermans and Rene Lagrou, set up a Flemish equivalent of the Allgemeine-SS in Antwerp. Hermans was a prominent member of the VNV, and began by enrolling 130 of his Party colleagues into the corps, which he called the Algemeene Schutsscharen Vlaanderen, or Flemish General SS. By March 1941 there were 1,580 active members, with a further 4,000 Patron Members or Beschermende Leden, who contributed financially like the German Fördernde Mitglieder. However, due to the constant loss of its men to the German armed forces, particularly the 'Westland' and 'Nordwest' regiments and Flemish Legion of the Waffen-SS, the strength of the Algemeene-SS Vlaanderen fell away considerably during 1941, although it was never less than 300.

In 1942, veterans returning from their voluntary service on the Eastern Front again built up the numbers of the Flemish SS. That October, in accordance with Himmler's policy of bringing all Germanic General SS formations within a single German orbit, the body was renamed the Germaansche-SS in Vlaanderen or Germanic-SS in Flanders. Those who were either too young, too old or not up to the physical requirements of the Germaansche-SS could enrol in its welfare association, known as the Vlaanderen-Korps. The policy of the Flemish SS was very much at odds with the cautious pro-Dutch attitude of the VNV, and it openly advocated total German control over Flanders. It published its own newspaper, *De SS Man*.

The black uniform of the Germanic-SS in Flanders was virtually identical to that of the Allgemeine-SS. The only points of difference were that the peaked cap featured a large elongated silver swastika instead of the SS eagle, and a black diamond bearing the SS runes was worn on the left upper arm instead of the swastika armband. The diamond was piped in black and silver for junior ranks and in silver bullion for officers. Rank insignia worn on the left collar patch was the same as that of the Allgemeine-SS, while the right collar patch was blank. On the lower left sleeve, a black and silver cuff title bore the legend 'SS-Vlaanderen', and the belt buckle featured the SS runes in a circle of oakleaves. Members of the Vlaanderen-Korps wore a similar black uniform, but were not entitled to sport the peaked cap or arm diamond. They had forage caps with a silver swastika on the left side, and their cuff titles read 'Vlaanderen-Korps'. Moreover, their belt buckles had only a semi-circle of oakleaves around the runes. In civilian clothes, members of the Germanic-SS in Flanders could wear a circular lapel badge with a white swastika on a black background, while Patron Members had their own diamond-shaped badge bearing SS runes and the letters 'B.L.'.

The nominal strength of the Flemish SS in June 1944 was 3,500. However, 1,600 of these were on military service with the Waffen-SS, 940 were with the NSKK and 500 were in the Vlaanderen-Korps, leaving only 460 active General SS members in Flanders, of whom 100 were still probationers. By the end of the year, most of Belgium had been liberated. There was only one significant exception — the important port of Antwerp, birthplace of the Flemish SS, which remained in German hands. The Senior SS and Police Commander in Belgium, SS-Gruppenführer Richard Jungclaus, linked the remnants of the Germaansche-SS in Vlaanderen and the paramilitaries of the VNV into a Security Corps or Sicherheitskorps of some 2,500 men. A battalion of this corps fought alongside the German defenders of Antwerp in a battle which lasted throughout September-November 1944. It was one of the rare examples of western European collaborators being used to fight against the British and Americans, most of their colleagues seeing service only in Russia.

At the end of the war, Belgium was more severe on its traitors than any other country except Norway, and over 4,000 sentences of death were pronounced for military collaboration during the 1940-45 period.

HOLLAND

Over 50,000 Germans lived and worked in Holland before World War 2, so it is not surprising that a number of pro-Nazi groups sprang up in the Netherlands during the formative years of the Third Reich. The most important of these was the Nationaal-Socialistische Beweging or NSB, the National Socialist Movement of Anton Adriaan Mussert. The NSB was a highly organised and fully uniformed Party with its own paramilitary section, the Weer Afdeelingen or WA, and in 1940 it was granted a political monopoly in the Netherlands under the controlling authority of the country's Reichskommissar, SS-Obergruppenführer Dr Arthur Seyss-Inquart.

In November 1940, following the Flemish example, the NSB took the bold step of establishing its own SS within the framework of the Party. The initiative came from the former leader of Mussert's personal bodyguard, Johannes Hendrik ('Henk') Feldmeijer who created what was known simply as the Nederlandsche-SS. Its uniform was the basic black one of the NSB, but ranks, worn on the left collar patch, were an exact facsimile of those of the German Allgemeine-SS, the names being merely literal translations into Dutch. Feldmeijer held the unique position of Voorman, and wore a three-

Plate 85   Badge worn by
Patron Members, or
Beschermende Leden, of the
Germanic-SS in Flanders.

Plate 86   Wolfsangel insignia
worn on the left upper arm by
members of the Germanic-SS in
the Netherlands.

legged trifos symbol on both collar patches. Others wore the regimental number on the right patch. A triangle bearing a silver wolfsangel on a red and black background was worn on the left upper arm, and a silver metal wolfsangel also appeared on the peaked cap in place of the SS eagle. On the right upper arm, the SS runes were worn on a black diamond, in silver bullion for officers and white cotton for lower ranks. All ranks wore blank cuff titles on the lower left sleeve.

In October 1942, the Nederlandsche-SS ceased to be a paramilitary formation of the NSB. It was renamed the Germaansche-SS en Nederland and became a part of the greater Germanic-SS under Himmler's orders. Mussert's control over it came to an end, and all Dutch SS men had to take a personal oath of loyalty to Adolf Hitler. The following year, Feldmeijer adopted the rank insignia of an SS-Standartenführer and thereafter called himself Standartleider. By that time, he had earned the Iron Cross 2nd Class and Wound Badge in Black while fighting as an SS-Hauptsturmführer with the Leibstandarte-SS 'Adolf Hitler' and 'Wiking' divisions in the Balkans and Russia, and Himmler had presented him with the SS Death's Head Ring. He had also secured for himself the rank of Standartenführer in the German Allgemeine-SS proper, holding SS number 440,001 and an attachment to Oberabschnitt Nordwest.

As in Flanders, the concept of Patron Membership was also adopted by the Dutch SS. Contributions of not less than one Florin per month entitled an individual to wear an oval badge with the SS runes surmounting a swastika and the letters 'B.L.' (Begunstigende Leden). By 1944, there were some 4,000 Patron Members in Holland.

The Germaansche-SS en Nederland had, on paper, a strength of five regiments plus an SS-Police regiment, and supported its own journal, *Storm SS*. However, its active membership — nominally 3,800 — was in fact constantly depleted by voluntary enlistments in the Waffen-SS. An affiliated guard unit set up by the HSSPf Nordwest, SS-Obergruppenführer Hanns Rauter, after the disbanding of the 'Nordwest' regiment, took the title SS-Wachbataillon Nordwest. It had four companies, one of which was used largely for ceremonial duties at SS Headquarters in The Hague. The others acted as guards at the concentration camps which were being established at Herzogenbusch, Vught and various other parts of the Netherlands. The SS-Postschutz in Holland also employed a number of over-age Dutch volunteers.

In addition to bringing in their own police, the German occupation authorities in Holland set about reorganising the Dutch police, and the SS were inevitably involved in the process. A new body, the Communal Police, replaced the various municipal forces and was trained under SS direction at the Police School at Schalkhaar. Members were kitted out in a uniform based upon that of the Allgemeine-SS but with a closed collar, and any Dutch police-

man who was also a member of the Germanic-SS could wear the SS runes below the left breast pocket of his tunic.

In March 1943, the NSB set up the Landwacht Nederland (Dutch Home Guard), in which all Party members between the ages of 17 and 50 were required to serve. The following October, it was renamed Landstorm Nederland and taken over by the SS. Members initially wore WA or Germanic-SS uniform, but later went into field grey. The Landstorm fought primarily against the Dutch Resistance, but was also engaged against the British airborne forces around Arnhem in September 1944. Two months later it absorbed the SS-Wachbataillon Nordwest, the staffs of various training establishments, and around 3,000 Dutchmen brought back from the Germanische Sturmbanne of the Allgemeine-SS in Germany, and became the SS-Grenadier Division 'Landstorm Nederland'. The division saw some minor defensive fighting before it surrendered in May 1945.

At the end of the war, Holland, like several other western countries, reintroduced the death penalty (abolished since 1873) to deal with extreme cases of collaboration. In all, 138 death sentences were pronounced. Mussert was executed on 7 May 1946, and Seyss-Inquart was hanged after the Nürnberg Trials. 'Henk' Feldmeijer had been killed in an air-raid towards the end of the war, and so cheated the gallows.

NORWAY

Unlike the other occupied western countries, Norway had only one collaborating Party of any importance, the uniformed Nasjonal Samling or NS (National Unity) movement of Vidkun Quisling. Quisling attempted to assume power immediately after the German invasion, but was ordered to step down and it was not until February 1942 that Hitler appointed him President of Norway, the only collaborator ever to achieve such high office in a German-occupied country. However, he was not entrusted with exclusive power. The real ruler of Norway was his arch-rival, Reichskommissar Josef Terboven, who operated a ruthless régime from his fortress at Castle Skaugum in Oslo.

In April 1941, Jonas Lie, Chief of the Norwegian Police, and Axel Stang, Minister of Sport and Chief of Staff of the Rikshird (the NS version of the German SA), saw service in Yugoslavia with the Waffen-SS division 'Das Reich'. Both received the Iron Cross 2nd Class. After his homecoming as a war-decorated hero, Lie at once set about intriguing with Terboven against their mutual foe, Quisling. With German complicity, Lie founded the Norges-SS, a Norwegian equivalent of the Allgemeine-SS recruited from the cream of the Rikshird. Quisling, who had not been consulted or forewarned, was furious, but there was little he could do for Himmler had given the Norwegian SS his blessing. The Reichsführer arrived in Oslo to preside over the oath-taking ceremony, and duly appointed Lie to command the unit with the rank of SS-Standartenführer.

The new SS men wore a curious uniform comprising a field-grey open-necked tunic with a khaki shirt and black tie. Rank insignia was that of the Rikshird, and the latter's black armband with sun cross and swords was also sported on the left sleeve. Before the Norges-SS could complete even its basic training, however, Hitler invaded Russia and 85% of its membership immediately volunteered for service with the Norwegian Legion in the East. The rest went into a Police Company under Jonas Lie, which took part in the siege of Leningrad.

In July 1942, many veterans returned from Russia and the Norges-SS was reactivated. A few months later, in accordance with Himmler's policy, it became the Germanske-SS Norge. The former Rikshird insignia was abandoned and a common scheme of ranks, based on those of the Allgemeine-SS and the other Germanic-SS formations, was adopted. The Germanic-SS in Norway severed all connections with its Rikshird parent and it was henceforth forbidden for members to belong to both organisations. A new oath of allegiance was taken, to Hitler rather than Quisling, and the German inspired motto 'Min aere er troskap' ('My Honour is Loyalty') was adopted.

The uniform of the Germanske-SS Norge was all black except for a brown shirt. It consisted of a ski cap (peaked caps were never worn by the Norwegian SS), an open-necked tunic, ski trousers or breeches and mountain boots. On the left upper arm the NS eagle holding a sun cross in silver and black was worn, above a cuff title bearing the legend 'Germanske-SS Norge'. Rank insignia appeared on the left collar patch with a silver sunwheel swastika on the right patch, while the commander of the Germanic-SS in Norway wore the sunwheel on both collar patches. SS runes on a black diamond were sported on the right upper arm. Daggers do not appear to have been worn, although Lie did carry a chained SS dagger on ceremonial occasions, as an officer of the Allgemeine-SS proper. In that capacity, he was attached to the staff of Oberabschnitt Nord and achieved the rank of SS-Oberführer in January 1944.

No Germanic-SS unit in Norway attained sufficient size to be regarded as a Standarte. The largest that could be mustered was a Stormbann or battalion, of which there were 12 in various parts of the country. It is possible that at least five of these existed only on paper and that all the others were consistently under-strength. This was not the result of a lack of volunteers so much as the fact that the Germanic-SS in Norway, as elsewhere, was part-time and often merely a stepping stone into the Waffen-SS or other branches of the Wehrmacht. So many Germanic-SS men did, in fact, volunteer for full-time Waffen-SS service that they were able to contribute an entire Company to the 'Nordland' regiment in the spring of 1943. At the same time, the Germanske-SS Norge established the SS-Wachbataillon Oslo which recruited another 500 Norwegians to act as guards at various installations in the city and elsewhere. Many of its volunteers came from the older age groups of the Germanic-SS.

The concept of Patron Members was introduced into Norway as in the other Germanic countries. These so-called Stottende Medlemner were entitled to wear a small oval badge in black enamel, with silver SS runes and the letters 'S.M.'.

Official figures published in Germaneren, the Norwegian SS paper, in September 1944 gave the strength of the Germanic-SS in Norway as 1,250 of whom 330 were on combat duty with the Waffen-SS and 760 in police units, including SS-Wachbataillon Oslo. That left only 160 Norwegians in the active Germanic-SS, so many units must have existed in a skeleton form only. At the same time, there were 3,500 Patron Members.

When the German forces in Norway capitulated, police files were opened by the resistance and some 90,000 Norwegians were branded collaborators. Mass arrests, retribution and summary justice followed. Quisling was executed and Jonas Lie died of a heart attack while awaiting trial. Terboven, however, managed to escape the hangman's noose in a most dramatic manner, blowing himself up with dynamite in the basement of his castle.

DENMARK

There were several pro-Nazi political Parties in Denmark before World War 2, the main one being the Danmarks National-Socialistiske Arbejder Parti or DNSAP under Frits Clausen. The DNSAP was highly organised, with its own Corps of Political Leaders, Youth Section, Labour Service and SA, which it called the Storm Afdelinger. In December 1939 the Danish SA could muster only 900 men, but by the beginning of 1941 this had risen to 2,500, many of whom were later sent on training courses to the Germanic-SS camp at Sennheim.

In April 1941, 200 Danes volunteered for service with the Waffen-SS 'Nordland' regiment, and after the invasion of Russia a further 1,200 joined the hastily-raised Freikorps Danmark to fight in the East. The Freikorps was commanded by Christian Frederik Count von Schalburg, a Danish aristocrat of Baltic-German origin and one-time leader of the DNSAP Youth who, until recently, had been serving as an SS-Sturmbannführer with the 'Wiking' division. The unit went into battle in May 1942 attached to the SS-Totenkopf-Division, and took part in the celebrated action at Demjansk where von Schalburg was killed on 2 June. He was given a State funeral by the Nazi authorities in Denmark.

The Freikorps ultimately suffered over 20% casualties, and was officially disbanded a year later.

Most of the Freikorps veterans were transferred, without much regard for their personal wishes, to the Waffen-SS division 'Nordland'. A few, however, including SS-Obersturmbannführer Knud Martinsen, the last commander of the formation, returned to their homeland to set up what amounted in all but name to a Danish branch of the Allgemeine-SS. In April 1943, with German support, Martinsen established the Germansk Korpset (Germanic Corps), which he shortly thereafter renamed the Schalburg Korpset or Schalburg Corps in memory of the Freikorps hero. Several Eastern Front veterans formed themselves into the cadre of the new unit, which opened its ranks to all young Danes of Nordic blood. The Corps was divided into two main groups, viz the active uniformed personnel, in five companies, and the non-regular patrons who gave moral and financial support. The latter came to be known as the Dansk-Folke-Vaern or Danish People's Defence, and practiced the use of small arms.

The Schalburg Corps adopted a black uniform virtually identical to that of the Allgemeine-SS, and rank insignia was also the same, although the nomenclature used was that of the Danish police. The main points of departure were that the SS cap eagle was replaced by a winged sunwheel swastika, and a sunwheel swastika also appeared on the right collar patch and on the belt buckle. A Danish heraldic shield, comprising three blue lions on a yellow field with red hearts, was worn on the upper left arm above a cuff title bearing the word 'Schalburg'. Five company cuff titles with the legends 'Herluf Trolle', 'Absalon', 'Skjalm Hvide', 'Olaf Rye' and 'Laessoe' were ordered into production, but it is not clear if they were ever issued. On ceremonial guard duty, a highly polished black German steel helmet was worn with a large white sunwheel swastika on the right-hand side. For more active purposes, the Corps was armed with light infantry weapons and supplied with a very practical khaki field uniform.

The Schalburg Corps adopted the same techniques as the partisan groups which it fought, and responded to each resistance assassination with one of its own. It was said that every act of sabotage provoked one of 'Schalburgtage'. A so-called Schalburg Cross bearing the Corps motto 'Troskab vor Aere' ('Our Honour is Loyalty') was instituted late in the war, and according to the Corps journal, Foedrelandet, at least one posthumous award was made to a Schalburg man killed by partisans.

After a General Strike in Denmark in July 1944, the Schalburg Corps was moved to Ringstad outside Copenhagen and incorporated into the Waffen-SS as SS-Ausbildungsbataillon (Training Battalion) Schalburg. Members were taught to use heavy weapons, in preparation for their defence of Denmark against the impending Allied invasion. Six months later the unit became SS Vagtbataillon Sjaelland or SS Guard Battalion Zealand. It never saw front line combat, however, and was officially disbanded in February 1945.

The Efterretnings Tjenesten or ET, the Intelligence Service of the Schalburg Corps, was withdrawn from its parent body in April 1944 and placed under the direct control of the Senior SS and Police Commander in Denmark, SS-Obergruppenführer Günther Pancke. On 19 September, as a consequence of what the Germans regarded as unreliable behaviour during the General Strike, the traditional Danish police organisation was stood down in its entirety and Pancke ordered the ET to form a new auxiliary police force in its place. This body, known by the Germans as the Hilfspolizei Korps or Hipo Corps, quickly acquired an ugly reputation and was responsible for the murder of at least 50 resistance suspects and the torture of hundreds more. In effect it became a Danish branch of the Gestapo. Some members wore a black uniform similar to that of the Schalburg Corps, but the majority operated in civilian clothes.

At the end of the war 12,000 Danes were arrested for collaboration and 112 death sentences were duly passed. Frits Clausen died of a heart attack while awaiting trial, and Knud Martinsen was executed in 1949.

THE GERMANIC-SS IN GERMANY

In addition to the Germanic-SS formations permanently based in Flanders, Holland, Norway and Denmark, the Allgemeine-SS established its own Germanische Sturmbanne or Germanic Battalions in the areas of the Reich where there existed large concentrations of workers imported from the Nordic countries. These foreigners numbered several hundred thousand by the end of 1942, and posed a major problem for German internal security. To assist in their control Flemish and Dutch SS officers and men, most of them fresh from frontline service in the East, were employed by German firms to engage upon a propaganda campaign in the factories. They succeeded in persuading such a large number of their compatriots to join the local Allgemeine-SS that seven Germanic Battalions were set up in the major industrial cities of Berlin, Brunswick, Dresden, Düsseldorf, Hamburg, Nürnberg and Stuttgart.

Service in the Germanische Sturmbanne was voluntary and unpaid, and was performed either during after-work hours or at weekends. Uniforms were supplied by the Allgemeine-SS, and comprised the standard black outfit, minus the tunic. Insignia was worn on the shirt, in the manner of the old SS Traditional Uniform. It is not known if members were permitted to wear any special badges indicative of their national origin, but it would appear doubtful.

By the end of 1944, the Germanic-SS in Germany was fully organised as an integral but distinctive

135

Plate 87 Himmler inspecting Norwegian volunteers for the SS-Standarte 'Nordland'. 9 February 1941. *IWM*

part of the regular Allgemeine-SS. Membership peaked at around 7,000 and SS-Obersturmbannführer Max Kopischke, formerly Gau Sports Leader in Bohemia and Moravia, held the post of Chef der Germanischen-SS in Deutschland (Chief of the Germanic-SS in Germany). Subordinated to him were several Reichsreferenten, officials for the various national groups into which the Germanische Sturmbanne were divided. Their Sonderstäbe or special staffs worked from the headquarters of the Oberabschnitte in which the battalions operated.

The cultural centre of the Germanische Sturmbanne was the Germanische Haus or Germanic House in Hannover, set up by the Germanische Leitstelle of the SS Hauptamt in May 1943 and subsequently moved to Hildesheim under the new title of Haus Germanien. It also served the social needs of associated Nordic workers, students and young people employed or holidaying in Germany, organising visits from their own national orchestras, singers, film stars and other celebrities. Copies of *Das Schwarze Korps* were distributed widely by the House, along with those of *De SS Man*, *Storm SS*,

Germaneren and *Foedrelandet*. As the war situation worsened, the House placed more emphasis on extolling the virtues of Germanic-SS men at the front, and by the end of 1944 it had become little more than a glorified recruiting office for the Waffen-SS.

GERMANIC-SS RANKS

The table below lists the standard Allgemeine-SS ranks and their Germanic-SS equivalents. With the exception of the Schalburg Corps, most units simply translated the German titles literally into their own language.

The four highest Germanic-SS ranks, ie those numbered 14-17, existed on paper only, as no formation ever grew large enough to accommodate them.

Members of the Germanic-SS in Germany used standard Allgemeine-SS rank terms, rather than their native equivalents.

	Germany		Flanders & Holland
1.	SS-Mann	1.	Man
2.	SS-Sturmmann	2.	Stormman
3.	SS-Rottenführer	3.	Rottenleider
4.	SS-Unterscharführer	4.	Onderschaarleider
5.	SS-Scharführer	5.	Schaarleider
6.	SS-Oberscharführer	6.	Opperschaarleider
7.	SS-Hauptscharführer	7.	Hoofdschaarleider
8.	SS-Untersturmführer	8.	Onderstormleider
9.	SS-Obersturmführer	9.	Opperstormleider
10.	SS-Hauptsturmführer	10.	Hoofdstormleider
11.	SS-Sturmbannführer	11.	Stormbanleider
12.	SS-Obersturmbannführer	12.	Opperstormbanleider
13.	SS-Standartenführer	13.	Standartleider
14.	SS-Oberführer	14.	Opperleider
15.	SS-Brigadeführer	15.	Brigadeleider
16.	SS-Gruppenführer	16.	Groepsleider
17.	SS-Obergruppenführer	17.	Oppergroepsleider

	Norway		Denmark
1.	Mann	1.	Schalburgmand
2.	Stormmann	2.	No equivalent
3.	Rodeforer	3.	Tropsforer
4.	Nestlagforer	4.	Overtropsforer
5.	Lagforer	5.	Vagtmester
6.	Nesttroppforer	6.	Overvagtmester
7.	Troppforer	7.	Stabsvagtmester
8.	Neststormforer	8.	Faendrik
9.	Stormforer	9.	Lojtnant
10.	Hovedsmann	10.	Kaptain
11.	Stormbannforer	11.	Major
12.	Neststandartforer	12.	Oberstlojtnant
13.	Standartforer	13.	Oberst
14.	Nestbrigadeforer	14.	No equivalent
15.	Brigadeforer	15.	No equivalent
16.	Stabsforer	16.	No equivalent
17.	No equivalent	17.	No equivalent

THE GERMANIC PROFICIENCY RUNE

Initially, SS personnel from Flanders, Holland, Norway and Denmark were entitled to compete for and wear the paramilitary sports badges awarded by their domestic pro-Nazi Parties, the VNV, NSB, NS and DNSAP. However, the formation of the Germanic-SS at the end of 1942 all but severed such links with home and consequently a new all-embracing sports award was called for.

On 15 July 1943, SS-Obergruppenführer Berger of the SS Hauptamt drew up draft regulations introducing just such a badge for the Germanic-SS. It was to take the form of two sig-runes, symbolic of victory and long the emblem of the German SS, superimposed over a sunwheel swastika, which was associated with the VNV, NSB, NS and DNSAP as well as with the Waffen-SS 'Wiking' and 'Nordland' divisions in which many west European volunteers were serving. The design was therefore representative of the union between the German SS and Germanic-SS. Approved and instituted by Himmler on 1 August 1943, the award was named the Germanische Leistungsrune, or Germanic Proficiency Rune.

The Germanic Proficiency Rune came in two grades, bronze and silver, differing only in the colour of the sunwheel. The tests leading to an award of the badge were on a par with those undergone by Germans in the SS to qualify for the German National Sports Badge and SA Military Sports Badge. They included running, jumping, swimming, rope climbing, throwing the hammer, shooting, completing an assault course, map reading, distance judging, observation, camouflage, first aid, signalling, verbal reporting and report writing. There were also written and oral examinations on National Socialist theories. Training requirements meant that at least 120hrs practice had to be completed every six months, and tests had to be passed annually in order to retain the badge.

The first tests and examinations took place in January 1944 at the training school of the Dutch SS at Avegoor near Arnhem. Over 2,000 members of the Germanic-SS presented themselves, but only 95 passed. They were decorated with the badge (18 silver and 77 bronze) by Himmler on 1 February. The following June, Berger decorated 20 Danes (6 silver and 14 bronze) at a ceremony at their training centre at Hovelte, and in August another 25 members of the Norwegian SS received their badges (10 silver and 15 bronze) from SS-Obergruppenführer Wilhelm Rediess, the HSSPf in Norway.

The Allied invasion of Western Europe undoubtedly prevented more widespread distribution, and it is believed that total awards numbered less than 200. Many badges were destroyed by their recipients at the end of the war, for obvious reasons.

The Germanic Proficiency Rune illustrated is one of only 10 original examples known to exist in collections worldwide. It is convex in form and measures 46mm in diameter. The sunwheel is of copper-plated zinc with an olive-bronze wash, and the sig-runes are black-enamelled tombak with silver-plated edges. The sig-runes are secured to the sunwheel by four round tombak pins bent over at the rear. The reverse has a slightly 'bubbled' appearance and there is no maker's mark. The pin bar is wide and flat. Construction and finish are typically German and of excellent quality. Because of its great rarity, the badge has been widely faked.

Since intended distribution was strictly limited, it is most probable that all original Germanic Proficiency Runes were produced at a single source. Unfortunately, due to the absence of manufacturer's markings, that source remains a mystery. However, it is more than likely that the badge was made 'in-house' by one of the many SS economic enterprises operating under the auspices of the WVHA.

Plate 88   The Germanic Proficiency Rune in Bronze.

138

12 The Waffen-SS

No history of the SS would be complete without mention being made of the Waffen-SS which, after 1939, rapidly outstripped the rest of the organisation in terms of manpower. In 1940, the traditional Allgemeine-SS numbered around 75,000 active regulars and the Waffen-SS about 100,000 men. By 1944, corresponding figures were 40,000 and 910,000 respectively. The Waffen-SS including its foreign volunteers and affiliated auxiliary units, ultimately came to account for 95% of the entire SS strength.

Many books about the Waffen-SS have been written since the end of World War 2, and that is the main reason why only brief coverage is necessary here. There is more than enough already in print on the subject of Hitler's 'Asphalt Soldiers', and various conflicting analyses have been presented. On the one hand, early works concentrated on the theme of crimes and criminality, describing how the racial indoctrination of the SS and the integration of the Totenkopfverbände into frontline SS units made the Waffen-SS susceptible to many kinds of inhumane warfare. During the Nürnberg Trials, for example, the Soviet Union made the charge that the Leibstandarte-SS 'Adolf Hitler' and the SS-Totenkopf-Division were responsible for the extermination of over 20,000 peaceful citizens in Kharkov, while the Western Allies made much of the SS massacres at Boves, Oradour-sur-Glane and Malmédy. Such incidents featured prominently in the first volumes on the Waffen-SS. More recent books, on the other hand, have tended to reappraise the Waffen-SS as an elite multi-national fighting force — even a forerunner of NATO — composed of soldiers like any others who frequently emerged victorious against overwhelming odds and earned the respect of their Wehrmacht comrades and of their enemies. The truth probably lies somewhere between these two extremes. Like all armies, the Waffen-SS had to weigh its substantial battlefield achievements against the undoubted atrocities which its men committed in the heat of war.

THE SS BAPTISM OF FIRE 1939-40

The SS, as the backbone of the projected Staatsschutzkorps, was primarily a civil police force which Hitler hoped would eventually maintain order not only in Germany but throughout Nazi-occupied Europe. The Führer decided that to do so, however, it would first have to win its spurs on the battlefield. As early as 1934 he told Himmler:

'In our Reich of the future, the SS and police will possess the necessary authority in their relations with other citizens only if they have a soldierly character. Through their past experience of glorious military events and their present education by the NSDAP, the German people have acquired such a warrior mentality that a fat, jovial, sock-knitting police such as we had during the Weimar era can no longer exert authority. For this reason, it will be necessary for our SS and police, in their own closed units, to prove themselves at the front in the same way as the army and to make blood sacrifices to the same degree as any other branch of the armed forces.'

Consequently, when Hitler formally reintroduced conscription in March 1935 he also issued an order for an increase in the size of his armed SS, which then comprised the Leibstandarte, two Standarten ('Deutschland' and 'Germania') of the SS-Verfügungstruppe, and the SS-Totenkopfverbände. The latter, which guarded the growing number of concentration camps, became a major area of SS expansion during the late 1930s, increasing from five Sturmbanne in March 1936 to four Standarten in April 1938. Members of these units wore army-pattern shoulder straps in conjunction with their regulation SS rank insignia. Himmler would have liked to dramatically enlarge the armed SS as a whole, but Hitler moderated his demands in the face of determined army opposition. The army remained a powerful force in German political life until the Blomberg-Fritsch scandal of 1938, orchestrated by Heydrich and the SD, which resulted in the retirement or posting of 60 generals and the transformation of the War Ministry into the Oberkommando der Wehrmacht with Hitler as Commander-in-Chief. This humiliation for the army was followed by the annexation of Austria, and the raising there of a third Verfügungstruppe Standarte, entitled 'Der Führer'. As the threat of war became ever more certain during the summer of 1939, the nucleus of an élite SS fighting force had emerged.

When German troops marched into Poland on 1 September 1939, the SS were split up among regular army formations dispersed along the invasion front. The Leibstandarte-SS 'Adolf Hitler' was attached to General von Reichenau's 10th Army, the SS-VT Standarte 'Deutschland' joined Generalmajor Kempf's 4th Panzer Brigade, and 'Germania' became part of the 14th Army under General List. The Leibstandarte had a hectic time around Warsaw and Bzura, while 'Deutschland' was actively engaged in the Battle of Brest-Litovsk and Totenkopf troops secured Danzig. During the campaign, these SS units were frequently grouped together for administrative purposes under the new term Bewaffnete-SS (Armed SS), and at the end of 1939 the abbreviated and definitive title Waffen-SS appeared for the first time on official documents. Simultaneously, army designations such as 'Bataillon' and 'Regiment' began to be used by the combat units instead of 'Sturmbann' and 'Standarte'.

The consolidation of the Waffen-SS during the 'Phony War' brought 'Sepp' Dietrich's Leibstandarte up to the strength of a superbly-equipped armoured regiment, and the three SS-VT regiments were formed into the first full SS division, the SS-Verfügungsdivision, under the overall command of SS-Gruppenführer Paul Hausser. Moreover, Himmler and Gottlob Berger partially overcame the Wehrmacht's monopoly on conscription and secured more young Germans for the Waffen-SS by means of an ingenious 'back door' method, namely the direct transfer of staff from other full-time branches of the SS organisation, men who would normally have been exempt from the call-up. In this way, three existing Totenkopf Standarten were grouped together under SS-Gruppenführer Theodor Eicke to become the SS-Totenkopf-Division, being replaced as guards in the concentration camps by older All-gemeine-SS reservists, and a third combat division, the Polizei-Division led by SS-Brigadeführer Karl Pfeffer-Wildenbruch, was created almost overnight by a mass transfer of uniformed police personnel.

The campaign in the West established beyond doubt the fighting reputation of the Waffen-SS and police. In May 1940, the Leibstandarte and 'Der Führer' were deployed on the Dutch frontier and had little difficulty in sweeping through Holland. The SS-Totenkopf-Division went into action in support of Rommel's 7th Panzer Division in southern Belgium and eastern France, duly committing one of the first recorded SS atrocities when 100 unarmed British prisoners of the 2nd Royal Norfolks were machine-gunned at Le Paradis. As the forces of Blitzkrieg advanced relentlessly, the Allies were compressed into an ever-decreasing pocket centring around Dunkirk. The Leibstandarte was heavily engaged in fierce fighting at nearby Wormhoudt, where 'Sepp' Dietrich nearly lost his life and a company of his men under Wilhelm Mohnke retaliated by killing 80 British POWs in cold blood. After the Dunkirk evacuation, the Waffen-SS was redeployed against the French army which was holding a line along the River Somme. While the ill-equipped horse-drawn Polizei-Division successfully battled it out in the Argonne Forest, other motorised SS units had little difficulty in smashing through enemy lines on 6 June and within a week the Leibstandarte had linked up with army panzers as far south as Vichy. The SS-Totenkopf-Division advanced on Bordeaux and the SS-Verfügungsdivision raced towards Biarritz. On 17 June, the French sued for peace and five days later the war in the West was over.

In recognition of their bravery and leadership during the Western campaign, the following seven SS men received the coveted Knight's Cross, at that time the supreme German military award:

25:06:40 – SS-Brigadeführer Heinz Reinefarth,
then serving as an army Feldwebel with
Infantry Regiment 337
04:07:40 – SS-Obergruppenführer 'Sepp' Dietrich,
commander of the Leibstandarte-SS
'Adolf Hitler'
15:08:40 – SS-Oberführer Felix Steiner,
commander of SS-Regiment
'Deutschland'

15:08:40 – SS-Oberführer Georg Keppler,
commander of SS-Regiment 'Der
Führer'
04:09:40 – SS-Hauptscharführer Ludwig
Kepplinger, 11th Company, SS-
Regiment 'Der Führer'
04:09:40 – SS-Obersturmführer Fritz Vogt, Staff
Reconnaissance, SS-Verfügungsdivision
04:09:40 – SS-Sturmbannführer Fritz Witt,
commander of 1st Company, SS-
Regiment 'Deutschland'

Many others were decorated with lower grades of the Iron Cross, wound badges and associated combat awards. The SS had won its spurs in convincing style.

YEARS OF EXPANSION AND CONQUEST 1941-43

Germany's victories in Western Europe opened up a new reservoir of pro-Nazi Volksdeutsche and Germanic peoples whom the Wehrmacht had no authority to conscript and whom Berger quickly set about recruiting into the Waffen-SS. With the consequent increase in SS numbers, the Leibstandarte was upgraded to a brigade and a completely new division was authorised, the bulk of its personnel being Nordic volunteers from Flanders, Holland, Norway and Denmark. Initially called 'Germania', the formation was soon designated SS-Division 'Wiking' and placed under the command of Felix Steiner. About the same time, the SS-Verfügungsdivision was renamed SS-Division 'Reich', and various Totenkopfstandarten were reorganised to become SS-Kampfgruppe 'Nord' and SS-Kavallerie Regiments. With the elevation of all Totenkopf units to combat status, their previous responsibility for security duties in occupied territory was delegated to the hastily-mustered Police Regiments, which have already been covered in Chapter 5: The SS and the Police.

On 6 April 1941, Germany invaded Yugoslavia and Greece to secure the southern flank before the long-awaited attack on Russia. SS-Division 'Reich' was in the forefront of the invasion force in Yugoslavia, and captured Belgrade on 13 April. In Greece, the Leibstandarte was engaged in a series of hard-fought battles culminating in the fall of Athens on 27 April. By the end of the month, the Balkan Blitzkrieg was effectively over. It had been another victory for the Waffen-SS.

On 22 June 1941, Hitler ordered his forces into Russia. The SS-Totenkopf-Division, the Polizei-Division and Kampfgruppe 'Nord' were assigned to Army Group North, SS-Division 'Reich' to Army Group Centre, and the Leibstandarte and 'Wiking' to Army Group South. The latter two formations in particular impressed their army counterparts with

Plate 89 Waffen-SS officer's 1937-pattern field cap, of typical crushed appearance. This example was manufactured to a private order by the firm of 'Successori Fare' of Milan, for an SS officer stationed in Italy during World War 2.

Plate 90 Soldiers of the Polizei-Division using a mortar during training, April 1940. Note the mixture of army, police and SS insignia. *IWM*

Plate 91 Himmler and SS-Brigadeführer Knoblauch reviewing Totenkopf troops in Russia, 1941. *Hoffmann*

Plate 92 Himmler greeting Waffen-SS cavalry officers on the Eastern Front, 24 July 1941. *Hoffmann*

Plate 93 The victors of Kharkov, April 1943. From left to right: SS-Hauptsturmführer Rolf Möbius; SS-Obergruppenführer 'Sepp' Dietrich; SS-Sturmbannführer Rudolf Lehmann; and SS-Sturmbannführer Hubert Meyer. Meyer commanded the 'Hitlerjugend' division for a short time at the end of 1944.

their aggression and skill in attack, while SS-Division 'Reich', later 'Das Reich', came to within a few kilometres of Moscow at the end of the year. The only real SS failure occurred on the Finnish front, when the second-rate troops of Kampfgruppe 'Nord' were thrown into a mass panic and routed on 2 July. The unit had to be withdrawn and completely overhauled, and was thereafter reinforced with seasoned veterans from the Totenkopf-Division, to become SS-Division 'Nord'.

In 1942, the Leibstandarte, 'Das Reich', 'Totenkopf' and 'Wiking' were upgraded to the status of SS-Panzergrenadier Divisions, and were now equal in terms of equipment to many full panzer divisions of the army. In September, the SS-Kavallerie-Division was formed, and three months later two new divisions, 'Hohenstaufen' and 'Frundsberg', were ordered into being. By the end of the year, Waffen-SS troops in the field numbered around 200,000.

The Soviet Offensive of December 1942 proved disastrous for the Germans. By early 1943 the 6th Army at Stalingrad was forced to surrender, and other German forces in the Caucasus region also faced the possibility of being cut off by the speed and depth of the Soviet penetration. In February, however, the commander of Army Group South, Generalfeldmarschall von Manstein, launched a counterattack in the Kharkov region. To spearhead the assault, an SS-Panzer-Korps comprising the Leibstandarte, 'Das Reich', and 'Totenkopf' was formed under the command of Paul Hausser. For the first time, a substantial body of Waffen-SS troops fought together and the result was a resounding victory. The Russians were thrown into disarray, Kharkov was taken, and the Germans were able to restore order in the south. To Hitler, who was increasingly disillusioned by army failures, it was proof of the capabilities of the Waffen-SS, which thereafter became the apple of his eye. Decorations were showered upon the SS as a token of gratitude, and the Führer arranged that his old favourite, Theodor Eicke, the 'Totenkopf' divisional commander, who had been killed during the early stages of the offensive, should be buried in the style of the ancient Germanic kings, with all the attendant Pagan ritual.

On 5 July, Hausser's SS-Panzer-Korps was deployed on the south flank at the Battle of Kursk. Again it fought well, despite being weakened by the removal of the Leibstandarte to bolster German forces in Italy following the Allied invasion of Sicily. Kursk was ultimately a strategic failure for the Germans, however, and for the rest of 1943 they fell back westwards across the Soviet Union. The three élite SS divisions, now redesignated as full panzer divisions, spent these hard months being sent from one danger area to another as the situation demanded. 'Das Reich' and 'Totenkopf' earned repeated praise from those army generals who had them under their command, and in November the Leibstandarte returned to the Eastern Front and retook Zhitomir.

The German position in Russia underwent an even more dramatic deterioration when the Soviets launched a massive offensive in the Ukraine on 14 December 1943. The battle lasted for four months, and culminated in the expulsion of the German forces from the south. 'Wiking', now under the command of SS-Obergruppenführer Herbert Gille, and Leon Degrelle's Belgian SS Brigade 'Wallonien' were caught in the Korsun-Cherkassy Pocket in a scene reminiscent of Stalingrad, but managed to smash their way out, suffering 60% casualties in the process. In a similar engagement, the Leibstandarte and elements of 'Das Reich' were trapped around Kamenets Podolsky and had to be rescued by 'Hohenstaufen' and 'Frundsberg'. Worn down and exhausted, the Waffen-SS formations were now increasingly unable to stem the advancing Russian tide.

THE FOREIGN VOLUNTEERS

Himmler always saw the SS developing as a primarily Germanic, rather than German, organisation and a small number of racially suitable foreigners had already been accepted into both the Allgemeine-SS and the SS-VT before 1939. With the conquest of Western Europe in 1940, the doors to greater expansion were thrown wide open and Berger's recruiting officers set to work in the occupied Germanic countries.

The first complete unit of foreign volunteers to be raised by the SS was the Standarte 'Nordland', from Norwegians and Danes. It was soon joined by the Standarte 'Westland', comprising Dutchmen and Flemings, and in December 1940 these two formations combined with the SS-VT Standarte 'Germania' to become SS-Division 'Wiking', a truly European formation. The main impetus to the recruiting of further so-called 'foreign legions' was the impending invasion of Russia, and in order to attract sufficient numbers of these troops the Germans reluctantly accepted that they would have to co-operate with the pro-Nazi political parties in each country, and that the new units would have to retain some of their own national characteristics. The idea of national legions was quickly extended from the Germanic countries to those ideologically sympathetic to Germany, like Croatia. However, during the early stages of the war at least, Himmler was not prepared to accept racially dubious volunteers into the SS, and so the eastern legions were assigned to the army.

During 1940-41, the SS-sponsored legions 'Flandern', 'Niederlande', 'Norwegen' and 'Freikorps Danmark' were raised. Their troops were distinguished from those in the German SS proper by special national badges, and by their oath, which committed them solely to the war against Communism. The recruitment programme immediately ran into difficulties, however, when the legionaries found that their German colleagues held them in low regard. Morale plummetted, particularly when 'Flandern' was decimated in Russia early in 1942 and had to be disbanded. The three other legions were reinforced and, at the end of 1942, amalgamated to form the 'Nordland' division of the Waffen-SS. A year later, the Dutch contingent was sufficiently strong to be removed and given the status of an independent brigade, which ultimately developed into the 'Nederland' division. Both 'Nordland' and 'Nederland' fought well in the defence of the Baltic States, taking part in the celebrated 'Battle of the European SS' at Narva in July 1944, before being destroyed in the final battle for Berlin the following year.

Despite the good fighting reputation quickly gained by the western volunteers, they were simply too few in number to meet SS requirements for replacing battle casualties, and so Berger turned to the Volksdeutsche scattered throughout Central and Eastern Europe. A sudden influx of volunteers from Yugoslavia after the invasion led to the formation in 1942 of the SS-Mountain Division 'Prinz Eugen', designed for anti-partisan duties against Tito's resistance movement. Later that year, the SS was given authorisation to formally conscript the Volksdeutsche, who fell outwith the remit of the Wehrmacht as they were not German nationals. In that way, an impressive numerical level of recruitment was maintained, but many of the conscripts were poor in quality and consequently the Volksdeutsche units tended to be second rate. They soon earned for themselves the reputation as specialists in perpetrating massacres against the civilian population and other soft targets. The associated policy of recruiting Croatian and Albanian Moslems into the 'Handschar', 'Kama' and 'Skanderbeg' divisions, to fight the Christian Serbs from whom many of Tito's partisans were drawn, was a total disaster and all three divisions had to be disbanded.

In the Soviet Union, the Germans made better use of local national groups opposed to Stalin's government, successfully persuading large numbers of the native population to enrol in the Schutzmannschaft for anti-partisan operations. The breakthrough for the Waffen-SS recruiters came in April 1943, when no less than 100,000 Ukrainians volunteered for a new SS division, of whom 30,000 were duly accepted. Over 80% of them were killed the following year, when the Ukrainian Division was trapped in the Brody-Tarnow Pocket. During 1944, many Armenian, Baltic, Caucasian, Cossack, Georgian and Turkestani volunteers were transferred en masse, for no good reason, from the hastily-mustered foreign legions of the German army into the Waffen-SS. The wide range of nationalities involved had some propaganda value, and the creation of so many new SS divisions at the end of the war undoubtedly increased Himmler's personal status. However, the actual performance of the eastern troops in combat left much to be desired. The Baltic divisions lived up to modest expectations, particularly when defending their homelands, but the remainder were poor at best, and at worst a complete rabble. Himmler regarded them merely as racially inferior auxiliaries, in effect expendable cannon-fodder. Their loyalty was always in question, and their horrific behaviour when set loose amongst the civilian population of Poland during the 1944 Warsaw Uprising led to frequent demands for their withdrawal, even by other SS commanders. Several units had to be disbanded, and many of their leaders were tried by SS courts-martial and executed for looting and other excesses.

RETREAT AND DEFEAT 1944-45

During the spring of 1944, increasing numbers of German troops were being stationed in the West in preparation for the expected Allied invasion. Among these were the Leibstandarte, 'Das Reich', 'Hitlerjugend', and 'Götz von Berlichingen' the latter division having been formed in France a few months earlier. When the Normandy landings struck on 6 June, 'Hitlerjugend' was the first SS formation to engage the enemy. The ferocity of the SS assault shocked the Allies, but their command of the air prevented proper deployment of the division and the attack ground to a halt. Two months of bloody fighting ensued. The Leibstandarte and 'Hitlerjugend' were immediately assigned the task of defending key positions around Caen. 'Götz von Berlichingen' was hindered by constant air attacks on its journey north from its base in the Loire Valley, and did not reach the invasion front until 11 June. 'Das Reich', travelling from Gascony, took even longer, being subjected to a series of ambushes carried out by the French Resistance. Frustrated at the consequent delays and loss of life, the division wreaked havoc upon the local population, whom it suspected of sheltering the partisans. The village of Oradour-sur-Glane was systematically destroyed, and 640 of its inhabitants killed, and all the male residents of the little town of Tulle were also shot. 'Das Reich' eventually reached its positions north of St Lô at the end of June, joining 'Hohenstaufen' and 'Frundsberg' which had been hurriedly transferred from the East.

Throughout July, the six SS divisions struggled ceaselessly to contain the Allies in their beachhead, taking a heavy toll of British and American armour. However, they were overwhelmed by the sheer weight of Allied numbers, and were frequently reduced to operating as ad hoc battle groups. By the middle of August, 19 German army divisions had become trapped around Falaise, and only determined efforts by 'Das Reich', 'Hitlerjugend' and 'Hohenstaufen' kept open a gap long enough for them to escape. Increasingly, while ordinary German soldiers were prepared to surrender to the Allies, it was left to the SS to fight on.

94

Plate 94 Waffen-SS 1943-pattern steel helmet.

Plate 95 The Flemish SS-Sturmmann Richard 'Remi' Schrijen, of 3rd Company, SS-Freiwilligen Sturmbrigade 'Langemarck', being paraded before his

fellow soldiers near Prague after receiving the Knight's Cross on 21 September 1944. He is accompanied by Konrad Schellong, the brigade commander, and adjutant Willy Teichert.

95

Plate 96 'Handschar' troops in festive mood, 1944.
IWM

Plate 97 Field-grey fez, with dark green tassel, as
issued to members of the short-lived Moslem
'Handschar', 'Kama' and 'Skanderbeg' divisions.

Plate 98 Pro-Nazi Cossack volunteers riding under the
flag of the Death's Head, 1944. *IWM*

97

98

Plate 99 Field-grey tunic as worn by an artillery Rottenführer serving with the 17th SS-Panzergrenadier Division 'Götz von Berlichingen', cApril 1944.

Plate 100 Camouflage tunic as worn by a Waffen-SS Infantry Obersturmführer, c1944-45. The unofficial display of insignia and decorations, the use of an Iron Cross 2nd Class as a 'Feldritterkreuz' or 'Frontline Knight's Cross', and the preference for the sturdier other ranks' belt buckle, typified the appearance of junior SS officers towards the end of the war.

Plate 101 SS-Sturmbannführer Christian Bachmann of the Totenkopf-Division, who won the Knight's Cross on 28 February 1945. Two weeks later, he was killed at Stuhlweissenburg in Hungary.

In September, the British airborne assault at Arnhem was countered and defeated by 'Hohenstaufen' and 'Frundsberg', in a battle noted for the mutual respect held by each side for the fighting abilities and fair play of the other. This victory, and the general slowing down of the Allied advance across France, persuaded Hitler to launch a major offensive in the West, in an attempt to repeat the successes of 1940. Two Panzer Armies were assembled to spearhead the attack, the 5th Panzer Army under General Hasso von Manteuffel, and the 6th SS-Panzer Army, the larger of the two forces, under 'Sepp' Dietrich. The nucleus of the latter Army comprised the Leibstandarte, 'Das Reich', 'Hohenstaufen' and 'Hitlerjugend'. On 16 December the offensive began in the Ardennes, but the hilly and wooded terrain naturally favoured defensive action and after only five days the German advance ground to a halt. SS frustration again translated itself into the committing of atrocities, this time the massacre of 70 American prisoners by Joachim Peiper's battle group at Malmédy. A subsidiary offensive in Alsace, led by 'Götz von Berlichingen', also came to nothing, and the division ended up trapped in Metz. With a virtual stalemate in the West, Hitler pulled his SS divisions out and sent them eastwards, where the situation had once more become desperate.

On 12 January 1945, a great Soviet attack was launched across Poland, in preparation for the final assault on Berlin. Even so, Hitler's main concern was to safeguard the tenuous hold he still maintained over the Hungarian oilfields. The SS cavalry divisions 'Florian Geyer' and 'Maria Theresa' were besieged in Budapest, and in an effort to relieve them 'Totenkopf' and 'Wiking' were transferred from their key positions on the German-Polish border. They made little progress, however, and the city fell to the Russians on 13 February. The 6th SS-Panzer Army was immediately moved in from the West, and on 6 March a German counter-offensive began. It was conducted by the largest aggregation of SS forces ever witnessed during the war, comprising the Leibstandarte, 'Das Reich', 'Totenkopf', 'Wiking', 'Hohenstaufen', 'Hitlerjugend' and 'Reichsführer-SS', the latter division having been transferred from Italy. At first the SS did well, but there were insufficient back-up resources and by mid-March their advance had been halted.

The failure of the Waffen-SS in Hungary had a devastating effect on Hitler, who had come to expect the impossible from them, and he openly accused Dietrich and his subordinates of betrayal. Despite that, SS troops carried on fighting as loyally as ever, as they slowly retreated into Germany. During the last week in April, when Soviet forces broke into Berlin, a hard-core of Waffen-SS including elements of the SS-Polizei-Division, 'Frundsberg', 'Nordland', 'Wallonien', 'Charlemagne' and 'Nederland', as well as some 600 men from Himmler's personal escort battalion, engaged in a life and death struggle defending the Führerbunker. However,

most other SS units had by then accepted the reality of the situation, and pushed westwards to surrender to the Anglo-American Allies, rather than risk capture by the Russians.

It is estimated that some 180,000 Waffen-SS soldiers were killed in action during World War 2, with about 400,000 wounded and a further 70,000 listed 'missing'. The entire establishment of the élite divisions, Leibstandarte, 'Das Reich' and 'Totenkopf', were casualties several times over, with only a few battle-hardened veterans surviving to train the continual injections of young Germans and Volksdeutsche fed in as replacements. By 1944-45, SS soldiers were normally in their late teens, and the average age of a Waffen-SS junior officer was 20, with a life expectancy of two months at the front. Moreover, it was not uncommon for divisional commanders to be in their early 30s, men like Kraas, Kumm, Meyer, Mohnke, Wisch and Witt, who had joined the SS-VT around 1934 and progressed through the ranks. The combination of youthful enthusiasm, political indoctrination and hard-bitten experience was a winning one, and went a long way to explaining how a division such as 'Hitlerjugend' could suffer 60% casualties over a four-week period in 1944 and yet still retain its aggressive spirit, thereby gaining for the entire Waffen-SS the admiration of friend and foe alike.

THE WAFFEN-SS ORDER OF BATTLE IN 1945

Although given suitably heroic names from an early date, Waffen-SS divisions were not numbered until 15 November 1943. Unit titles and designations were frequently altered, either to acknowledge a change in status or, particularly late in the war, to camouflage a formation's true identity and confuse enemy intelligence. The 'Das Reich' division was a typical example, and had its nomenclature altered no less than 11 times, as follows:

09:39	– Panzerverband Ostpreussen/Panzer Division 'Kempf'
10:10:39	– SS-Verfügungstruppe-Division (Motorised)
04:04:40	– SS-Verfügungsdivision
01:12:40	– SS-Division 'Deutschland'
28:01:41	– SS-Division (Motorised) 'Reich'
05:42	– SS-Division (Motorised) 'Das Reich'/Kampfgruppe 'Ostendorff'
14:11:42	– SS-Panzergrenadier Division 'Das Reich'
15:11:43	– 2nd SS-Panzer Division 'Das Reich'
24:02:45	– Ausbildungsgruppe 'Nord'

Divisions staffed by Germans were known as 'SS-Division' while those comprising mainly Volksdeutsche or Germanic personnel, whether volunteers or conscripts, were called 'SS-Freiwilligen Division'. Units composed primarily of East Europeans or Russians came into the category of 'Waffen Division der SS', a term of inferiority which denoted attachment to, rather than actual membership of, the Waffen-SS.

Most divisions numbered above 20 were merely upgraded regiments, or even battalions, flung together in a hurry and given grandiose titles.

The following table lists all the Waffen-SS divisions which had been mustered, at least on paper, by 1945. The number of Knight's Crosses awarded is a good indication of the effectiveness and general battle experience of each division.

Title	Granted Divisional Status	Primary Composition	Knight's Crosses Awarded
1st SS-Panzer Division Leibstandarte-SS 'Adolf Hitler'	1940	German volunteers with Hitler's SS bodyguard regiment as the nucleus	58
2nd SS-Panzer Division 'Das Reich'	1939	German volunteers with the SS-Verfügungstruppe as the nucleus	69
3rd SS-Panzer Division 'Totenkopf'	1939	German volunteers with the SS-Totenkopfverbände as the nucleus	47
4th SS-Polizei Panzergrenadier Division	1939	German Police transferees	25
5th SS-Panzer Division 'Wiking'	1940	German/West European volunteers	55
6th SS-Gebirgs Division 'Nord'	1940	German volunteers with Totenkopf regiments as the nucleus	4
7th SS-Freiwilligen Gebirgs Division 'Prinz Eugen'	1942	Yugoslavian Volksdeutsche volunteers	6
8th SS-Kavallerie Division 'Florian Geyer'	1942	German volunteers with SS-Kavallerie regiments as the nucleus	22
9th SS-Panzer Division 'Hohenstaufen'	1943	German volunteers and conscripts	12
10th SS-Panzer Division 'Frundsberg'	1943	German volunteers and conscripts	13
11th SS-Freiwilligen Panzergrenadier Division 'Nordland'	1943	West European volunteers, many from the disbanded SS foreign legions 'Niederlande', 'Norwegen', and 'Freikorps Danmark'	25
12th SS-Panzer Division 'Hitlerjugend'	1943	German Hitler Youth volunteers	14
13th Waffen Gebirgs Division der SS 'Handschar'	1943	Yugoslavian Moslem volunteers	4
14th Waffen Grenadier Division der SS	1943	Ukrainian volunteers	1
15th Waffen Grenadier Division der SS	1943	Latvian volunteers, many transferring from the Schutzmannschaft and Police Rifle Regiments	3
16th SS-Panzergrenadier Division 'Reichsführer-SS'	1943	German/Volksdeutsche volunteers and conscripts with Himmler's escort battalion as the nucleus	1
17th SS-Panzergrenadier Division 'Götz von Berlichingen'	1943	German/Volksdeutsche volunteers and conscripts.	4
18th SS-Freiwilligen Panzergrenadier Division 'Horst Wessel'	1944	Hungarian Volksdeutsche volunteers and conscripts	2

Title	Granted Divisional Status	Primary Composition	Knight's Crosses Awarded
19th Waffen Grenadier Division der SS	1944	Latvian volunteers, many transferring from the Schutzmannschaft and Police Rifle Regiments	12
20th Waffen Grenadier Division der SS	1944	Estonian volunteers, many transferring from the Schutzmannschaft and Police Rifle Regiments	5
21st Waffen Gebirgs Division der SS 'Skanderbeg'	1944	Albanian Moslem volunteers	0
22nd SS-Freiwilligen Kavallerie Division 'Maria Theresa'	1944	German/Hungarian Volksdeutche volunteers and conscripts	6
23rd Waffen Gebirgs Division der SS 'Kama' (disbanded late 1944 and number '23' given to next division)	1944	Yugoslavian Moslem volunteers	0
23rd SS-Freiwilligen Panzergrenadier Division 'Nederland'	1944	Dutch volunteers, many formerly of the SS foreign legion 'Niederlande'	19
24th Waffen Gebirgs Division der SS	1944	Italian Fascist volunteers	0
25th Waffen Grenadier Division der SS 'Hunyadi'	1944	Hungarian volunteers	0
26th Waffen Grenadier Division der SS	1945	Hungarian volunteers	0
27th SS-Freiwilligen Grenadier Division 'Langemarck'	1945	Flemish volunteers, many formerly of the SS foreign legion 'Flandern'	1
28th SS-Freiwilligen Grenadier Division 'Wallonien'	1945	Walloon volunteers, many formerly of the German army's Wallonische Legion	3
29th Waffen Grenadier Division der SS (disbanded late 1944 and number '29' given to next division)	1944	Russian convict volunteers	0
29th Waffen Grenadier Division der SS	1945	Italian Fascist volunteers	0
30th Waffen Grenadier Division der SS	1945	Russian volunteers, many transferring from the Schutzmannschaft and Police Rifle Regiments	0
31st SS-Freiwilligen Grenadier Division	1945	Czechoslovakian Volksdeutche volunteers and conscripts	0
32nd SS-Freiwilligen Grenadier Division '30 Januar'	1945	German conscripts and SS training school personnel/ Volksdeutsche volunteers and conscripts	0
33rd Waffen Kavallerie Division der SS (destroyed early 1945, and number '33' given to next division)	1945	Hungarian volunteers	0
33rd Waffen Grenadier Division der SS 'Charlemagne'	1945	French volunteers, many formerly of the German army's Französisches Legion or LVF	2

Title	Granted Divisional Status	Primary Composition	Knight's Crosses Awarded
34th SS-Freiwilligen Grenadier Division 'Landstorm Nederland'	1945	Dutch volunteers, many formerly of the Landwacht Nederland	3
35th SS-Polizei Grenadier Division	1945	German Police transferees	0
36th Waffen Grenadier Division der SS	1945	German/East European volunteers, including a large number of convicted criminals	1
37th SS-Freiwilligen Kavallerie Division 'Lützow'	1945	Hungarian Volksdeutsche conscripts and remnants of the 'Florian Geyer' and 'Maria Theresa' divisions	0
38th SS-Grenadier Division 'Nibelungen'	1945	German volunteers, conscripts and SS training school personnel	0

102

Plate 102 Leon Degrelle with men of his Walloon Division in Pomerania, 9 March 1945. The SS-Unterscharführer in the foreground is a Frenchman, Jean Lejeune. *Ullstein*

13 The Fall of the SS Empire

THE LAST DAYS OF THE THIRD REICH

By the autumn of 1944, the SS had seized almost total political, military and economic power in Germany, and there were only two men who really mattered in the whole of the Reich — Adolf Hitler and Heinrich Himmler. The Swedish Press was already referring to Himmler as 'Dictator of Germany', and with Göring long since disgraced it seemed to many that the Reichsführer-SS was merely waiting for Hitler's death to place himself at the head of the Nazi régime. As Commander-in-Chief of the Home Army, it was Himmler who drew up plans for the last ditch defence of the Fatherland, and threatened that every deserter would be punished not only by his own execution but also by that of his entire family. Flying Waffen-SS courts-martial swung into action, and began hanging their victims from trees and lamp-posts as a warning to others. Allgemeine-SS men serving in the Wehrmacht and Volkssturm increasingly kept their ears to the ground for defeatist talk, and reported whether the sentences passed on offenders by regular military courts-martial measured up to Himmler's severe standards. In November, Himmler's power reached its peak, and on the 9th of the month he was granted the unique and symbolic privilege of taking Hitler's place for the delivery of the traditional beer hall speech commemorating the Munich Putsch.

In the background, however, lurked a shadowy rival in the power struggle. Martin Bormann, Head of the Party Chancellery and Hitler's closest adviser, was an SS-Obergruppenführer, but felt only jealous hatred towards Himmler and longed for his downfall. Bormann knew that the Reichsführer was no military tactician, and in an effort to discredit him persuaded Hitler to nominate the SS Chief to the vacant post of Commander of Army Group Upper Rhine in early December. As expected, Himmler the arch-policeman failed miserably in his new soldierly role, and did no better when reassigned to take charge of Army Group Vistula in January 1945. Haunted by the spectre of defeat, unable to cope with his massive military responsibilities, and no longer sure of Hitler's favour in those volatile times, Himmler went on extended sick leave with 'severe influenza' and took refuge in the SS hospital at Hohenlychen. On 20 March, a disillusioned Führer relieved him of his army command on the Vistula.

Having suddenly lost face, and consequently all realistic hope of the succession, Himmler now determined to save his own skin and that of his SS comrades by opening secret peace negotiations with the Western Allies, using important concentration camp inmates as bargaining counters. At the beginning of April, Count Folke Bernadotte, Vice-President of the Swedish Red Cross and agreed intermediary in the talks, paid his second visit to Himmler at Hohenlychen to discuss the possibilities of arranging a German capitulation on the Western Front. Bernadotte was prepared to appeal to Eisen-

hower only if Himmler would declare himself Hitler's successor, dissolve the NSDAP, and release all Scandinavian prisoners held in Germany. Himmler, however, was unable to make up his mind. He dreamed of himself as the new saviour of Nazi Germany, but still could not wrench free from Hitler's overpowering psychological influence. As late as 13 April, he personally denounced his old adjutant Karl Wolff as a traitor, when Wolff opened up his own independent peace negotiations with the Allies in Switzerland. The situation worsened dramatically when other notable SS leaders panicked and began to abandon the sinking ship in considerable numbers. Three SS-Obergruppenführer, Felix Steiner, Curt von Gottberg and Richard Hildebrandt, seriously considered a plan to assassinate Hitler as a means of swiftly putting an end to the war, and even Ernst Kaltenbrunner of the RSHA plotted the surrender of Austria. The general consensus among the SS was that their postwar interests would best be served if Himmler was Head of State, and able to negotiate on their behalf.

On 19 April, SS-Brigadeführer Walter Schellenberg, Kaltenbrunner's subordinate, implored Himmler for the last time, on behalf of a growing section of the SS leadership, to depose Hitler and make peace. The Reichsführer wavered, but his courage evaporated once again. The following day, he journeyed to the Chancellery Bunker to pay his respects on his master's birthday, and tried unsuccessfully to persuade Hitler to quit the capital and continue the battle from an alpine redoubt in Southern Germany. After the meagre birthday celebrations, Himmler bade a final farewell to Hitler and left Berlin for his field headquarters at Hohenlychen.

On 28 April, news was relayed to the Führerbunker that Schellenberg, supposedly acting on behalf of the Reichsführer-SS, had offered the Western Allies the conditional capitulation of Germany, which they had duly rejected. Himmler had probably never officially sanctioned Schellenberg's offer, but Hitler was nonetheless paralysed by the apparent revelation of 'der treue Heinrich's' betrayal. He immediately ordered SS personnel in the bunker to leave his presence, and thereafter issued instructions for Himmler's arrest, simultaneously expelling him from the NSDAP and all his government offices. Hitler then appointed SS-Obergruppenführer Karl Hanke, Gauleiter of Lower Silesia, as the new Reichsführer-SS. Hanke, however, never received word of his promotion, having already abandoned his post in the besieged city of Breslau, and flown off in one of the few helicopters then in operation.

Forty-eight hours later, Hitler was dead and the Third Reich was at an end. In its stead, confusion and chaos reigned. Grand Admiral Dönitz, head of the rump Nazi government, confirmed that he had no place for Himmler in his short-lived administration. SS officers and men from all branches of the organisation, fearful of the reprisals which they were sure would be directed against them, burned their uniforms, files and identity papers, gathered what loot and booty they could, and fled into hiding. Those captured were put to work clearing up the mess, pending a de-Nazification process and possible criminal proceedings. The dreaded day of reckoning had arrived.

THE FATE OF HIMMLER AND THE SS LEADERS

For Himmler, the cease-fire concluded by Dönitz on 5 May 1945 marked the end of the road. All the Wehrmacht officers who had hastily gathered around the Grand Admiral, desperate to avoid charges of war crimes being levelled against them, now shifted the blame for Nazi Germany's conduct totally on to the SS and the person of the Reichsführer. On 6 May, Himmler mustered his remaining entourage including his brother Gebhard, Hans Prützmann, Leon Degrelle, and various Hauptamt Chiefs, police generals, and Waffen-SS leaders, and gave a final farewell speech. He ended by handing out prepared false identity documents, and advising his followers to 'submerge in the Wehrmacht'. Each then went on his way. Himmler furnished himself with the papers of a former sergeant in the Geheime Feldpolizei named Heinrich Hitzinger, who had earlier been executed by the SS for defeatism. He also carried two phials of cyanide, and had holes drilled in his molars to accommodate them. There was no doubt in his mind about his fate and that of his chief accomplices should they fall into enemy hands.

On 10 May, Himmler set out on foot from Flensburg for Bavaria. He was escorted by Obersturmbannführer Werner Grothmann and Hauptsturmführer Heinz Macher, both in army uniform. Grothmann, only 29 years old, had been the Reichsführer's personal adjutant since 1943, and was one of his most loyal subordinates. Macher, although four years younger, was a hardened combat veteran and had won the Oakleaves to his Knight's Cross in 1944 while serving with 'Das Reich' in Russia. It was Macher who had blown up Wewelsburg Castle the previous month on Himmler's direct instructions, to prevent its capture by the Allies, and he had also been charged with the task of burying the castle's treasures, including its stock of Death's Head Rings.

Protected by these two stalwarts, Himmler intended to join the many other SS and NSDAP leaders who had fled southeast to the Alps. On 21 May, however, the three men were arrested by the British at a routine checkpoint between Hamburg and Bremen. Two days later they arrived at an interrogation centre at Barfeld, near Lüneburg, where the former Reichsführer's identity was confirmed. As his elated captors began to question him, Himmler bit on one of his cyanide capsules and was dead within minutes, thus escaping the humiliation of a show trial and certain fate of a hangman's noose. He was subsequently buried in an unmarked grave on Lüneburg Heath, and his few meagre possessions were distributed amongst the attendant Allied intelligence personnel as souvenirs. His death mask was put on display at the Imperial War Museum, London, where it can still be seen.

Only a small number of SS leaders followed Himmler's example by committing suicide. Among them were Hans Prützmann, Philipp Bouhler, Herbert Backe, Leonardo Conti, Odilo Globocnik, Friedrich-Wilhelm Krüger, and Ernst-Robert Grawitz, the latter blowing both himself and his family up with hand grenades. Christian Weber, the old Stosstrupp veteran, was killed in action in Bavaria at the end of the war, and Karl Hanke, the last Reichsführer-SS was beaten to death by Czechs a couple of months later. Many SS officers, including the Gestapo chief Heinrich Müller, the Concentration Camp Inspector-General Richard Glücks, and the infamous Dr Josef Mengele, simply disappeared underground as Himmler had recommended.

During the second half of 1945, the victorious Allies engaged upon a concerted effort to root out and round up all former members of the SS, which they declared had been an illegal and terrorist organisation. Their primary objective was to put the leaders before a military tribunal, to answer charges of war crimes. Mass arrests followed, and 32,000 ex-SS men were incarcerated at Dachau alone by the end of the year. Franz Breithaupt died at Prien soon after being taken into British custody, and Maximilian von Herff suffered a similar fate at Cornshead Priory POW camp on Lake Windermere in September, the same month as Walter Schmitt expired in Dablice as a captive of the Czechs. Those who were duly put on trial at Nürnberg and elsewhere during 1946-47 received a variety of sentences. Ernst Kaltenbrunner, Oswald Pohl, Arthur Greiser, Karl Hermann Frank, Kurt Daluege, Karl Gebhardt, Friedrich Jeckeln, Karl Brandt and Albert Forster, along with a further 18 less well-known SS and police generals, were condemned to death and executed for their involvement in the Nazi extermination policy. Large numbers of more junior personnel who had staffed concentration camps, served in Einsatzgruppen, or taken part in Waffen-SS atrocities were similarly dealt with. Gottlob Berger was sentenced to 25 years imprisonment, Werner Lorenz and Hans Lammers each received 20 years in jail, Wilhelm Keppler got 10 years, and Walter Buch was condemned to five years hard labour before committing suicide. Gustav-Adolf Scheel and Walter Schellenberg were each given five years imprisonment, and Otto Dietrich one year. Erich von dem Bach, a prime candidate for the death sentence, saved his skin and avoided extradition to Poland by acting as a witness for the prosecution at Nürnberg. The majority of these men served out their terms of imprisonment, which were often reduced on appeal

Plate 103 Hitler greets 'der treue Heinrich' at Führer Headquarters, Rastenburg, on 7 October 1943. Bormann lurks in the background. *Hoffmann*

Plate 104 Himmler after his suicide, 23 May 1945. *Ullstein*

Plate 105 A chart depicting the organisation of the RSHA is displayed at Nürnberg, 20 December 1945. *Ullstein*

or for good behaviour, and went on to enjoy comfortable lives in postwar West Germany. Indeed, for years thereafter, Allied intelligence agencies frequently sought the advice of Schellenberg and his former RSHA colleagues, and paid handsomely for the benefit of their expertise in espionage and interrogation techniques.

As for the other former SS commanders and notable personalities, Franz Xaver Schwarz succumbed to ill-health in Regensburg internment camp in 1947, while Ulrich Greifelt died in February 1949 at Landsberg, also after a long illness. Ulrich Graf perished a pauper in Munich in March 1950, followed by Richard Hildebrandt in 1951. Richard Walther Darré expired from liver failure two years later, Rudolf Diels accidentally shot and killed himself during a hunting expedition in November 1957, and Max Amann died in poverty the same year after having had all his wealth confiscated by a de-Nazification tribunal. Heinz Reinefarth, the first SS member to win the Knight's Cross and the man who crushed the Warsaw Uprising in August 1944, was luckier, taking up a career in local government and rising to the post of Bürgermeister of Westerland in 1958. His close police associate Alfred Wünnenberg died in Krefeld in 1963. Karl Wolff built up a successful public relations business until he received a belated 10-years prison sentence in 1964, following revelations at the Eichmann trial. Hans Jüttner died at Bad Tölz in 1965, and in 1966 four former Waffen-SS generals, 'Sepp' Dietrich, Georg Keppler, Herbert Gille and Felix Steiner, all succumbed to various illnesses. Julius Schaub pursued his profession as a Munich chemist until his demise in 1967, while Karl Fiehler and Jakob Grimminger both died in obscurity in 1969. Emil Maurice, holder of SS membership No 2 (Hitler held No 1), lived until 1972, the same year as 92-year-old Paul Hausser, the revered 'Father of the Waffen-SS', was laid to rest in the presence of hundreds of his ex-soldiers. Werner Lorenz died in 1974, Gottlob Berger in 1975, and August Heissmeyer in 1979. The last surviving Hauptamt Chief, Karl Wolff, gave up the ghost at Rosenheim in 1984. With his death, the former top ranking SS leadership and the lingering Old Guard of the organisation was finally extinguished.

ODESSA AND HIAG

While the majority of the very highest SS leaders were too well-known to avoid detection and arrest by the Allies at the end of the war, there were many more anonymous and rather faceless individuals who quite easily evaded capture. Prominent among such men were Heinrich Müller, Richard Glücks and Dr Josef Mengele, whose associations with the extermination programme earned them death sentences 'in absentia' from the Nürnberg Tribunal.

Hundreds of junior SS officers and NCOs from concentration camp guard units, policemen who had served with Einsatzgruppen in the East, and foreign volunteers such as Leon Degrelle who were regarded as arch-traitors in their own countries, managed to flee to the safety of sympathetic nations and set up new and comfortable lives for themselves after 1945. Their ability to do so was due entirely to the assistance provided by a vast and typically efficient escape network organised by the SS in its terminal stages.

At the end of 1944, Himmler ordered the RSHA to prepare false identity documents and passports bearing fictitious names, which were subsequently distributed to selected leading members of the SS and NSDAP. After the armistice was signed, many top Nazis went into hiding, or operated openly under their new pseudonyms. In front of the very eyes of the Allied administration, valuable contacts were established between high-ranking Nazis in prison and new underground groups outside, using secret codes devised by the SD before the collapse of the Third Reich. The initial overall organisation which co-ordinated these activities was called 'Spinne' or 'Spider', and was restricted to operating within Germany itself. Most important ex-SS men did not want to hang around the homeland for too long, however, and by 1946 they decided that the time had come to set up a worldwide escape network. As a result, the ODESSA (Organisation der SS-Angehörigen, or Organisation of SS Members) came into being the following year.

In a surprisingly short time, using the expertise of its RSHA veterans, ODESSA built up an efficient system of couriers who managed to smuggle wanted SS men and other Nazis out of the country. A few enterprising individuals even secured jobs driving US Army trucks on the Munich-Salzburg autobahn, and hid fugitives in the backs of the vehicles, which were seldom searched by the American military police, to get them safely across the Austrian border. Every 40 miles or so, an ODESSA Anlaufstelle or reception centre was established, run by at least three but not more than five people, who knew only the Anlaufstellen on either side of them along the route. These relay points covered the entire German-Austrian frontier, with the most important ones being situated at Ostermiething in Upper Austria, Zell-am-See in the Salzburg District, and Igls near Innsbruck in the Tyrol. Many SS men on the run ended up at either Bregenz or Lindau, both on Lake Constance, from where they crossed into Switzerland and thereafter boarded civil airline flights to the Middle East or South America. ODESSA also ran a so-called Monastery Route, between Austria and Italy, where sympathetic Roman Catholic priests, particularly Franciscan Friars, passed hunted SS men down a long line of religious 'safe houses'. Moreover, the organisation had connections with professional smugglers in all frontier areas, and cultivated valuable contacts in the Spanish, Egyptian, Syrian and numerous South

American embassies, in various European capitals. One of the main organisers was Obersturmbannführer Franz Roestel, formerly of the Waffen-SS division 'Frundsberg'. Although not on the 'wanted' list himself, he operated under the assumed name of Haddad Said, and found places for many of his ex-colleagues as military advisers to the governments of developing Arab states.

All this cost money, a resource which ODESSA conveniently had in virtually unlimited supply. The huge profits amassed through the SS economic enterprises, the substantial donations received over many years from members of the Freundeskreis RfSS and the Fördernde Mitglieder, and the cash raised by the sale of confiscated Jewish property and art treasures looted from the occupied territories, had filled the wartime coffers of the SS to the point of overflow. Early in 1945, the WVHA and RSHA conspired to liquidate all remaining SS assets and transfer the bulk of its money into bank accounts opened in neutral countries. These were subsequently used to establish and finance over 750 SS-sponsored companies which sprang up all over the world, including 112 in Spain, 58 in Portugal, 35 in Turkey, 98 in Argentina, 214 in Switzerland, and 233 in various other countries. Trusted former SS officers suddenly and unexpectedly had substantial sums deposited into their personal bank accounts, which explains how so many of them became 'successful businessmen' in later life. One ex-Obersturmbannführer paid a visit to his bank in 1947 to discover that his account, which had stood at a modest 12,000 Marks the previous week, had risen abruptly to over 2,600,000 Marks! He had no idea where the additional money had come from, until he recalled a mysterious visit he had in the autumn of 1944 from two senior SS officers, who wanted to know the number of his bank account and asked for a specimen of his signature on two blank sheets of paper. Although no reason was given at the time, they had evidently been preparing the ground-work for the distribution of SS funds.

ODESSA derived additional income from its illegal trade shipping scrap metal to Tangier and Syria, and its transfer to the Middle East of weapons stolen from US ammunition depots in Germany. Its contact men also procured import and export licences and sent strategic goods through holes in the Iron Curtain, particularly Vienna which acted as a gateway to Czechoslovakia.

It has been estimated that between 1945 and 1948 the SS managed to hide the present-day equivalent of around £900,000,000 worth of money and assets in various parts of the world. The six lists of people authorised to dispose of and benefit from these funds are probably the most important undiscovered documents of the Third Reich. Two were in the hands of the men who organised ODESSA in 1947, two are said to be in the safe-keeping of banks, and one of the remaining two is believed to be lying at the bottom of Lake Töplitz in Austria, where a large quantity of Nazi loot was hurriedly sunk in 1945. The vast majority of those named on the lists will now be dead, but their children live on. There can be little doubt that many respected family businesses currently operating successfully across the globe owe their origins and continued existence to the funds of ODESSA.

While ODESSA was always a secret network, geared towards securing the escape of SS war criminals and the continuance of Nazi ideology, a second well-publicised organisation for ex-SS men was established about the same time. It was the Hilfsgemeinschaft auf Gegenseitigkeit der Soldaten der ehemal Waffen-SS, or HIAG, the Welfare Association of Former Soldiers of the Waffen-SS. HIAG consistently denied any connection with ODESSA, but the latter undoubtedly financed it in the early days. Its avowed purpose was to campaign for and achieve the payment of State benefits to ex-servicemen of the Waffen-SS, particularly the war wounded, who did not qualify for regular Wehrmacht disability pensions. In that aim, it was moderately successful. Over the years, as its original membership progressively died off, HIAG dwindled in importance, and it is currently only a pale shadow of its former self, devoted almost entirely to the running of a small publishing house, Munin-Verlag GmbH of Osnabrück, which produces literature celebrating the combat achievements of SS field troops during World War 2. The 1990s will inevitably see the complete dismemberment of HIAG, the last acknowledged active remnant of the SS.

Almost 70 years after its modest foundation, Himmler's Black Corps is only now finally passing into the history books.

Bibliography

PRIMARY SOURCES

Archiv der Reichsführer-SS und Chef der Deutschen Polizei. Presently stored within the National Archives, Washington DC

Das Schwarze Korps : Zeitung der Schutzstaffel der NSDAP, Organ der Reichsführung-SS. (Zentral Verlag der NSDAP, Munich, 1935-45). The official newspaper of the SS

Der Dietrich. (Various issues). The bulletin of the Leibstandarte-SS 'Adolf Hitler'

Dienstaltersliste der Schutzstaffel der NSDAP (SS Personalhauptamt, Berlin, various editions). The SS Officers' List

FM-Zeitschrift : Monatschrift der Reichsführung-SS für Fördernde Mitglieder. (Zentral Verlag der NSDAP, Munich, 1935-45). The journal of the SS Patron Members Organisation

Organisationsbuch der NSDAP. (Zentral Verlag der NSDAP, Munich, various editions 1934-45). Includes the development of SS uniforms and insignia

Schutzstaffel der NSDAP : Kleiderkasse Preisliste. (SS Verwaltungsamt, Berlin, various dates). The official SS uniform and equipment price list

SS Personnel Files and Records. Several million of these are preserved by the US military authorities at the Berlin Document Centre

The General SS (SHAEF Counter-Intelligence Sub-Division, 1944). Comprehensive Allied Intelligence report on the Allgemeine-SS

SUGGESTED FURTHER READING

d'Alquen, G.
Die SS (Berlin, 1939). Official pamphlet produced by the Reichsführung-SS, detailing the origins and functions of the SS organisation. German text
Angolia, J.R.
Cloth Insignia of the SS. (Bender, San Jose, 1983). Lavish illustrative history of the development of SS badges
Barker, A.J.
Waffen-SS at War. (Ian Allan, Shepperton, 1982). Good coverage of Waffen-SS battles during World War 2
Bender, R.J. and Taylor, H.P.
Uniforms, Organisation and History of the Waffen-SS, Vols 1-5. (Bender, San Jose, 1969-83). A good reference on unit histories and insignia, for the first 20 Waffen-SS divisions

Borsarello, J. and Lassus, D.
Camouflaged Uniforms of the Waffen-SS, Vols 1 & 2. (ISO, London, 1986-88). Photographic study of SS camouflage
Buss, P.H. and Mollo, A.
Hitler's Germanic Legions. (McDonald & Jane's, London, 1978). An illustrated history of the Western European Legions of the Waffen-SS, 1941-43
Cooper, D.J.
Using the Runes. (Aquarian Press, Wellingborough, 1987). A comprehensive introduction to the ancient art of runecraft
Davis, B.L.
Waffen-SS. (Blandford, Poole, 1985). A basic photographic history
Eelking, Freiherr von.
Die Uniformen der Braunhemden : SA, SS, Politische Leiter, Hitlerjugend, Jungvolk & BDM. (Zentral Verlag der NSDAP, Munich, 1934). Illustrates early SS uniforms. German text
Frutiger, A.
Der Mensch und seine Zeichen. (Weiss Verlag, Dreieich, 1978). The design and meanings of signs and symbols. German text
Gilbert, A.
Waffen-SS. (Bison, London, 1989). An excellent illustrated history
Hamilton, C.
Leaders and Personalities of the Third Reich. (Bender, San Jose, 1984). Mini-biographies of all the main Nazi leaders
Harms, N. and Volstad, R.
Waffen-SS in Action. (Squadron/Signal, Texas, 1973). A general pictorial account.
Höhne, H.
Der Orden unter dem Totenkopf. (Verlag der Spiegel, Hamburg, 1966). The standard history of the SS. German text
Holzmann, W.K.
Manual of the Waffen-SS. (Bellona, Watford, 1976). Basic reference on Waffen-SS uniforms and equipment
Hunt, R.
Death's Head. (Hunt, Madison, 1979). A combat record of the SS-Totenkopf-Division in France, 1940
Jurado, C. and Hannon, P.
Resistance Warfare, 1940-45. (Osprey, London, 1985). Includes coverage of the Germanic-SS and associated units in the West
Krausnick, H. and Broszat, M.
Anatomy of the SS State. (Paladin, London, 1970). A scholarly account of the concentration camp system and the persecution of the Jews

Kumm, O.
Vorwärts Prinz Eugen! (Munin-Verlag, Osnabrück, 1978). An illustrated history of the SS division 'Prinz Eugen'. German text

Lehmann, R.
Die Leibstandarte. (Munin-Verlag, Osnabrück, 1977). An illustrated history of the Leibstandarte-SS 'Adolf Hitler'. German text

Littlejohn, D.
Foreign Legions of the Third Reich, Vols, 1-4. (Bender, San Jose, 1979-87). Includes sections on the Germanic-SS and non-German units of the Waffen-SS

Littlejohn, D.
The Hitler Youth. (R.L. Bryan, Columbia, 1988). Good coverage of the relationship between the SS and the Hitler Youth

Lucas, J. and Cooper, M.
Hitler's Elite. (McDonald & Jane's, London, 1975). The story of the Leibstandarte-SS 'Adolf Hitler'

Mollo, A.
A Pictorial History of the SS, 1923-45. (McDonald & Jane's, London, 1976). Excellent photographic record of the SS

Mollo, A.
Uniforms of the SS, Volumes 1-7. (Historical Research Unit, London, 1969-76). The best series of books available on the subject of SS uniforms

Mund, R.
Der Rasputin Himmlers. (Vienna, 1982). Biography of SS-Brigadeführer Karl Maria Wiligut-Weisthor, Himmler's expert on Germanic culture and runic symbolism. German text

Padfield, P.
Himmler : Reichsführer-SS. (McMillan, London, 1990). The ultimate biography of Heinrich Himmler

Pallud, J.P.
Ardennes 1944 : Peiper and Skorzeny. (Osprey, London, 1987). The SS involvement in the Battle of the Bulge

Passmore, M.
SS Porcelain Allach. (TLO, Oxford, 1972). A history of the SS porcelain and ceramics industry

Pia, J.
SS Regalia. (Ballantine, New York, 1974). Includes good colour illustrations of SS collectables.

Quarrie, B.
Hitler's Samurai. (PSL, Cambridge, 1983). A history of the Waffen-SS

Quarrie, B.
Hitler's Teutonic Knights. (PSL, Cambridge, 1987). A history of the Waffen-SS panzer divisions

Quarrie, B.
Waffen-SS in Russia. (PSL Cambridge, 1978). A photographic account of the SS on the Eastern Front

Quarrie, B.
Weapons of the Waffen-SS. (PSL, Cambridge, 1988). Covers all types of weapons from small arms to heavy artillery

Reider, F.
L'Ordre SS. (Editions de le Pensee Moderne, Paris, 1980). A good general account of the SS. French text

Reitlinger, G.
The SS: Alibi of a Nation. (Heinemann, London, 1956). The first detailed history of the SS

Russell, S. and Schneider, J.
Heinrich Himmlers Burg. (Heitz & Höffkes, Essen, 1989) A chronicle of Wewelsburg Castle, 1934-45. German text

Schneider, J.
Their Honour Was Loyalty. (Bender, San Jose, 1977). An illustrated and documentary history of the Knight's Cross holders of the Waffen-SS and Police

Stein, G.
The Waffen-SS : Hitler's Elite Guard at War. (Cornell, New York, 1966). A scholarly account of the Waffen-SS

Stephen, A. and Amodio, P.
Waffen-SS Uniforms in Colour Photographs. (Windrow & Greene, London, 1990). Imaginative reconstructions of Waffen-SS uniforms in wear

Stöber, H.
Die Sturmflut und das Ende. (Munin-Verlag, Osnabrück, 1976). Illustrated history of the SS division 'Götz von Berlichingen'. German text

Sydnor, C.
Soldiers of Destruction. (Princeton, 1977). The story of the SS-Totenkopf units, 1933-45

Thomas, N. and Abbott, P.
Partisan Warfare, 1941-45. (Osprey, London, 1983). Includes coverage of SS anti-partisan engagements on the Eastern Front

Time-Life Books (Various authors)
The SS. (Time-Life, Alexandria, 1988). An illustrated history of the SS

Weidinger, O.
Division Das Reich. (Munin-Verlag, Osnabrück, 1979). An illustrated history of the SS division 'Das Reich'. German text

Wilson, K.
SS Headgear : A Collector's Guide. (Reddick, Texas, 1990). Many colour photographs of SS peaked caps, field caps, steel helmets, etc.

Windrow, M.
The Waffen-SS. (Osprey, London, 1982). A general history of Waffen-SS units and campaigns